"Frank Miniter is one of the finest writers and investigative journalists I know. He does a remarkable job describing the context and history of firearms in America, and then delves into their contemporary lawful and positive use. And in analyzing the criminal use of firearms and the effect the government restriction of gun rights has had on our society, this book makes a dramatic impact on the national debate. Woven into his narrative is the history and big picture of firearm manufacturing in the United States (guns kick-started the Industrial Revolution) and what effect technological developments are having and will have on firearms in the near future."

—Mark A. Keefe IV, editor in chief, *American Rifleman*

"*The Future of the Gun* is an interesting, honest, thought-provoking treatment that you won't want to put down. I would expect no less from my amigo Frank Miniter."

—Jim Wilson, senior field editor, *Shooting Illustrated* and Texas sheriff (ret.)

"*The Future of the Gun* is an insightful look into gun politics and policy, written with Frank's trademark wit. An important read for every American."

—Chris W. Cox, chief lobbyist, National Rifle Association

"I first met Frank at the Supreme Court covering the *Heller* case. From his work there, I knew he was a top-notch reporter, and he shows his writing chops in *The Future of the Gun*. He's taken two centuries of the gun in our culture and boils it down to give the backstories on guns in America. He uses that foundation to offer an informed, yet highly readable look into our future. And he's done it all in under three hundred pages."

—Jim Shepherd, editor and publisher, The Outdoor Wire Digital Network, including The Shooting Wire, and founding member of CNN

THE
FUTURE OF
THE GUN

THE FUTURE OF THE GUN

FRANK MINITER

REGNERY
PUBLISHING

A Salem Communications Company

Library of Congress Control Number: 2014942665

ISBN 978-1-62157-240-4

Published in the United States by
Regnery Publishing
A Salem Communications Company
300 New Jersey Ave NW
Washington, DC 20001
www.Regnery.com

Manufactured in the United States of America

10 9 8 7 6 5 4 3 2 1

Books are available in quantity for promotional or premium use. For information on discounts and terms, please visit our website: www.Regnery.com.

Distributed to the trade by
Perseus Distribution
250 West 57th Street
New York, NY 10107

Appendix photos credit: NRA Museums, NRAmuseums.com, except for the Remington R-51 photo, which is courtesy of Remington Arms.

By the rude bridge that arched the flood,
Their flag to April's breeze unfurled,
Here once the embattled farmers stood,
And fired the shot heard round the world.

—Ralph Waldo Emerson, "Concord Hymn"

Contents

American Guns: Freedom's Tool

Among the many misdeeds of British rule in India,
history will look upon the Act depriving
a whole nation of arms as the blackest.
—Mohandas Gandhi, *An Autobiography*

In a way, the future of gun ownership in America is about what happens to Mike K.

He grew up in an inner city without a father, joined a gang, stole cars, had a felony conviction at eighteen, and odds are should have been incarcerated or shot dead by twenty-one. He's a linebacker-sized black man whose first experiences with guns were with illegal semiautomatic handguns tucked into pants and stuffed into puffy jackets. Yet it was guns that eventually saved him from all the bad stuff. We met so he could tell me his story.

We're seated in little plastic chairs made for middle school students. There is a small wood school desk between us. Mike is now in his mid-thirties and drives a truck to pay the bills. He has tattoos on his arms of his three children's names. Two of the names are in the shape of a crucifix on his left forearm and the third is on his right bicep. The two making the cross are wrapped in ivy, his wife's name. He can't own a gun, because of his youthful felony conviction. "It was nothing really. Just a stupid thing," he tells me, but then he pauses. I sense he knows he's paid a hefty price for his mistakes—and is grateful to be alive and in a better place.

He tells me slowly, warily, "You know, I'd be dead or locked up if John didn't teach me to handle a gun."

John is John Annoni, who is speaking in a nearby classroom to thirty kids, most of whom are in middle school. The kids are here for Camp Compass, an after-school program designed to save inner-city kids from the bad influences of rough neighborhoods. The kids are friendly, respectful, and courteous and will shake your hand when you meet them and call you sir or ma'am. John has found a way to save these kids by using guns as a carrot at the end of a long stick.

The classroom is not in a public school. We're actually in an upstairs room of Joe Mascari's Carpets & Rugs in Allentown, Pennsylvania. If you're wondering what we're doing in a carpet store, so is Joe Mascari. He never thought he'd give up floor space to a program for inner-city kids. It all started when the public school where John teaches and began this after-school program told him he couldn't use guns as a teaching device, because guns are a bad influence. John says guns helped save him when he grew up in a bad neighborhood; and guns, he says, are part of these kids' lives, though too often in bad ways. Teaching them about guns in the right way is what, he thinks, makes his after-school program so effective.

Like a lot of kids from these asphalt-and-brick neighborhoods, John grew up without a father. His grandmother raised him. On weekends he went to his mother's apartment in the projects. "It was a violent and abusive place," he says, "so I started going out behind the projects and hiding in this little woodlot. I'd sit there in the woods where nobody could hurt me. Pretty soon I saw a squirrel and I started to stalk it. As time goes on I got better at stalking and tracking game around that little woodlot. I was safe and happy there until I had to go back to the apartment—Mother Nature was saving me. Later an uncle took me hunting and I found a real connection to the outdoors. Guns, in this very different culture from [what] I knew on the streets, helped save my life."

John says he found himself between two cultures, so he decided to take good parts from both. "A lot of students wonder where I grew up and what color I am," he often tells people. "New students sometimes ask me, 'What are you?' I think they're looking for a role model they can relate to by skin color, so I reply by asking them, 'What do you think I am?' After they guess, I tell them, 'I'm half-black and half-white but I look Spanish and I eat Chinese food.' They laugh. I let them all know I'm just like them."

A friend of John's introduced him to Joe Mascari. At first, when John broached the idea of having his after-school programs there, Joe said, "Are you nuts? This is a carpet store." But John kept talking and pretty soon Joe gave him these rooms to use for free.

Joe's wife was killed by a knife-wielding murderer. "Most people would say he shouldn't be helping us because of that," says John, "but he gets it. He gets that if she had a gun she might be alive. He gets that something is rotten in this inner-city culture and he gets that we're doing something about it. He even says if that thug had come to Camp Compass he never would have done such an evil thing. So he helps us use guns to teach responsibility, to grow upstanding adults."

Mike K., sitting across from me, tells me that two of his close boyhood friends are in jail for "shooting at cops" and that others are dead. He waves his tattooed right arm at the city streets of Allentown, Pennsylvania, and says, "People blame guns for all that bad stuff out there. I tell 'em it's not guns. I tell them how John used guns to save my life."

He leans closer, puts his hands on the little school desk between us, and says, "The only way to save people like me is with good examples and by not lying to them about guns and all that. Those politicians who blame guns are making the streets worse. They're sentencing kids to death and jail 'cause they just don't understand." He shakes his head and says, "All those counselors I saw." He pauses again. His eyes tell me he's repressing a lot of things he doesn't want to get into. He says, "Only John told me the truth. Only John cared enough to do that. You tell the truth like he does in your book and, I dunno, maybe it'll make some difference."

He takes a deep breath and continues, "Back in 1995 I was getting into fights, stealing, getting suspended from school and all that. Mentor after mentor quit on me. I was a lost cause in their eyes, someone that would either end up in jail or dead by twenty-one. Let me tell you I was ready to give up, too. But then I was introduced to John. Sure, I knew of John from elementary school. I remember walking by his classroom, always seeing smiling faces and hearing laughter. It was such a positive atmosphere. But I thought he was going to be another mentor to quit on me. But then weeks had passed and John was still there. He took me out to do positive things. He showed me life!

"It was weird. Guns in my neighborhood were bad things. The guys who had them got them because a gun made them powerful. Guns made them cool. Most of my friends got handguns. No one taught them about guns. Most of their dads weren't around. All they knew was a gun tucked in their pants made them feared, made them dangerous."

"But you know," Mike says, "John took me out to a gun range and taught me to shoot a shotgun, then a rifle. He showed me how to unload a gun and to shoot safely by keeping my finger off the trigger until I'm gonna shoot and teaches me to keep the barrel in a safe direction and all that. He teaches me responsibility. He shows me how a real man handles a gun. He trusted me. No one ever did that. I didn't want to let him down."

Mike shifts his feet and says, "So I stopped getting in trouble and got my grades up. John took me hunting. Soon I'm back in the neighborhood showing my friends the picture of the deer I got and they think it's so cool. So all I want to do is go hunting. It was so good, so far away from the streets and in my hands was this great responsibility, this gun, and all I had to do was handle it right, like a man does, and I'd be right and good and maybe get a deer or whatever.

"But looking back now, I know something else was going on. When John took me hunting in those days we'd sit and talk about what was going on in my life and ways to make things better. I connected with John because I looked at him as a big brother, not as some social worker and because he was showing me something I never saw before—how guns are tools and that when you do things right they're good and you're good. I finally found someone to look up to and a way to prove myself with the very thing my friends feared and respected most—guns. I had to earn everything I did with John. I had to learn discipline by hunting and shooting."

He pauses again and his eyes go down to the wood table before coming back up again, and he tells me that some of his friends from the streets wanted to pull him back. They thought those hunting photos were pretty cool, but they wanted him to hang out and do all that bad stuff he was getting away from. Mike says, "Eventually, John and I spent less time together. I was finally happy with myself, with my life, and I owed that to John. But then one day I was with a group of friends and they decided to rob some kids standing on a street corner. Not thinking, I stayed in the car instead of leaving. Naturally, we got arrested. I thought my life was over because I was the only one of adult age—the blame fell squarely on my shoulders. I didn't know what to do or who to turn to. I never had a father figure. My friends were all I had. I couldn't call John. I was scared. I didn't want to disappoint him. Besides, I hadn't spoken to John in months, why would he help me? Although every bone in my body didn't want to, my heart told me to call him. John took me in with open arms. He sat me down just like in the beginning of our relationship and we came up with a plan to get myself back on the correct path. I have been on that same path ever since."

Mike shifts his weight in his little plastic chair, frowns, and his eyes get emotional as he explains that he's now trying to get his gun rights back after that awful mistake almost twenty years ago. He didn't get any jail time for that robbery, just probation. Nevertheless, he has a felony conviction so he can't own a gun. Now his wife can't have a gun because, as a felon, Mike can't be in the same house with a gun. That's eating away at him. "She's not safe when I'm out driving the truck. She's not safe because of me," he says. He has a lawyer helping him try to get his Second Amendment rights back. He hopes he can have his freedom again. He only wants to live free and to protect his family and for his wife to be safe when he's away driving trucks, but the law is stopping him.

He got mugged recently when he pulled his truck into a loading dock to make a delivery. The guy jumped on his truck's running board, pointed a pistol in his face, and said, "Sorry man, I gotta eat. Give me whatever money you got."

"Right there my life was in this guy's hands," says Mike. "He didn't want to shoot me and I gave him my wallet and he ran away, but it made me think about my wife and kids alone at home and that drives me crazy."

Mike pauses, looks at the floor, and then back at me as he says, "In my time on the streets I've seen what gun laws do. They ban handguns. So then all my old friends have handguns anyway, but the law-abiding people don't. What good does that do? You want to make the streets safer, you need to let law-abiding people carry if they want. That way you'll have people who're responsible being, you know, good examples. They'll show kids by example how guns should be treated. There are too many guns out there to just ban them. I can take you to places right now where you can buy an illegal handgun no problem. You want this to get better, you want a brighter future, then enforce the gun laws—let me tell you they're not—and let good people carry concealed if they want to. That would have stopped me from doing a lot of the bad stuff I did all those years ago. It would reduce violence now."

Mike's story is powerful, but he's far from alone. I talk to other people from the rougher parts of town who were saved by John.

Andrew M. is twenty-two years old and of Egyptian descent. He is about to graduate from college and become a teacher, like John. He says, "When I was in the sixth grade the police came and took my father away. It was in all the papers. The whole street knew they were arresting my father. He was convicted of rape and is still in jail. My father used to walk me to school, but now we had to move and I was in a new school in a tough neighborhood. So suddenly I'm all alone—

just a little scared sixth grader. John sees me there and he knows all about it. He says, 'Don't worry, it's my first day, too.' It wasn't, of course, but he knew just what to say. Right away he welcomes me into Camp Compass. He saves my life. I'd be dead or in jail now if John didn't take me in and use guns and hunting to show me how to be a positive, hard-working adult."

Two others join me. Tiffany S. and Mike M. Tiffany is white and Mike is black. They tell similar stories. They say the only way to make the streets safer is with good examples, with people like John. Tiffany tells me about the guns she saw in high school. She went to a rough inner-city school with gang problems; illegal guns were easily had and were used to victimize people. "You take the freedom to own a gun away and you get what John saved us from on these streets. You do that and all you have left is the bad," says Tiffany. She's twenty-four years old now and has a college degree that helped her get a job in a hospital.

Tiffany has always had health issues. They make her weak. They used to make her feel helpless. She says, "When John took me shooting and hunting I learned confidence. He gave me this rite of passage to become a good adult."

Most of the people I talk to tell me they don't hunt anymore. Many don't even own guns. But they all back gun rights.

I wish those who back "gun-free zones" could meet these people and spend time on their streets. Murder and violence took place before the invention of guns, and they will continue to take place—and have taken place, at high rates—even in localities with stiff gun-control laws. Guns don't cause violence. What guns can do in the hands of honest people is equalize the odds between a one-hundred-pound woman and a two-hundred-pound potential assailant, or between the good guys and the bad guys.

There are two wildly different gun cultures in America—the freedom-loving, gun-rights culture that upholds the responsible use of guns for hunting, sport, and self-defense, and the criminal culture that thrives in spite of, or even because of, government attempts at restricting gun rights. Those two cultures lead to two different futures. The path we take will determine the future of the gun and the future of our freedom.

PART I

Future Glock?

CHAPTER ONE

Every American Should Hear This

Like history it repeats itself.
—A 1904 ad for the Winchester Automatic Rifle,
a semiautomatic .22 rimfire rifle[1]

I say, swallowing a laugh, "Just tell me what you really think about America's love affair with the gun, Phil. Don't let me stop you."

Phil Schreier, the senior curator for the NRA's National Firearms Museum, and I are standing right in the middle of the biggest gun museum in all the world, and he's just said, "Since David killed Goliath, the person with the more advanced weapon, not the guy with biggest muscles, has always won the fight."

He says this as we're looking at the "Mayflower gun," a wheel-lock carbine brought to America on the Mayflower by John Alden in 1620. Alden was one of the Pilgrim leaders of Plymouth Colony, so his gun was certainly at the first Thanksgiving.

"From the beginning," says Phil, "handheld guns led to individual liberty. When this translates to an armed society, it tends to lead to a freer people. Trace the history of the gun and you'll find out how European feudalism was finally ended. They don't teach that fundamental part of history in grade school, do they?"

I'm smiling as I say, "Not in the New York public school I went to."

Phil grimaces and says with a sad look in his brown eyes, "Yeah, if school kids were just taught that the 'shot heard 'round the world' was fired through an American-forged and -rifled barrel, they might know a damn thing about American ingenuity and how we really won our freedom. That way they might just have a clue what our freedom is all about."

Before I ask him to unpack all that, he says, "School kids—hell, even the adults—often don't even know what the British were after. The Redcoats were coming to seize a weapons depot. They were coming for the peoples' guns. They wanted to disarm the colonists before a rebellion began."

Phil points to a flintlock rifle and says, "This just might be the gun that fired the shot heard 'round the world. It's from that period and region. It was the type of muzzle-loading rifle many of the colonists had."

I look from Phil to this old flintlock rifle, and the connection between guns and freedom becomes as vivid as burned black powder. Phil, you see, is one of those short, heavyset guys who moves so continuously and quickly you can't understand how they stay heavyset. But you soon forget about that because what he has to say is so authoritative. Phil knows more about the history of American guns than anyone. The History Channel calls him when they need an expert. When historians at the Springfield Armory, a museum run by the National Park Service (NPS) on the grounds of the original armory founded by George Washington, were stumped about a particular Springfield Model 1903, they called Phil and he dug up the original records for them. That's the kind of history-loving, truth-telling, fact-ridden gun nut he is.

That's why I'm here in this gun museum with Phil for a hands-on history lesson of the American gun. I'm thankful he's here to teach it, as this history is so politically incorrect that few are exposed to it. Yet this history is fundamental to understanding American freedom. More than that, if we don't understand our freedom's connection to the gun from 1775 to today, we're sure to lose our liberty.

Phil keeps rolling along with the excited tone of a gifted teacher: "If you looked down the muzzle of that flintlock rifle, you'd see grooves. That's rifling as you well know, and the rifling grooves in this gun were cut by hand by a New England gunsmith in the early 1770s."

After a pause for effect, he starts into a speech that gets him so worked up his arms begin to flail. He explains that, sure school kids learn that on the night of April 18, 1775, hundreds of British troops marched from Boston to nearby towns. And yes, they learn that Paul Revere and others sounded the alarm and that colonial militiamen mobilized to confront the Redcoat column. They are even taught that an initial confrontation on the Lexington town green started the fight that led to a British retreat from a large force of Americans at Concord. "However," Phil says, "one small but pretty important fact few learn about that battle is the colonists actually had more-advanced arms than the British troops.

"What those young minds aren't taught is that some of the Americans had rifles, whereas the British had Brown Besses—smoothbore muskets. The Americans' rifles could hit a man-sized target at two hundred and perhaps three hundred yards, whereas the Brown Bess was only accurate to maybe seventy-five yards. And those New Englanders were hunters. They needed to kill squirrels and rabbits to eat, so they'd learned to be marksmen. They used these skills and their rifle technology by lying behind rocks and trees and shooting the Red Coats dead long before the British got close enough to use their .75 caliber smoothbore muskets."

Phil points to an older flintlock made in Germany and says that though barrel rifling is thought to have been invented in Augsburg, Germany, at the end of the fifteenth century, American gun makers improved on previous designs by making the American Longrifle (what later became known as the "Kentucky rifle"). By looking at the German rifle and the American Longrifle, there is no doubt that the American Longrifle is quite a bit longer. By looking at features and designs of seventeenth- and eighteenth-century flintlocks, gun historians today can tell where each rifle was likely made. Like schools of art, different regions of the colonies used various stock designs and other features.

Even though the American rifles were more accurate, the British, Phil explains, preferred the smoothbore Brown Bess because it lobbed a big bullet and because it is faster to load than a muzzleloader with a long-rifled barrel—you have to twist a bullet down a rifled barrel, and that takes time. Redcoats were geared for close-quarter engagements between masses of troops. But the Americans at Concord didn't fight that way. They impolitely used their rifles to fire before the Redcoats could get close enough to take advantage of the firepower from their less-accurate muskets.

There were downsides to American Longrifles, Phil adds. They were comparably expensive to make and their production rate was slow, as small-arms makers produced them one at a time. So though

General George Washington made significant use of snipers, most American revolutionaries were later armed with smoothbore muskets—many of them made in France.

"Nevertheless," Phil says, "small, private rifle makers in the colonies made it possible for the war to begin on good footing for the colonists. This helped to get the public behind the revolution and, as a lot of British officers who were targeted during the war found out, it damn well helped American troops throughout the war."

After a pause, Phil's voice grows smaller as he says inwardly, "Thus began the long and lovely relationship between American citizens, American gun makers, and the U.S. military. A relationship still ongoing, a relationship that keeps us free, a relationship some are trying to end. If they succeed our freedom will follow, as real freedom is linked to the gun in ways most don't comprehend."

His serious expression grows into a Cheshire cat grin. We are just getting started, and he's excited to teach this stuff. This beneficial relationship didn't stop with the American Revolution, he explains. After the war, George Washington established the Springfield Armory in Springfield, Massachusetts. The armory was founded to produce and develop arms for the military. The armory began making flintlocks in 1795. From then until its closing, in 1968, the armory made weapons for the U.S. military. James Woolsey, superintendent of the Springfield Armory, a man who looks a bit like Ranger Rick in his National Park Service (NPS) uniform, told me when I visited there in October 2013 that "though most people aren't aware of this today, the civilian gun market and the government have always worked together. Now, of course, all our arms come from the private sector."

When I ask why the armory closed, Woolsey frowns as he says, "The army flubbed the launch of the M14. Meanwhile some savvy entrepreneurs in a California aircraft factory were using new materials and manufacturing techniques to perfect the AR-15—the precursor to the M16. Soon the U.S. government's Springfield Armory fell behind technologically. This isn't politically correct to say," he adds, "but today a very innovative civilian gun market is what's keeping America's armed forces prepared and better equipped than other militaries."

From 1777 until it was converted into a technical college in 1968, the Springfield Armory was the largest manufacturer of firearms for the U.S. military. There is a fascinating museum on the property showcasing America's history of firearms. From muskets used in the American Revolution to the Trapdoor Springfield, first produced in 1868 (the 1952 film *Springfield Rifle*, starring Gary Cooper, shows what a big deal it was), to bolt-action Model 1903s used in World War I, to semiautomatic M1 Garands used in World War II, and later to M14s, the armory's firearms were all designed for the military.

"The thing is," says Woolsey, "civilians simultaneously used these firearms types, too. In fact, civilian gun designers, like Samuel Colt and John Browning, influenced and often collaborated with the U.S. military to design new and better firearms."

Semiautomatic designs were so popular with civilians in the early twentieth century that a 1907 magazine ad for the Savage Model 1907 (known as the "Savage Automatic Pistol") read: "Her property—her little ones—her own life—she knows are safely protected when she has a Savage Automatic in her home. She knows its ten sure shots are at her command—quick or slow, as she chooses—one to each trigger pull."

Mark A. Keefe IV, editor of *American Rifleman*, says, "What's really interesting is that from about 1900 to 1940 semiautomatic rifles were more often used by civilians than the U.S. military. It was the civilian market that drove and tweaked semiautomatic rifle designs that made it possible for the M1 Garand."

Phil adds to this by saying, "History teaches us that without the civilian gun market, gun innovation would fall on its face. Government procurement contracts come bureaucratically slow. If gun companies had to solely rely on them, most would stop innovating. This would let America fall behind the world. Pretty soon we'd be dependent on other nations for our military's firearms, and our American people wouldn't know how to use them. Our military would lose the great advantage that comes from recruiting from a populace in which a substantial percentage knows how to shoot. Making sure Americans know how to shoot is, of course, why the NRA was founded, in 1871."

I knew what he meant, as I've interviewed Special Forces soldiers to find out if civilian gun ownership helps prepare citizen-soldiers. Greg Stube, a former Special Forces sergeant who fought in Afghanistan, put it best when he told me, "In my experience, a lot of training time in the Special Forces is used to teach those who don't have gun experience. To put it plainly: The Special Forces are in the business of creating country boys."

Stube adds, "I've toured the Smith & Wesson plant in Springfield, Massachusetts. I saw firearms headed for law enforcement and for the civilian market coming off the same lines. This is how America has always worked. It's how it should and must work. I saw again and again in training and on the battlefield that soldiers who grew up hunting and shooting recreationally are better soldiers. As I said, the Special Forces is in the business of creating country boys. If our free citizens are barred from using firearms similar to those used by the military, then we won't be as prepared as a nation.

"Also, my experience in war taught me," says Stube, "that law-abiding people shouldn't be put in a position where they're potentially less armed than those who might prey on them. I saw horrific things that the Taliban did to unarmed civilians in Afghanistan, things I don't want my children ever to see."

Steve Adelmann, a retired SOF Operator and owner of Citizen Arms, agrees with Stube. He tells me, "America's firearms culture helps the military and law enforcement. When I trained new snipers for my team, I always found the best shooters had been raised with a gun in hand. In fact, drill sergeants and other instructors spend much of their limited range time trying to get young men and women with little or no gun experience up to par with troops who grew up hunting or target shooting. In particular, people who come from urban areas use a disproportionate amount of training time just learning to sight in their rifles and hit targets at close range.

"I've also seen a difference in the abilities of other armed forces," says Adelmann. "I've trained with and fought alongside allied soldiers from many nations. Soldiers from firearms-friendly places like Israel and Scandinavian countries acquit themselves very well with a wide variety of arms. Conversely, soldiers from nations with severe gun restrictions like England and Australia are far less familiar with firearms and generally don't have the same comfort levels as Americans. They're very good with the weapons they are issued but the battlefield requires enough flexibility to adapt quickly to a wide variety of firearm types."

Adelmann now builds custom AR-15s for private citizens. He asks every customer what they intend to do with their modern sporting rifle. He says, "Ninety percent of them list hunting and home defense as their first two reasons for ownership. ARs are supremely accurate hunting rifles and utilitarian home-defense firearms," he says. "If they're banned we'll lose an effective tool for the citizen while military and law enforcement entities will suffer down the road. Also, many advances in firearm technology come from the civilian market, especially competition shooting. If manufacturers can no longer sell ARs to citizens, much of that innovation will grind to a halt."

To add an exclamation point to the experiences and views articulated by Stube and Adelmann, consider a letter written by retired Army Special Forces Master Sergeant Jeff Hinton and signed by 1,100

Special Forces operators. Hinton wrote that banning AR-15s and "high-capacity" magazines will "only provide us with a false sense of security." He argues that we need to do away with gun-free zones and to empower citizens to be the line of defense they've historically been, whether it was against British Red Coats attempting to enforce tyrannical laws, or hostile Indians on the frontier, or dangerous criminals.

Phil explains this from a historian's perspective. He notes that the AR-15 (what the media has dubbed an "assault weapon") is merely the latest example of private citizens using and helping to develop a firearm type that is closely related to those used by the military. As he points to various firearms in the museum, he explains that every major firearm type used by the U.S. military has also been owned and used by civilians. This goes for lever-action Winchesters, bolt-action Krags, pump-action shotguns from Browning, and the modern AR-15. "Anti-gun politicians who're fond of saying that 'weapons of war have no place in civilian hands' are either unaware of American history or are dishonest," says Phil.

He then grounds the point historically by explaining that in 1836 Samuel Colt perfected and patented a revolving handgun by bringing together features from previous guns and fashioning them into a mechanically reliable revolver. Colt even thought of developing an assembly line to manufacture his product. School textbooks often call Henry Ford's use of an assembly line nearly a century later (in the late 1920s) a major innovation, as Ford used an assembly line to make the Ford Model T. But a gun maker a century before had this idea. Colt wrote in a letter in 1836 that the "first workman would receive two or three of the most important parts and would affix these and pass them on to the next who add a part and pass the growing article on to another who would do the same, and so on until the complete arm is put together."[2]

The English gave Colt a patent for his revolver. The United States also gave Colt a patent for a "revolving gun" on February 25, 1836. These early revolvers were used by Texas Rangers to defeat Comanches. In previous fights, frontiersmen had to get off their horse to use a flintlock rifle to fire one shot at a Comanche, a tribe renowned for swiftly shooting arrows from horseback. Even if the frontiersman killed one Comanche, he'd be killed by others before he could load powder and ball down his muzzleloader, prime the firearm, cock it, aim, and fire. When armed with a Colt revolver, however, a Ranger could fight from horseback and fire multiple shots. This changed the nature of Indian fighting on the frontier.[3]

Colt didn't know his revolving handgun was proving so effective for Texas Rangers. His Patent Arms Company went bankrupt and ceased operation in 1842. One constant problem for Colt was the government. The Militia Act of 1808 required that any arms purchased by a state militia had to be in current service in the U.S. military. This Act standardized arms, but it prevented state militias from spending money on guns that might be better suited to their needs or terrain. To try to make a sale to the U.S. military, Colt presented his revolver to President Andrew Jackson, and though Jackson saw the military advantages, the meeting didn't lead to orders from the U.S. government.[4]

The assets from Colt's Patent Arms Company had been sold at auction. Colt was trying other ideas, including using electric current from galvanic batteries to detonate underwater explosives. The U.S. government was interested in this concept. They gave Colt funding to continue his work for possible use in harbor defense.[5]

Meanwhile, Captain Sam Walker of the Texas Rangers wanted to purchase revolvers from Colt to arm five hundred Texas Rangers who had been absorbed into the U.S. Army during the Mexican-American War. Walker had been in a troop of fourteen Rangers led by Captain

John Coffee Hays on June 9, 1844, when they had used Colt's early Paterson revolvers to win the Battle of Walker's Creek (not named after Sam Walker) against a much greater number of Comanches.[6]

"Walker wrote to Colt," says Phil. "He didn't know Colt had gone out of business. Walker had been given a blank check to purchase arms for Texas Rangers who would fight in the Mexican-American War. Walker wanted one thousand revolvers from Colt."

Walker and Colt met in New York City in 1847.[7] As great a revolution as the Paterson revolver was, Walker felt it had shortcomings. He told Colt the revolver was too fragile and too difficult to reload. Colt seems to have welcomed the criticism. He agreed to modify his revolver according to Walker's suggestions. As they collaborated, Walker said he would get the government to buy them.[8]

Phil explains, "Not having a factory to complete the order, Colt made a deal with the Whitneyville Armory, run by Eli Whitney Jr., son of the famed inventor of the cotton gin, to produce the new revolvers."[9]

As Colt worked, Walker went to Washington. Walker was a famous Texas Ranger, and his fame helped him secure a meeting with President James Polk. After hearing Walker explain the new handgun Colt could produce, President Polk and Walker went to the office of William Marcy, the secretary of war. President Polk ordered him to purchase the weapons. Marcy passed the purchase order for one thousand revolvers at twenty-five dollars each to Lieutenant Colonel George Talcott, the ordnance chief.[10]

From Colt's new design, Eli Whitney Blake (Eli Whitney's nephew) produced one thousand "Walker Colts." Fully loaded, the revolver weighed almost five pounds. Unlike the Paterson, which fired five shots, the Walker fired six. The Colt Walker was the most powerful handgun then made. It used 60 grains of blackpowder to shoot .44 caliber lead balls.

With the money Colt made from the sale of the Walkers and a loan from his cousin, banker Elisha Colt, Colt later bought the machinery and tooling from Blake to build his own factory—Colt's Patent Fire Arms Manufacturing Company, in Hartford. The first revolving-breech handguns made at the new factory were called "Whitneyville-Hartford-Dragoons" and became so popular that the word "Colt" soon became a synonym for "revolver." Meanwhile, as Colt produced revolvers, people out on the frontier and in the cities thought it a pretty good thing that Colt had invented a gun that could rapidly fire six shots. No politician thought about passing laws to stop him. To everyone it was progress.

Left to work without bureaucrats wagging their fingers, Colt kept advancing manufacturing processes by making guns with interchange-able parts (made by machine and assembled by hand).

"When he did this," Phil explains, "Colt revolutionized the idea of how products are made by making a product with truly inter-changeable parts. Colt traveled to the first World Fair in London in 1851 and amazed people there by completely disassembling a half dozen revolvers, putting the parts in a bag and shaking them up, and then putting the guns back together. This doesn't seem like a big deal now, but at the time it was jaw-dropping revolutionary. Machine parts had to be filed and fit at the time to fit individual products. But Colt had found a way to make the parts interchangeable. This means any-one could repair one of his guns by simply replacing a part. This reduced labor costs and expertise."

Soon this novel idea caught on and began to fuel America's Indus-trial Revolution. All along Colt was also spreading freedom; for example, in 1860s Colt Manufacturing would famously run newspa-per ads showing women with Colt revolvers and touting, "God made man, but Samuel Colt made them equal." So more than a half century before women got the right to vote, Colt was doing something real for women's rights by making them equal to bigger, stronger men—and no one thought that controversial either.

To make this point even clearer, Phil moves us to another display case, this one with revolvers from Horace Smith and Daniel B. Wesson. In 1852 they formed a company to produce a lever-action handgun nicknamed the "Volcanic Pistol." After it failed, Smith and Wesson came out with a revolver in 1856—the Smith & Wesson Model 1. This was the first revolver that fired a fully self-contained cartridge.

Phil points out a Smith & Wesson Model 1, a blackpowder handgun. He then walks me over to the Smith & Wesson handgun Clint Eastwood used when he played Dirty Harry and says, "This revolver, of course, shoots smokeless powder, self-contained cartridges." It is famously chambered in .44 Magnum (the "most powerful handgun in the world"). Except it's not the most powerful anymore; it has been far surpassed by Smith & Wesson's .500 and by others. That's the thing about American innovation—it keeps evolving to please more consumers, unless the government bans it.

We next moved to self-loading (semiautomatic) pistols. Phil points to a Model 1911 and says, "People think of semiautomatic pistols as being space-age technology, but the truth is perhaps the greatest pistol ever invented, one still carried by cops, civilians, and some in the military, is the Model 1911, a gun designed when the Wright brothers were still selling bicycles in Ohio."

The semiautomatic pistol is actually a late nineteenth-century invention made for both civilians and the military. After Hiram Maxim (1840–1916) introduced his recoil-powered machine gun in 1883, several private gunsmiths set out to apply the same principles to handguns. The first model to gain commercial success was from Hugo Borchardt (1844–1924). His C-93 hit the market in 1894. The C-93 was too bulky to receive widespread acceptance, but its design helped other inventors. In 1896, Paul Mauser (1838–1914) introduced his first semiautomatic pistol, the Mauser "Broomhandle." These and other innovations quickly led to the Model 1911, a single-action, semiautomatic, magazine-fed, recoil-operated pistol chambered in .45 ACP (Automatic Colt Pistol).

The Model 1911 pistol was the result of a search for a suitable self-loading pistol that would replace the variety of revolvers then in service. Designed by John Browning (1855–1926), this gun came to be after the need for a new and more powerful semiautomatic pistol became clear to the U.S. military when American units fought Moro guerrillas during the Philippine-American War (1899–1902). The U.S. forces were using the then-standard Colt Model 1892 revolver chambered in .38 Long Colt. The Moros frequently used drugs to numb themselves to pain, and the .38 Long Colt cartridge didn't have enough knockdown power to stop them. Also, the revolver was slower to reload than new semiautomatic pistols. The U.S. Army briefly reverted to using the Model 1873 single-action revolver in the .45 Colt; its heavier bullet was more effective against charging tribesmen, but there was better pistol technology becoming available. This prompted then–chief of ordnance, General William Crozier, to authorize further testing for a new service pistol.

In 1906 this search for a better handgun led to military test trials. Six firearms manufacturing companies submitted pistols. Of the six, three were eliminated early on, leaving a Savage, Colt, and DWM (a German arms manufacturer) chambered in .45 ACP cartridge. These three handguns still needed tweaks, but only Colt and Savage resubmitted their designs. Field tests from 1907 to 1911 were held to decide between the Savage and Colt designs. Six thousand rounds were fired from single Colt and Savage pistols over the course of two days. When the guns began to grow hot, they were simply immersed in water. The Colt passed with no reported malfunctions, while the Savage designs had thirty-seven.[11] The Colt Model 1911 was then adopted by the U.S. Army on March 29, 1911, thus gaining its designation, Model 1911. It was adopted by the U.S. Navy and Marine Corps in 1913.

Originally manufactured only by Colt, the Model 1911 was in such high demand in World War I that it was also manufactured in the government-owned Springfield Armory, making it yet another civilian invention that was picked up and manufactured by contract by the U.S. government.

The Model 1911 pistol was subsequently widely copied. It quickly became popular with civilian shooters in competitive events. Soon full sized and compact variants were made available for civilians as carry guns. The Model 1911 would serve as the standard-issue side-arm for the U.S. Armed Forces from 1911 to 1985. In total, the U.S. military bought around 2.7 million Model 1911 and 1911A1 pistols. The Model 1911 was replaced by the 9mm Beretta M9 pistol as the standard U.S. sidearm, but due to its popularity, the Model 1911 has not been completely phased out.[12]

After going through this history, Phil points me to another part of the museum and says, "The next big leap forward came from civilians working for a private aeronautics company."

We stop in front of display cases showcasing the AR-15 and its relations. These firearms are what many in the media now call "assault weapons." This deserves a clarification, as the media often interchange the terms "assault weapon" and "assault rifle." According to Bruce H. Kobayashi and Joseph E. Olson in the *Stanford Law & Policy Review*, "Prior to 1989, the term 'assault weapon' did not exist in the lexicon of firearms." "Assault weapon" is a political term developed by antigun advocates to convince people that some guns are too, well, scary, effective, ergonomic, or something, for U.S. citizens to own. The technical term "assault rifle" includes full-auto military firearms such as the M4A1 carbine. The AR-15 is not an assault rifle—it's not full-auto; it's semiautomatic (when you pull the trigger, it goes *bang* once). "AR" doesn't stand for "assault rifle." It stands for the first two letters of the original manufacturer's name: ArmaLite Corporation. AR-15s can't be configured to be fully automatic. Assault rifles, being full-auto machine guns, are already heavily restricted.

The term "assault weapon" is a relative term used by some to include a growing number of firearm makes and models some want to ban. To see how this century-plus-old technology suddenly became a target for antigun groups and politicians, we need to look back to the late 1980s. In 1988, antigun activist Josh Sugarmann, who was the communications director for the National Coalition to Ban Handguns and is currently the executive director and founder of the Violence Policy Center (VPC), recommended that gun-control groups use public ignorance and fear to ban everything they can stuff into the phrase "assault weapon" when he wrote, "Assault weapons ... are a new topic. The weapons' menacing looks, coupled with the public's confusion over fully automatic machine guns versus semi-automatic assault weapons—anything that looks like a machine gun is assumed to be a machine gun—can only increase the chance of public support for restrictions on these weapons.... Efforts to restrict assault weapons are more likely to succeed than those to restrict handguns."[13] Rich Lowry, editor of *National Review*, has rightly called the term "assault weapon" a "manufactured term."[14]

The political shift to dubbing these semiautomatic rifles "assault weapons" led to the 1994 Assault Weapons Ban (a federal law that expired in 2004) and to state bans, such as those in California, Connecticut, and New York. Public education from the NRA and many other gun-rights groups—including the fact that such firearms are rarely used in crimes—has made it politically difficult to pass another federal ban on "assault weapon" semiautomatic rifles. According to FBI crime statistics, only 2.5 percent of murders were committed by a killer using a rifle in 2011. AR-15-type rifles make up an even smaller fraction of that percentage.[15] Almost four times as many murderers used knives (323 used rifles whereas 1,694 used knives or another sharp object in 2011) to kill someone. Also, the data show that the number of people shot and killed with semiautomatic "assault weapons" didn't change appreciably during the ten-year period (1994–2004) that those firearms were banned from being sold.[16] Specifically, reports submitted by state and local law-enforcement agencies to the FBI and published annually in its "Uniform Crime Reports" indicate that firearms-related murders and the non-negligent manslaughter rate per 100,000 people decreased from 6.6 for 1993 to 3.6 for 2000. The rate held steady at 3.6 for 2001 and fluctuated thereafter between a high of 3.9 in 2006 and 2007 and was a low 3.2 in 2010 and 2011.[17] No matter how someone plays with these statistics, they don't show any correlation with the 1994–2004 ban.

Actually, the true story behind the invention of this class of firearms is very American.

"The AR-15, and its offspring the M16, got their start in an American aeronautics company. Some smart engineers wanted to use new materials and technology to make guns for the public," says Phil. "Soon after World War II, one of the most remarkable conversations in the history of the American gun is said to have taken place when an aeronautical engineer named George Sullivan spoke with a Brussels-based arms dealer named Jacques Michault. Michault entertained Sullivan with stories about the Germans' making lighter guns faster from stamped parts. This made Sullivan realize that guns could benefit from the aviation industry's use of new materials and manufacturing techniques. Sullivan, who was a self-described gun nut, understood that guns were still largely stuck in the nineteenth century—they still had heavy wood stocks and blocky, machined steel parts. He saw a huge opportunity."

A few years later, in 1953, Sullivan convinced the Fairchild Engine and Aircraft Corporation to establish a division that would invent gun designs by utilizing new materials and manufacturing processes then being perfected for airplanes.[18] Sullivan met Paul S. Cleveland, Fairchild's corporate secretary, at a meeting of an aircraft industry committee and discussed using new materials to bring guns up to date. Cleveland took this idea to Richard S. Boutelle, Fairchild's president and a long-time gun enthusiast. Boutelle loved the idea and hired Sullivan to create a branch of the company that would develop space-age small arms.

Sullivan named the Fairchild subsidiary "ArmaLite." The division became known as "George's Backyard Garage" and was located in Hollywood, California.[19] The idea was that Sullivan would create gun prototypes by utilizing lightweight, modern alloys and plastics that the company would then license to firearms manufacturers. The initial plan was to produce sporting firearms for the commercial market. They hoped that some of the concepts would eventually be used by the military. Shortly after Fairchild established its ArmaLite division, ArmaLite was invited to submit a rifle to the U.S. Air Force as a replacement for the then-standard survival rifle. ArmaLite submitted the .22 AR-5, which was adopted and designated the MA-1 Survival Rifle, but few were made, as the gun fell out of favor.

Nevertheless, the initial success with the AR-5 led Fairchild to reverse strategy and focus on the military market. The decision to forgo the average consumer for the military turned out to be a great miscalculation. But at the time, Fairchild was flush with revenue from other parts of its vast business. For a while this enabled Sullivan to experiment freely without worrying about making a profit.

As he developed new gun designs, Sullivan brought his experimental firearms to the Topanga Canyon Shooting Range for testing. This led to the next fortuitous meeting that would change the future of the gun. At the range, Sullivan happened to see Eugene Stoner, a former U.S. Marine who had served in Aviation Ordnance during World War II, shooting what looked to be a homemade rifle. Stoner was then a design engineer making dental plates. Sullivan and Stoner started talking. Before long, Stoner joined Sullivan's team as chief engineer for ArmaLite.[20]

For the next five years, almost all ArmaLite's activity was focused on developing military firearms. Stoner had been working on small arms independently since World War II, and his patents formed the basis of much of ArmaLite's work. From the beginning, another man, Charles Dorchester, directed and coordinated all development programs, first as general manager of the ArmaLite Division of Fairchild, later as president of ArmaLite, Inc. The combined efforts of these three individuals quickly resulted in revolutionary changes in combat-weapon concepts.

In 1955 ArmaLite submitted a gun design, the AR-10, devised by Stoner but based on Sullivan's concepts using anodized aluminum, a plastic butt stock, and other materials, to the U.S. Army. The army was then searching for a new service rifle. The AR-10 looked like the later AR-15 and then M16, but the AR-10 used the larger 7.62 mm chambering, a .30-caliber cartridge used by NATO. The chambering wasn't novel, but the AR-10 was a modern, modular-looking rifle, using space-age materials. The AR-10 might have looked awkward at first, but it lightly fit into a person's shoulder and pointed well. It also weighed 7.25 pounds without a magazine—about two pounds lighter than the M14 it was competing with.

The army, however, was skeptical. *Time* magazine profiled the AR-10 and called it a new "aluminum rifle" produced "at no cost to the taxpayer" and said the rifle "gave promise of being superior."[21] At the time, the Springfield Armory was still making guns for the U.S. military, as it had since George Washington founded it. Sure, civilian gun designers had always collaborated with the armory and often pushed new designs into the hands of soldiers and citizens alike, but if this rifle was accepted, it could mean the end to the armory, as the armory was counting on making the M14 and didn't have the know-how to make plastic stocks and rifles with anodized aluminum parts. Some of the U.S. Army's leadership were also reportedly turned off by ArmaLite's media blitz.[22]

The AR-10 didn't win a military contract for these and other reasons; however, in 1955, U.S. Army Colonel Henry Nielsen and General Willard Wyman got together and discussed the possibility of the AR-10 being chambered in a lighter caliber to truly make it a rifle for the future. Both were intrigued with the potential of this new rifle design. So intrigued that in 1956 both Nielsen and Wyman visited Stoner at ArmaLite to discuss the idea of chambering the AR-10 in a cartridge that would shoot a .22-caliber, 55-grain bullet at 3,250 feet per second at the muzzle.[23]

Stoner went to work and soon developed the AR-15, a lighter, 5.56 mm version of the AR-10. More military trials came as Wyman found ways to give the AR-15 a chance to win a military contract in 1957. Meanwhile, the secretary of the U.S. Army, Wilber Brucker, announced the adoption of the M14 as the new service rifle. The M14 had gone through years of manufacturing delays and bureaucratic problems but was finally ready for full production. Meanwhile, both Wyman and Nielsen, ArmaLite's biggest fans, retired in 1958. After more machinations from the military's bureaucracy, and after ArmaLite's parent company, Fairchild Engine and Aircraft Corporation, hit hard times financially, a decision was made to unload ArmaLite. In January 1959 the AR-15's design and manufacturing rights were sold to Colt for the rock-bottom price of $75,000 and a 4.5 percent royalty on future sales.

Colt's experienced firearms engineers went to work and quickly tweaked the AR-15's design—the biggest change they made was relocating its charging handle from under the carrying handle to the rear of the receiver. Colt then started a public-relations campaign that knocked the M14 for being too old school as they talked up the benefits of the lighter AR-15. The AR-15, with its lighter .223-caliber round, gave an infantryman the ability to carry as much as three times the amount of ammo as a soldier carrying an M14 chambered in .308 Winchester. The original AR-15 also weighed less than 6 pounds without a magazine, whereas the M14 weighed on average 9.2 pounds when empty.

Phil says, "A lot of people thought of the .223 as a varmint round. These people didn't think the AR-15's chambering in the puny .223 cartridge was a good choice for the military, as the lighter caliber wouldn't have the same stopping power as a .30-caliber round."

An article in *American Rifleman* in 1959 reported that "[c]aliber reduction is in line with past development. Adoption of a breech-loading rifle by the United States brought a reduction in caliber from .58 to .50 and then to .45, and adoption of smokeless powder brought a further reduction to .30. Each of these steps was accompanied by a marked increase in effective range and power. However, further caliber reduction would entail a marked reduction in range and power."[24]

The shift to the much smaller .223 cartridge almost derailed the AR-15 and might have if it wasn't for its success in the coming Vietnam War. This caliber choice is still hotly debated. As Phil tells me all this in the National Firearms Museum, a U.S. Border Patrol agent standing nearby interjected, "The .223 is proven. It's a high-velocity round that lets you stay on target longer to make multiple hits."

The U.S. military still considers chambering its standard-issue rifles in a heavier caliber as bullet designs and propellants evolve. To see what a touchy topic this is, try raising it at any gun range, military or private, and you'll run into sound, passionate, and entrenched positions from every guy who calls himself a rifleman. Phil points out that pretty soon *American Rifleman* was also praising the AR-15's attributes. In its May 1962 issue, *American Rifleman* reported: "It is not at all impossible to conceive of such a small bore military rifle. The United States Navy rifle was a 6 mm. (.236) for a number of years following 1895. Studies were made by most nations, including the United States, of cal. .22 military cartridges, sometimes even smaller. Rifles of cal. 6.5 mm. (.256) were adopted by several nations before the beginning of this century. The fact that they were adopted by very few major military powers, and even by those users were not considered fully successful in the test of World War II, need not prevent renewed consideration of small bores under requirements of the present."

Though the NRA and conservatives in the U.S. military were still somewhat critical of a "varmint round" being used by the U.S. military, support for the AR-15 gained traction during weapons testing. In 1963 the U.S. military finally ordered eight-five thousand AR-15s for the army and nineteen thousand for the air force.[25] On July 1, 1964, the U.S. military ceased production of the M14. Soon, the full-auto military version of the AR-15 was dubbed the M16. It would become the iconic gun of the Vietnam War.

Colt had already begun selling semiautomatic AR-15s to U.S. consumers in 1963. The November 1964 issue of *American Rifleman* reported, "A semi-automatic model of the Colt AR-15 cal. .223 (5.56 mm.) automatic rifle is now offered by Colt's. Designated Colt AR-15 Sporter, it is made for semi-automatic use only, its magazine has a removable spacer which limits capacity to 5 rounds, and its bolt carrier assembly has a Parco-Lubrite finish. In other respects, it is the same as the AR-15 automatic military rifle produced by Colt's for the Army and Air Force."

The article further explained, "Design of this sporter is such that parts required for fully-automatic fire cannot be installed, and the Alcohol and Tobacco Tax Div., Internal Revenue Service, U.S. Treasury Dept., does not consider the rifle a 'Firearm' in the machine gun category."

Fast-forward a half century and we find American gun enthusiasts in an AR craze. According to the research firm Southwick Associates, Inc., in 2012 one in five rifles sold was chambered in .223—most of these are AR-15-type rifles. Today the AR-15 and its variations are manufactured by a long and growing list of companies. ARs are popular with civilians and law enforcement around the world because they're accurate, light, portable, and modular. Its design also allows it to be accessorized. A civilian can buy after-market sights, vertical forward grips, lighting systems, night-vision devices, laser-targeting devices, muzzle brakes/flash hiders, bipods, and more, making the AR the most versatile rifle platform. It's also easy to shoot and has little recoil, making it popular with women.

The AR-15 is so user-friendly that a group called "Disabled Americans for Firearms Rights," which has about twenty thousand members, says the AR-15 makes it possible for people who can't handle a bolt-action or other rifle type to shoot and protect themselves. Also, its .223 caliber makes it safer to use as a home-defense gun because this lighter caliber is less likely to travel through walls.

Phil adds, "Politicians who say the AR-15 is a 'weapon of war' that civilians shouldn't be allowed to own are ignorant of our history or are lying. Historically, Americans have always owned similar gun types to those used in the military. Besides, semiautomatic AR-15s for sale to civilians are internally different from the full-automatic M16. Sure they look similar, but their hammer and trigger mechanisms are different designs. The bolt carrier and internal lower receiver of semiautomatic versions are even milled differently so that their firing mechanisms can't be interchanged."

Phil leads me to the vault located beneath the National Firearms Museum and we handle American guns from every era. As he gives me this hands-on lesson, he says, "The mainstream media doesn't tell this important story about guns and our freedom. Sure, many of them don't know it—why would they, as it's not taught. But the thing is, they're also not curious enough to ask. This leads me to conclude they'd rather the American people didn't know this history. When people understand the gun's link to freedom they tend ... [to cherish] their right to keep and bear arms, a freedom men and women fought and died for here and on foreign battlefields."

It's a freedom that's at risk today, even as gun technology continues to advance in ways that can benefit not only the U.S. military but the individual American citizen, as we'll see.

CHAPTER TWO

The Rifle Grows a Brain

When I was a sniper I always critically considered new technologies. They can offer a lot of benefits, but their capabilities can often be over-hyped. I do, however, see digital shooting systems as the future of small arms.

—Steve Adelmann, a retired SOF operator who spent twenty-two years in the U.S. Army and who currently owns Citizen Arms

"**S**o this is the future of the gun?"

"Of the rifle anyway," says Paul Merz, plant manager of Remington Arms' factory in Ilion, New York, as he nods at a dusty glass display showcasing the Remington 2020, a shooting system that can make long-range marksmanship video-game easy. Remington has a website that says its 2020 is "The Only Scope That Lets You See the Future."[1] Seeing it here, in this out-of-the way spot in America's oldest gun factory, is like finding Buck Rogers's rocket pistol in your grandfather's gun cabinet.

I laugh at this juxtaposition of past and future.

Paul shrugs at my apparently incongruous laughter and tries to impress me with the seriousness of this technology by saying very slowly, "The Remington 2020 is a video shooting system with a built-in ballistics computer that combines readings from a laser rangefinder, three gyroscopes, accelerometers, and temperature and air-pressure sensors to calculate a shooting plan."

His engineer voice is so monotone serious that I really have a hard time stopping myself from laughing. And regardless, I know all this. I also know this is just the beginning of what's happening right now with firearms technology. The truth is gun innovations are just starting to make a tentative but nevertheless giant leap into the digital age. Meanwhile, gun-control advocates haven't a clue what's going on. I ask Paul to open the display case.

Paul's eyes twinkle. He pulls a dungeon-master-sized set of keys from his pocket. As he tries one key, then another, he brags he can unlock anything in this aged industrial complex of brick buildings. I find this almost as astonishing as the shooting system behind the dusty glass. This multi-level series of brick buildings is filled with row after row of humming computer numerical controlled (CNC) machines and grating, pounding, half-a-century-old, grease-stained lathes and barrel reamers. Located near Utica in upstate New York, this old soot-soiled factory is the beating heart of Ilion and nearby Mohawk. It's America's oldest factory that still makes its original product—guns. In October of 2013, about 1,400 employees were making 4,900 guns per day in this factory.

They've been making guns here for a long time. This factory is right where Eliphalet Remington began the company as E. Remington and Sons in 1816. Upstate New York used to manufacture everything from guns to typewriters to bicycles—in fact, all of those were made in this factory. Many of the redbrick factories still frame the edges of towns in New York and southern New England, but their windows are shattered, the roofs are falling in, and their smoke stacks haven't belched in generations. Remington has outlived almost all of them. This place has kept making its increasingly politically incorrect products through almost two centuries. And it hasn't stopped innovating. This factory now makes Marlin lever-action rifles, Bushmaster AR-15s, and Model 1911 pistols. Some of their designs are at the pinnacle of firearms innovation, others are age-old designs made for hunters and shooters who are nostalgic for walnut stocks and blued metal.

Started when James Madison was president of the United States, the factory has grown into a complex series of buildings and floors that would give an architect an anxiety disorder. You can walk from one building to another and change floors without using stairs or an elevator or even getting the notion you're going up or down. The Remington Arms factory is not only an architectural marvel, it is a working museum and a state-of-the-art manufacturing facility—within its walls one can witness the past, present, and future of the gun. Business remains brisk; Remington invested about $20 million in this factory between 2011 and 2013. It is one of the few businesses still thriving in upstate New York, and the work here pays well: In 2012 the average Remington employee made $47,000. Meanwhile, in Herkimer County, where Ilion is located, the median home price was just $92,300, according to the U.S. Census Bureau.

While touring the factory, I can't help but think that this was what New York was like when it was at the center of the American Industrial Revolution. The state, of course, has since lost most of its machine shops and manufacturers to states with lower taxes and to countries with cheaper labor. Remington has stubbornly stayed on.

It's kept alive by military contracts for sniper rifles, by orders for Model 870 pump-action shotguns from police departments and other government entities, and from a long list of firearms sold to millions of hunters and shooters who've nostalgically nicknamed Remington "Big Green."

It has also benefitted from the efforts of New York state to keep the factory in Ilion and see off rival states that have tried to lure it away. It's not uncommon for states to use tax breaks, grants, loans, and other economic incentives to keep jobs within their borders, but it can be controversial when those companies make guns.[2] For example, in January 2013—a month after the Newtown shooting put "assault weapons" back in the news—the Maine Center for Public Interest Reporting dug into tax records and found that five companies that make semiautomatic firearms had received more than $19 million in tax breaks in the last few years.[3] This $19 million figure didn't just go to Remington. Kimber, which makes rifles and pistols in Yonkers, received $700,000 from Empire State Development in 2009. And a Lewis County–based company called Otis Products, which makes gun-cleaning equipment, received $2.2 million from the state and the local industrial development agency, according to the Maine group.

Even New York's antigun politicians help Remington when it's politically beneficial to them. In March 2011 New York's senior U. S. senator, Democrat Charles Schumer, boasted on his website that he had "joined Remington officials and plant employees to announce that Bushmaster Firearms is relocating a manufacturing facility from Windham, Maine, to Ilion, NY, bringing over forty new jobs to Central New York in the process. Schumer has been a long-time supporter of manufacturing at the Remington plant, urging top army officials to open up competition for the army's small arms contracts to other U.S. manufacturers and domestic producers across the country like the Ilion, New York-based Remington. Today, Schumer applauded

Remington's decision to add new jobs to the productive and capable work force already making the factory an economic powerhouse in the Mohawk Valley."[4]

Bushmaster makes AR-15s, which Schumer calls "assault weapons" and wants to ban nationally, but no one in the mainstream media accuses him of hypocrisy.[5] Liberal politicians like Schumer support gun industries for supplying jobs, but they, along with liberal pundits and bureaucrats, are simultaneously the gun industries' most dangerous menace. For instance, after sociopath Adam Lanza took a Bushmaster AR-15 into Sandy Hook Elementary in December 2012 and murdered twenty children and six adults, the California State Teachers' Retirement System, which then held a 2.4 percent interest in Remington Outdoor Company (ROC), pressured ROC's owner, Cerberus Capital, a private-equity firm located in New York City, to put Remington and its other gun companies up for sale.

The political vulnerability of ROC—Remington, Marlin, Bushmaster, DPMS, Barnes Bullets, and many more gun and ammo companies—prompted former New York governor Eliot Spitzer to publish a column at Slate.com saying, "While Cerberus, whose array of holdings is vast, is generally immune to public pressure and the opprobrium of trafficking in products that while legal may be marketed in a loathsome way, Cerberus would not be immune to pressure brought by its own investors.... Cerberus' investors are indirect owners of Bushmaster, the company that made the weapon that brought evil to Newtown, Conn. It is time to determine pension fund by pension fund who has invested in Cerberus and bring pressure on those investors either to get out of Cerberus or have Cerberus change the way it runs the gun industry."[6]

Spitzer has always been a political opportunist with red-light-district ethics. Perhaps the most obnoxious hit came from John MacIntosh, formerly a partner with a global private equity firm. He wrote a mean-spirited op-ed for CNN that called for then–New York City mayor Michael Bloomberg, billionaire George Soros, and others to pay "'whatever it takes' to acquire control of [ROC]" and then, if a "'moral turnaround'" of the gun companies isn't feasible, to commit "corporate euthanasia" of Remington, Marlin, Bushmaster, and all the rest. He seemed to think the U.S. military, law-enforcement agencies, hunters, and millions of other gun owners would be better off buying guns and ammo from foreign manufacturers than from the men and women in New York state.

New York governor Andrew Cuomo responded to Newtown with what he calls the "toughest gun control in the nation." It actually might be the stupidest. Cuomo rushed to be the first governor to use the massacre at Sandy Hook Elementary to massively restrict gun rights, and he got his way. The hastily written SAFE Act passed the New York State Senate on Monday, January 14, 2013, and the State Assembly on Tuesday, January 15. Cuomo signed the bill into law a half hour after it passed the legislature.

The next Saturday (January 19, 2013) thousands of gun owners gathered in Albany, the state's capital, to protest. Though they were too late, the pushback has since been unprecedented. At least fifty-two of New York's sixty-two counties passed official resolutions in direct opposition to the New York SAFE Act—some of these counties directed their law-enforcement officials not to enforce the SAFE Act. More than 325 local municipalities throughout New York voiced public opposition to the law. The New York State Sheriffs' Association issued a letter criticizing the law. The sheriffs noted, "The new definition of assault weapons is too broad, and prevents the possession of many weapons that are legitimately used for hunting, target shooting and self defense." Dozens of organizations, including sportsman's clubs, the American Legion, the New York State Association of County Clerks, the New York State Association of Psychiatric Rehabilitation

Services, the New York State Conservation Council, the U.S. Department of Veterans Affairs, and others, publicly denounced the law.

If the breadth of this opposition from New Yorkers surprises you, it is worth noting that New York state isn't all skyscrapers and Manhattan scenes seen from *Seinfeld* episodes. By size New York state is thirtieth among the fifty states. By population it is third. By population density it is seventh. In 2012 New York state's population was estimated to be 19,570,261, of which 8,336,697 live in New York City (NYC). That means 42 percent of New York state's population lives in New York City. Millions more live in the metropolitan areas around NYC, anchoring New York state in deep-blue political waters. But upstate New York is different. More than 581,000 New York residents hunt deer each year. Gun ownership is common upstate.

Cuomo rushed through the SAFE Act because he didn't want opposition from upstate, as well as from a lot of freedom-loving citizens in the downstate metropolitan areas, to galvanize. Instead of looking for real solutions by getting recommendations from police, citizens, gun company employees, and more to see how the state could better stop bad guys from getting and using firearms, Cuomo shoved an ideological, antigun-rights package through the legislature; as a result, some of his law's mistakes quickly required amendments and postponements, while still more are clearly unconstitutional. Among the mistakes in the hastily written law was a provision that barred police officers from carrying their pistols (the legislature ended up passing an exemption for law enforcement). Another provision (now postponed) tried to force buyers of ammunition to undergo FBI background checks (illegal under federal law). Another part of the law so strictly limited magazine sizes (to seven rounds) that it would have amounted to a de facto ban on most popular handguns. In *District of Columbia v. Heller* (2008), the U.S. Supreme Court reaffirmed that the Second Amendment protects commonly owned firearms. So

Cuomo and his allies tweaked the law to allow New York residents
to have ten-round magazines but stipulated they could only load seven
rounds into a magazine unless they "are at an incorporated firing
range or competition, in which case you may load your magazine to
its full capacity." On December 31, 2013, Judge William M. Skretny
of the U.S. District Court for the Western District of New York issued
a decision invalidating the SAFE Act's requirement that magazines be
loaded with no more than seven rounds. Judge Skretny determined
the seven-round limit to be "arbitrary" and noted that because the
law allowed for possession of ten-round magazines, the limit could
"disproportionately affect law-abiding citizens." As this book was
being written, this decision was being appealed.

Incredibly, the SAFE Act even gives "licensed clinical social workers" the power to anonymously report someone they think should
have their guns taken away. The state police are then required to use
the information provided to determine if the person has, or has applied
for, a firearms license or has a registered "assault weapon." If the
person in question has such a license or firearm, the state police will
relay that information to the "local firearms licensing official, who
must either suspend or revoke the license." Law enforcement will
likely then use a search warrant to seize the firearms in question. This
portion of the law also includes immunity from civil liability for the
social worker, nurse, or other designated person who decides a gun
owner can't be trusted with his Second Amendment rights. All that is
done without even a court hearing. Why a constitutional right should
be left to the whim of some anonymous and unaccountable person
will take a very creative lawyer to explain if the legal challenge to this
law reaches the U.S. Supreme Court.

Of course, all that is just the beginning. The SAFE Act also broad-
ens the already-erroneous use of the phrase "assault weapon" to
include a lot of popular, commonly owned, and American-made rifles,

handguns, and shotguns that are semiautomatic. To accomplish this, the SAFE Act replaces a "two features" test the state previously used with a "one feature" test. Rifles that are semiautomatic, with a detachable magazine, and that have at least one of the following characteristics are banned: a folding or telescoping stock; a pistol grip; a thumbhole stock; a second handgrip or a protruding grip that can be held by the nontrigger hand; a bayonet mount; a flash suppressor, muzzle break, or muzzle compensator; and a lot of other cosmetic features. Ask for the wrong customization on your Ruger 10/22 and you could break the law in the state of New York.

The SAFE Act uses similar criteria to ban shotguns as "assault weapons." As a result, it actually bans Remington's Model 1100 shotgun—a gun first sold in 1962 that has since been very popular with hunters and clays shooters—if the shotgun has a thumbhole or pistol-grip stock. Will this ban really reduce the murder rate? What crime studies show that semiautomatic shotguns are a crime weapon of choice?

The law also uses a list of features to ban pistols the state now considers to be "assault weapons." More than forty of the firearms made in Ilion can't be purchased by the people who make them. They can be manufactured there, the state can tax their sale, but the guns must be sold in another state or country.

This is fodder for higher courts because, as the Supreme Court made clear in *District of Columbia v. Heller*, the arms protected by the Second Amendment are those weapons "of the kind in common use ... for lawful purposes like self-defense." In fact, applying this "common use" test, *Heller* struck down the District of Columbia's handgun ban. This makes the SAFE Act very vulnerable to a court challenge that in early 2014 was being led by the New York State Rifle & Pistol Association (NYSRPA) and backed by the National Rifle Association (NRA).

The SAFE Act also bans undefined categories of firearms, such as those that are "a semiautomatic version of an automatic rifle, shotgun or firearm," but it doesn't say what a "semiautomatic version" is. Does this only ban semiautomatic firearms made by manufacturers that also make automatic firearms with similar designs? If so, what designs or features constitute their ban? The only way Remington Arms, which makes semiautomatic and automatic firearms (for the U.S. military) in Ilion, could answer such questions is by speculating. The Due Process Clause of the Fourteenth Amendment was written and passed to protect us from having to speculate about such things.

Also, the law orders gun owners to discard or permanently modify "high-capacity" magazines, but it never explains how such magazines can be legally modified. This leaves gun owners in jeopardy of being found guilty of a felony at the discretion of any given judge—a felony that would take away their Second Amendment rights for life. These and many other undefined areas of this law leave gun owners and dealers guessing what is legal and what is a felony. This potentially turns manufacturers and individuals who think they're following the law into criminals.

If Cuomo had simply stepped into any gun store in America, he would have seen that semiautomatic technology is not unusual or uncommon. The first successful design for a semiautomatic rifle is attributed to German-born gunsmith Ferdinand Ritter von Mannlicher, who unveiled the design in 1885.[7] The Model 85 was followed by other innovative semiautomatic rifles from Mannlicher. Although Mannlicher earned his reputation with his bolt-action rifles, he also produced a few semiautomatic pistols, including the Steyr Mannlicher M1894. A few years later, American gunsmith John Moses Browning developed the first successful semiautomatic shotgun, the Browning Auto-5. The Auto-5 was first manufactured in 1902 by Fabrique Nationale d'Herstal and sold in America under the Browning name.

In 1903 and 1905, the Winchester Repeating Arms Company introduced the first semiautomatic rimfire and centerfire rifles designed especially for the civilian market. Also, by the early twentieth century, several manufacturers had introduced semiautomatic .22 sporting rifles, including Winchester, Remington, Fabrique Nationale, and Savage Arms. In 1906, Remington Arms introduced the Remington Auto-loading Repeating Rifle. Remington advertised this rifle, renamed the "Model 8" in 1911, as a sporting rifle.

Today, semiautomatic firearms account for about 20 percent of the estimated three hundred million privately owned firearms in the U.S. and this percentage is rising, as semiautomatics now make up about half of all new firearms bought in the United States—Americans bought about five million new semiautomatic firearms in 2012 alone.[8]

Semiautomatic firearms are not going away. But, fortunately for New Yorkers, large portions of the SAFE Act might be. Given the Heller and McDonald rulings, it is extremely likely that it will be found at least partly unconstitutional by the U.S. Supreme Court.

In December 2013, after a year of weathering a political storm, George Kollitides, chairman and CEO of Remington Outdoor Company, sent his employees a memo stating that instead of selling the company (worth more than a billion dollars), he and others would buy out unhappy stockholders. David Keene, editorial page editor of the *Washington Times*, later told me, "Kollitides is trying to save a small town in New York. He could [sell or] move Remington, but it would kill that little town."

Saving the Remington plant in Ilion, New York, seems to me a tremendous thing, as Paul Merz, plant manager of the Remington Arms factory, finds the right key and slides open the glass case beneath which lie two historic rifles. One is a Remington Model 700, a bolt-action rifle first introduced in 1962. The other is a Bushmaster AR-15 developed in the late 1950s. Both rifles, however, have been brought into the future, topped with riflescopes packed with computerized brains that calculate shooting solutions.

I pick up the AR-15 and say, "So New York just banned this rifle—semiautomatic technology developed when the Wright Brothers were still fixing bicycles in Ohio—and," as I nod at the video scope, "this cutting-edge electronic gizmo that calculates long-range shooting solutions is still quite legal."

Paul shrugs and says, "More of those politicians really should visit our museum."

I hold the AR-15 up to my shoulder and look at its video scope, which is made by a Texas-based company named TrackingPoint. I'd first seen the Remington 2020 in January of 2013 at the SHOT Show (which stands for the "Shooting, Hunting, Outdoor Trade Show") in Las Vegas. After it was introduced, some pundits immediately began saying it's so scary it should be banned. Even *Field & Stream*'s rifles editor, David E. Petzal, is still making up his mind about this technology. David is arguably the top magazine writer on rifles today. He also cohosts a TV show on the Outdoor Channel called *Gun Nuts* and writes a blog by the same name. He told me, "My own personal feeling is these devices are going to be a PR catastrophe for hunters once the general media becomes aware of them."

Here's why he feels so strongly about this shooting system. The TrackingPoint's product is a video-screen scope (you don't look through its scope; instead you see a video image of what's downrange). It uses a laser rangefinder to measure the distance to the target and other instruments to measure temperature, barometric pressure, incline/decline, cant, air density, magnus effect drift (spin drift), target movement, and Coriolis effect drift from the spinning of the Earth.

The riflescope's computer then takes all that data and uses stored ballistic and firearm information including lock time, ignition time, rate and direction of barrel-rifling twist, muzzle velocity, and ballistic coefficient to calculate a shooting solution. Basically, the scope figures out where the rifle needs to be held for the bullet to hit the target.

To put all that in motion, the shooter places a "tag" on a target by centering a crosshair on it and pushing a red button located on top of the scope. The tag then starts the calculation, which is automatically updated fifty-two times per second. The scope calculates the ballistic solution and adjusts the image on the video screen with a digital zoom to compensate for yardage so the shooter can see the target clearly.

Now here's the cool-scary part. The system TrackingPoint sells directly—not the one sold on the Remington rifles—marries a rifle's trigger with the digital scope, so that when someone pulls the trigger, the rifle won't fire until the crosshair is precisely in line with the tag. This theoretically takes shooter error out of the equation. With a traditional rifle/scope, a marksman has to learn to breathe properly and to apply pressure to a trigger perfectly so that the gun goes off at precisely the right moment—even your heartbeat can make the rifle shake noticeably at extreme long range—but with TrackingPoint's system none of that matters. A novice can use this shooting system to hit targets placed ten football fields away with very little training.

Remington's 2020 is a little different. It has the same video scope and all that software, but it's not integrated with the rifle's trigger. With the Remington 2020, the rifle will still go *boom* even if the sight isn't perfectly aligned with the target that has been tagged. Instead, you still tag a target, but now the crosshair will go from blue to red when it's aligned with the tag. The shooter can still jerk the trigger, flinch, or make any number of other errors and thereby pull the shot. Still, the system—when all the data is properly input and the wind calculation is correct—can put a novice shooter on target at extreme long range with very little learning curve.

Bryce Towsley, a gun writer who reviews rifles and optics for *American Rifleman* and many other publications, told me: "I let my fifteen-year-old nephew try out the Remington 2020. He was on target so fast it shocked me. He's not an experienced long-range marksman; in fact, his mother is antigun. But he had no problem hitting ten-inch steel targets at three hundred yards. He said, 'Uncle Bryce, this is so easy. It's just like a video game.'"

TrackingPoint is a tech company formally located in Austin, Texas. Soon after these digital sighting systems were introduced, the company had so much media buzz that management decided to relocate to a bigger facility. So they took their then–one hundred employees to a forty-eight-thousand-square-foot building in nearby Pflugerville, Texas. TrackingPoint's new facility includes what they say will be the world's longest underground shooting range.

In mid-2013 TrackingPoint's former CEO, Jason Schauble (also a former Remington vice president), told me, "There are a number of people who say the gun shoots itself, but it doesn't. The shooter is always in the loop, as you have to tag a target and pull the trigger." Schauble is hard not to like. He's a former U.S. Marine captain who was wounded in Iraq. His right hand is partially paralyzed from being shot by an insurgent using an AK-47. He still wears black "kill bracelets" commemorating dead friends. While as of early 2014 a military contract was still eluding TrackingPoint, Schauble says, "From a patriotic standpoint and as a veteran, I would love every soldier to be better armed today, and this technology could get them there."

The founder and chairman of TrackingPoint is John McHale, a serial entrepreneur who has started several companies that were ultimately sold to Cisco, 3Com, and Compaq. Early in his career, he worked on weapons accuracy systems for tanks. The idea for

TrackingPoint came to McHale while he was on safari. He was frustrated by his inability to shoot a gazelle at three hundred yards. He decided the technology was now available to make a better sighting system for rifles, and he was just the entrepreneur to do it. Soon he hired John Lupher, whose electronics design firm, Austin Ventures, had designed software for Motorola's DVR box and Siemens' cordless handsets. Lupher at first thought McHale just wanted a rifle for personal use. He used a Remington Model 700 rifle and hooked it up to a laptop. It came together so well that Lupher jumped ship with eleven other employees to build "Precision Guided Firearms."

Schauble, given his experience at Remington, was hired to be CEO. They soon began using custom rifles from Surgeon Rifles in Prague, Oklahoma, and adding on their shooting system. Before long they were selling shooting systems, and the TrackingPoint was used to kill a wildebeest in South Africa at 1,103 yards.

The system wasn't perfect, but because the scope records video, customers were able to send in videos documenting their problems, which helped the company respond quickly. The main complaint was that some of the guns weren't accurate in extreme hot and cold temperatures, which the company addressed by tweaking the optical system.

Lupher told me at the SHOT Show in January of 2014 that "all new companies go through growing pains and a learning process," but that the company, while hoping for that elusive big government contract, is "finding ways to get our products into the hands of more people."

That is precisely what worries antigun activists. The idea that a psychopath with no shooting skills could become a lethal assassin using TrackingPoint technology is chilling—at least for people who don't know much about guns and who buy into marketing hype.

Long-range shooting is difficult even with TrackingPoint technology, because you need to establish a clear line of sight and the system can't automatically account for bullet wind drift. You have to toggle in an estimated wind drift. You can use a handheld device to gauge wind speed and direction, but real-world factors are still hard to overcome.

If, say, a rifle is chambered in .338 Lapua Magnum—some TrackingPoint rifles come in this caliber because it is a long-range caliber popular with Special Forces snipers—and is shooting a heavy and stable 250-grain MatchKing bullet, well, that bullet will still drift 12.2 inches at 500 yards from a light 10 mph crosswind and 57.1 inches at 1,000 yards from that same wind. You can use a toggle button to input wind speed into the scope, but winds are rarely consistent. Ridges, flats, and other terrain that hunters contend with when shooting at game over long distances have variable air currents and moisture contents that will push a flying bullet like turbulence pushes an airplane. In a military context, in urban fighting, there would be crosswinds from side streets, thermals rising from heating asphalt, and many other factors to challenge the best marksman.

At long range, any shooter would likely have only short windows of opportunity at a moving target. This makes it hard to "tag" a target and then make the shot. Also, the scope uses a laser rangefinder that needs a reflective target in order to achieve a reliable reading at long range. This is never a given. As a hunter I use laser rangefinders constantly. Even the best rangefinders need ideal conditions to work at ultra long range and often fail at moderate ranges. The TrackingPoint scope also uses an optical system with a digital zoom that can be hard to see in daylight and that gets even harder to see at long range.

For these reasons and others, while TrackingPoint's sophisticated system is a tremendous technological advance, it is not a clear and present danger to the public. An aspiring murderer would need about $25,000 to buy such a gun and then would need stable conditions, a unique opportunity, and a lot of expertise to reliably put rounds on a man-sized target at extreme long range.

———————

The Remington 2020 costs $5,000. That's a lot less than the TrackingPoint's price tag of $22,500 to $27,500, but it's more than a week in Saint Thomas. TrackingPoint introduced new price points at the 2014 SHOT Show, but the system is still very high-end. Obviously, average hunters and shooters won't buy many of these advanced rifle systems until they become more affordable, but as with most technological advances, that seems inevitable. Does that mean we ought to ban it? A lot of engineers, gun writers, and self-described gun nuts have been telling me the TrackingPoint is just one big step into an entirely new breakthrough—taking firearms technology into the digital age. The guns of the future are going to be lighter, more accurate, and ergonomic mechanical wonders. There is no reason to stop this progress, which will ultimately make firearms not only more effective but safer, as we'll see later.

At the Side Street tavern in Mohawk, I attend the late-afternoon happy hour, after Remington's first shift has left the factory. I order a beer from the twenty-one they have on tap and notice that the man on my right is wearing a t-shirt beneath an open jacket that says, "Cuomo Made Me a Criminal."

I ask, "How'd our governor make you a criminal?"

He takes a sip from a long-necked bottle of Bud and looks me over. After a long pause, he replies with a megaphone voice broadcast to attract an audience: "The Second Amendment enshrines my God-given right to tote my Remington." He pulls back his jacket. On his right hip around the side of a bulging stomach is a Model 1911 pistol. He says, "The state makes me get a concealed-carry permit to utilize a basic human right that's protected from government infringement by the Second Amendment. So I get their damn permission. I apply and get my permit," he growls as he turns to face me. "Took them a year to approve me even though I've never had more than a speeding ticket. They fingerprinted me and made me pay to use my rights. But okay, so I comply. Now Cuomo tells me I can only put seven bullets in this gun." He taps the pistol with his right hand as he holds his beer with his left. Men and women all around him are holding beers and smiling, enjoying the show. "If I load eight rounds of .45, I'm a criminal. That's how our governor made me a criminal."

I ask if he made the gun.

"No," he says, "but a friend made me this beauty."

"I was just in the factory and saw Bushmasters being made. Must be strange making semiautomatic guns you can't legally buy in this state."

A man beside him who has a gray beard and deep lines beneath brown eyes says, "Pisses us off. Remington has been making semi-autos for more than a century. Now they go and ban the most popular rifle type being sold today and they want us just to obey and pay taxes?"

Others weigh in and want to know who I am and where I come from, but I ignore the questions. Instead, I ask a group of guys at the bar, "What about micro-stamping? You think you should have to do that?"

"Those people running Albany are crazy," says the bartender as she puts a beer on the bar and scurries off.

"It would drive Remington from New York once and for all," says the man with the "Cuomo Made Me a Criminal" t-shirt.

Micro-stamping is a patented process that uses a micro-laser to engrave a firearm's make, model, and serial number on the tip of the gun's firing pin so that, in theory, it will imprint the information on a cartridge's primer. With a semiautomatic firearm, this info would theoretically be discharged on the cartridge case and maybe left at a crime scene. Sounds ingenious, but the trouble is it doesn't work in real-world manufacturing. Studies have found it's unreliable in the best conditions. A study done by the National Academy of Science determined that "[f]urther studies are needed on the durability of micro-stamping marks under various firing conditions and their susceptibility to tampering, as well as on the their cost impact for manufacturers and consumers."[9] A study done by the University of California at Davis said, "At the current time it is not recommended that a mandate for implementation of this technology be made. Further testing, analysis and evaluation is required."[10] The thing is, even if it works, it's expensive, and it can be removed with one swipe of a file. Criminals can be stupid, but this is a no-brainer. Nevertheless, some New York state legislators try every year to make micro-stamping mandatory for New York's gun manufacturers.

I ask about a shooting that took place just around the corner, at a barbershop, in March 2013. The gunman killed four people and wounded two others, including a man retired from Remington Arms. John Seymour, a barber who was shot twice by sixty-four-year-old Kurt Myers of Mohawk, was quoted saying from his hospital bed, "There's nothing wrong with guns. This is an unfortunate situation that happened in a small town where they happen to make a lot of guns. It gives people the wrong idea that guns are bad."[11]

"Crazy stuff can happen anywhere, even here in small-town America. People also drive drunk and smoke crack while pregnant and who the hell knows what else," says the man with the "Cuomo Made Me a Criminal" t-shirt.

Myers, who was broke and had maxed out his credit cards, had snapped. He used a shotgun to kill two customers at the barbershop. He then drove about a mile to Gaffey's Fast Lube in Herkimer and killed two more men. Myers then ran into an abandoned bar in Herkimer. Police killed him there in a shootout the next morning. The whole bloody thing rocked this area, a county that didn't have a single murder between 2001 and 2011.[12]

"Are you a reporter or something?" asks an older gentleman.

"Yeah, I'm here to report the truth about guns in America."

He rolls his eyes and says, "Reporters don't tell the truth about guns."

The evening wears on and the beers keep coming. Later another Remington employee tells me if he were there at Newtown, armed as he likes to be, "that Lanza kid wouldn't have had a chance."

Others condemn the murderer's late mother: "What kind of a mother gives a sick kid like Adam Lanza the combination to a gun safe?"

They'd like to know why the actions of such a clueless mother and her troubled son, a twenty-year-old diagnosed with Asperger's syndrome who kept a spreadsheet in his bedroom rating mass murders, should be used as an excuse to take away a constitutional right. And why should the actions of a psychopath be allowed to imperil America's oldest gun factory?

"Lanza's mother promised to buy him a CZ 83 semiautomatic pistol for Christmas," I add.

"At least it wasn't a Remington," one says.

The man with the "Cuomo Made Me a Criminal" t-shirt says, "Yeah, I heard that. She really had no clue what she was doing. If government wants to do some good, why don't they work with the NRA and teach gun-safety courses. That way maybe she'd have met people who would've taught her how to treat guns. What she did was like giving an alcoholic the keys to a car."

———————————

In the end, the Remington Outdoor Company finally decided that its new expansion wouldn't take place on its historic ground in Ilion, New York. Instead, the company bought the old Chrysler building in Huntsville, Alabama, where the company expected to create more than two thousand new jobs within a decade. CEO George Kollitides said, "Remington was careful about exploring all the options when considering what could be their home for our next 200 years." Then, in May 2014, Senator Schumer lost his "assault weapons" jobs. ROC announced it would be moving its Bushmaster rifle and Remington Model 1911 pistol production lines from its nearly two-hundred-year-old plant in Ilion to its new facility in much more gun-rights-friendly Huntsville. The future of the gun looks brighter in Alabama than it does in New York.

CHAPTER THREE

Technology Perfects the Pistol

The pistol took a giant leap into the future with the Glock 17. Polymer-framed pistols can now fit anyone's hands—an NFL player and a ballerina can often use the same pistol by just changing grips.
—Mark A. Keefe IV, editor of *American Rifleman*

The know-it-all voice from my GPS declares I've arrived at Beretta's factory in Accokeek, Maryland. I can't see how. I'm in a little parking lot with a single-chair barbershop on my right. On my left is a six-lane thoroughfare clogged with commuters on their way to Washington, DC.

As I dig for a paper map, a barber steps out of the little shop and asks, "You lookin' for Beretta?"

I nod, and he points with his scissors down what looks like a driveway, but a short minute later that tiny road takes me behind a grove of leafless oaks to a small reception area at the front of a modern gun factory. This facility employs more than three hundred people. They come in on three shifts to make semiautomatic handguns, machine guns, and shotguns. Just another minute passes before I'm in this bustling factory trying to hear Richard Grimes, Beretta's director of manufacturing operations, raise his voice over the steady hum of CNC (computer numerical controlled) machines: "We have three shifts working around the clock. The machines never stop making guns. Nevertheless we're having trouble keeping up with orders."

Beretta's factory is in suburban Maryland because of its contracts with the Pentagon. Beretta's Maryland factory started making M9 pistols for the military in 1987. In 2012 Beretta announced the U.S. Army awarded it another contract for up to one hundred thousand M9s. As of September 2012, more than six hundred thousand Beretta 9mm pistols had been delivered to the U.S. military since the late 1980s.[1]

Like many U.S. gun makers, Beretta's factory in Maryland makes guns for law-enforcement, the U.S. military, and civilians from the same CNC machines. Though the products Beretta makes are not politically palatable to the media elite, their guns are iconic to millions of Americans. Beretta shotguns are works of art that might be an over/under with a grainy walnut stock, blued metal, and engravings of a bird dog and maybe a pheasant on its receiver. Or it might be a semi-automatic Benelli (a Beretta-owned company that also manufactures in Maryland) with a carbon-fiber stock and inertia-driven action. In either case, the Beretta man stands with his back straight and the shotgun in the crook of his arm. He is wearing a shooting vest and shooting glasses. He has class. He is how James Bond would look if he went skeet shooting. He's sophisticated, but hardly a snob. He has what the Spanish call *duende*, a characteristic James Michener said is almost indefinable, as it means to have taste, refinement, beauty, perfection, and elegance all in just the right proportion and with no showiness at all.[2] He is what the Japanese mean when they use the word *shibui*, which is something a samurai tried to embody but only could manage in fleeting moments when life and art met before again separating with a bad gesture or misstep.

Naturally, the Beretta man isn't any more real than James Bond. But what archetype is? He's an American icon men want to be. He's an ideal never reached, but, if you do everything right, you might be him for just a manly moment when you shoot a perfect round and thereby master yourself. Beretta supplies guns and also fashion for the shooting man and woman.

Beretta was founded in 1526 and is still family owned. Matteo Recanatini, web and social media manager for Beretta in the United States, tells me, "The Beretta family approves every clothing design, every tweak to every firearm. They're conscious that the Beretta image is iconic, an ideal. Everything has to perfectly fit that image and to function flawlessly."

The Beretta man doesn't see firearms in a negative way. To him they're cool. To him they're a blast to shoot. To him (and increasingly her), semiautomatic guns have been the ultimate home-defense guns since they were first designed, more than one hundred years ago. To the Beretta man, using a firearm properly is a sign of responsibility, of maturity.

During my visit to Beretta's factory in Maryland, we stop by their underground gun range. They let me shoot a full-auto ARX-160, a gun Beretta makes for law enforcement and some militaries. This assault rifle is certainly a gun Ian Fleming would have had Bond use when the need arose (Bond carried a Beretta 418 semiautomatic pistol in the first five novels before he switched to a Walther PPK).

Shooting short bursts from it was pretty damn fun. That feeling, the feel of a gun smoothly operating as you handle it safely and well, is what drives gun sports; and it's something that many antigun advocates don't understand.

Grown men shoot in Cowboy Action competitions and so own six-guns and lever-action rifles. Americans hunt for deer and waterfowl and other animals and have specialized firearms for the job. Some men and women shoot AR-15s, semiautomatic shotguns, and pistols in 3-gun competitions. They see guns as a responsibility, as a means of self-defense, and as a tool—for competition and for hunting. More than one hundred million Americans now own guns, and surely most of them resent it when politicians treat them as criminals because they want to shoot recreationally and own guns to protect themselves and their families.

———————

Richard Grimes, Beretta's director of manufacturing operations, tells me he "can't find enough qualified engineers. Our engineering shop has literally tripled in size in the last few decades and America is no longer graduating enough engineers. All the new products and tweaks to the process take a lot of know-how from a lot of skilled engineers." Engineers have changed the way guns are manufactured. It used to be that every component of a gun was dependent on the skill of an individual worker. But now guns are made with simple interchangeable parts. Grimes lets me assemble a Beretta Px4 Storm Sub-Compact pistol. I don't own a Px4 and had never broken one down before. Nevertheless, I have no trouble assembling a pistol in a few minutes.

If the antigun fearmongers had their way, this development might never have happened. In the 1980s Glock quickly redefined the pistol with its series of polymer-framed, short recoil operated, locked-breech semiautomatics. Despite initial worries that a "plastic gun" would be fragile and unreliable—and propaganda from antigun groups that Glocks would be invisible to metal detectors at airports—police departments swiftly discovered the superiority of the Glock to their age-old revolvers. By 2007, Glock commanded 65 percent of the market share of handguns for U.S. law-enforcement agencies.[3]

The truth is Glock pistols, and all their competitors, still contain many vital components made of metal (such as the slide, barrel, and ammunition). They can be detected by conventional screening technologies, but the fear did lead to legislation (The Terrorist Firearms Detection Act), and in 1988 Congress banned the manufacture, import, or sale of any firearm with less than 3.2 oz of metal in it. In December 2013 Congress extended the ban for another ten years. The National Shooting Sports Foundation (NSSF), the trade association representing firearms manufacturers, backed the extension.

Glock's founder, engineer Gaston Glock, had no experience with firearm design or manufacture at the time his first pistol, the Glock 17, was being prototyped (before that he'd been making curtain rings). Glock did, however, have extensive experience in advanced synthetic polymers.[4] Glock also introduced ferritic nitrocarburizing into the firearms industry as an anticorrosion surface treatment for metal gun parts.

Glock got his start by competing for a military contract. In 1980, the Austrian military announced it was seeking a new, modern duty pistol to replace its World War II–era Walther P38.[5] The Austrian Ministry of Defence formulated a list of criteria for the new-generation service pistol. But Gaston Glock wanted to go beyond the basics. He assembled a team of handgun experts from military, police, and civilian sport shooting circles to define the most desirable characteristics of a combat pistol. Several samples of the prototype Glock 17 (so named because it was based on the seventeenth set of technical drawings) were submitted for trials in early 1982.

The Glock was revolutionary because its design and engineering improved the pistol's ease of maintenance and manufacture. Its extensive use of polymer made it lighter, and unlike most pistols then available, you didn't need a gunsmithing course to take one apart. It didn't have all the pins, springs, and lathed bits of steel many pistols were then using. The Glock's simple design made it easy to clean and maintain, and far from being less durable or reliable, it was more so.

The Glock 17 was adopted into service with the Austrian military and police forces in 1982 as the P80 (Pistole 80), with an initial order for twenty-five thousand guns.

By 2002 some two million Glocks had been sold in more than forty-five countries. In 2007 Glock passed the five million milestone.[6] Meanwhile, the Glock revolution influenced the designs and materials used by other pistol makers. Since the Glock takeover began in the 1980s, firearms have gotten both simpler and more sophisticated. The pistol Gaston Glock submitted to the Austrian military for testing weighed just twenty-three ounces, while the next lightest gun in the competition was a model from Heckler & Koch that weighed thirty-three ounces. The Glock 17 had only thirty-four components. The other pistols in consideration were much more complex—a Sig Sauer in the running had fifty-three parts; a Heckler & Koch had seventy-seven parts; a Beretta had seventy parts.[7]

The advances Gaston Glock made have continued. And Beretta is as much a beneficiary of these advances as any gun manufacturer.

When I interviewed Matteo Recanatini in December 2012, I asked him if labor costs or politics might prompt Beretta to move its factories to a more gun-friendly state. He told me, "Beretta is about five hundred years old and still strong because they invest in people. We have a skilled workforce here in this 'blue' state so we're staying and investing in the future."

That optimism was about to change.

<hr>

The day after I left Beretta's factory in Maryland, Adam Lanza, a twenty-year-old resident of Newtown, Connecticut, killed his mother before shooting his way into Sandy Hook Elementary. His evil actions ignited a national debate that would change the fortunes of many of America's gun makers and gun owners.

On February 9, 2013, a few months after the Newtown murders, Sarah Merkle, who was then a fifteen-year-old Maryland resident, was finishing her homework just before midnight. But something else was keeping her up too. She was upset that state legislators were considering a gun-control bill that might ban her Bushmaster AR-15. She knew there was a public hearing on the bill in Annapolis the next day. She went online and checked to see if there was an age limit for speakers. She didn't see one. Any person who signed up could get three minutes at the podium.

She thought about this. She'd been shooting since she was eight years old. She started with a shotgun. At eleven years old, she graduated to an AR-15. To do that she had to prove to her dad she could hold it. She'd been competing with the rifle ever since. Because of its light recoil, she thought of it as a "girl-friendly gun" and was rated "expert" with it. As a member of the Maryland Rifle Team, her next goal was to reach the "master" level, but this legislation might stop her from continuing to progress as a marksman and competitor.

It might also hurt her in other ways. She knew there were shooting scholarships at some colleges. The state might ban her dream of competing in shooting sports and trying for a rifle team scholarship. She was so wound up, she wrote a speech.

She finished around 2:00 a.m. and fell asleep. A few hours later, her alarm woke her for school. During breakfast she told her dad, Mike, she wanted to speak at the public hearing. She asked, "It's today. Can we go? I've written a speech and everything."

Her father knew better than to doubt her. When she was thirteen years old, he put her name forward as a good fit to be the secretary of the Maryland Rifle Club, a five-hundred-plus-member club that has one-hundred- and two-hundred-yard rifle ranges, handgun ranges, and more. It's one of those stalwart clubs that quietly trains people to be safe and responsible gun owners. The Maryland Rifle Club was founded in 1933. The official mission of the club is to encourage "organized rifle and pistol shooting among members of our community, with a view toward a better knowledge of the safe handling and proper care of firearms, as well as improved marksmanship." The club also decided its mantra should be to develop "honesty, good fellowship, self-discipline, team play and self-reliance which are the essentials of good sportsmanship, and the foundation of true patriotism."

At first the club leadership was skeptical about letting a thirteen-year-old be its secretary. But those who knew Sarah said they were sure she could handle the responsibility.

"I'm like really organized," says Sarah. "I keep everything sorted in separate folders on my computer. It's just easier when you know where everything is."

She convinced them, and they changed the club's bylaws to allow a person her age to fill the post. She's been reelected since. No one doubts her now. She keeps the minutes at the club's meetings, responds to emails, and handles club applications, among other duties. "I love doing it," she says, "but maybe I'll be too busy to keep it up later in high school or when I go to college or something. We'll see."

Bill Perry, the club president, knew Sarah could handle the job. Perry says, "A number of years ago, I think when she was eleven, I heard this girl screaming during a competition, 'Close the range. Close the range.' We shut down the range and then I see this little blonde girl running out onto the two-hundred-yard range. She stops next to one of the targets and picks up this little box turtle and moves it off the field. She saw the little thing and couldn't bear the thought that it might get shot. She's quite the girl."

Yeah, quite the girl. The whole country was about to find that out. Her father agreed to take her to the hearing. He would have to take the day off work. Her mother, Karen, was coming too. They decided to leave right away.

They arrived at 7:30 a.m. and had to wait until 8:00 a.m. for the doors to open. They were still waiting at 9:00 a.m. when the sign-up sheet to speak was brought out. "I was the second person in line, and by the time I left there was already quite a crowd behind me," says Sarah. "We had never been there before so we weren't sure how much time we really had, but by then we were all hungry so we headed down the street to find something to eat."

When they got back, a pro-gun rally at Lawyer's Mall was beginning to form around 11:00 a.m. They found out that the hearing in the Miller Senate House wouldn't begin until 1 p.m., so they decided to attend the rally.

Sarah began talking to people, and before she knew it she was being introduced to Republican Maryland state delegate Kathy Szeliga. "Szeliga liked what I had to say, so she put me up on the podium at the rally in front of what I was told to be a crowd of four thousand people," says Sarah.

Sarah spoke for a minute and finished by saying, "Martin O'Malley, you can't take my guns, you can't take my rights."

She left to cheers and weaved through the crowd to her parents. She still had to wait all afternoon and into the evening before she would get her three minutes at the podium in the Maryland State House, the oldest state capitol in continuous legislative use. It's also the only state house that served as the U.S. capitol. The Continental Congress met in the Old Senate Chamber from November 26, 1783, to August 13, 1784. Today, the Maryland State House is where the Maryland General Assembly convenes for three months each year. On February 6, 2013, Maryland's lawmakers had debated all afternoon—in the very place George Washington resigned his commission as commander of the Continental Army—whether to deny Marylanders their Second Amendment rights.

Sarah told me, "You only get three minutes so you have to stay on message and be careful with your words. If you get off topic at all you won't have a chance to say what you came to say. So I made sure I could say what had to be said in three minutes."

Of course, she didn't know her speech would go viral, getting more than three million views on YouTube after the Maryland Minutemen posted it, in March 2013. She simply wanted to use her First Amendment rights to defend her Second Amendment rights.

The room hushed as she read her speech: "I'm fifteen years old and I've been shooting for almost eight years. I've also been a part of the Maryland Rifle Club and Maryland State Rifle Team since I was eleven. Because of this, I have become eligible for various shooting scholarships around the country to a wide array of even the most prestigious colleges that have shooting teams. Achieving stricter gun-control laws would obliterate any opportunity I could've had to attend a decent college on a shooting scholarship. Ever since I first learned how to shoot, the issue with gun violence around the nation became clear; guns are not the problem, people are. Purging our society of violence and murder cannot be done through gun-control legislation. By signing this legislation you are not signing away gun violence but instead confiscating American citizens of our constitutional rights."

She continued: "You are not eliminating guns from society but eliminating our ability to protect our lives, liberty and pursuits of happiness. Chicago, Illinois, has had some of the strictest gun-control laws in America enacted for the past few years and it is currently more than twice as likely for you to be killed in Chicago as in the Afghani War. For the past eleven years and four months in the Afghani War, 2,166 people have been killed. Now, in only eight years in Chicago, 4,265 people have been killed and 3,371 of them were from being shot. Is that really something we want to model our state laws after?"

She finished her three-minute speech by saying, "To abolish or severely limit the right of the Maryland residents as a whole to bear arms, which is the intent of the proposed legislation, is to essentially defeat the purpose of our own U.S. Constitution. The entire foundation of the United States was formed on the principle that the government, our government, is a government of the people, for the people, by the people, and taking away the people's right to bear arms is taking away the people's power in the government. The Second Amendment, which grants citizens the right to secure their natural rights, is the backbone of our democratic American society."

She was too focused on her speech to remember if the legislators were sneering or simply baffled by the politically incorrect truth she was dishing out. Outside the legislature, her remarks resonated nationally. Millions watched her speech on YouTube, and she soon found herself on *Fox & Friends* being interviewed by Gretchen Carlson and on Sean Hannity's show on Fox News.

Nevertheless, on April 3 the Firearm Safety Act of 2013 (Senate Bill 281) received final approval in the House of Delegates by a 78 to

61 vote. On the House floor, the bill was made even worse as delegates stripped out a committee amendment that would have exempted active-duty military and veterans under age twenty-one from the handgun licensing and training requirements. The Maryland Senate passed the bill and Democrat governor Martin O'Malley signed the legislation. O'Malley said in a statement that the bill strikes "a balance between protecting the safety of law enforcement and our children, and respecting the traditions of hunters and law-abiding citizens to purchase handguns for self-protection." But Republican Maryland Senate minority leader E. J. Pipkin countered, "The fact is the Firearm Safety Act of 2013 provides no safety. It says, if you own guns, we're coming for you. That's the message."

What the legislation certainly does is ban the sale of forty-five types of semiautomatic rifles (what the media call "assault weapons"), require citizens who follow the law to be fingerprinted and more before they can purchase a handgun, limit magazine capacity to ten rounds, require gun owners to report lost or stolen firearms to police, and empower state police to audit gun dealers.

As this book was going to press, opponents of the bill had joined with the NRA to mount a legal challenge to the law's constitutionality.

═══════

To find out if this Maryland law is really helping law enforcement, as Governor O'Malley claims, I spent a day with a Maryland sheriff who had also testified against the bill that day in Annapolis. I thought he'd give a cop's perspective. I didn't realize Sheriff Mike Lewis of Wicomico County would show me the moving line between two gun cultures, between two viewpoints now shaping America's future of the gun.

In November 2013 I drove south of Washington, DC, to Salisbury, Maryland, to meet Sheriff Lewis. Lewis retired as a sergeant after twenty-two years with the Maryland State Police in July 2006, was elected sheriff that November, and along with running the sheriff's department is a certified instructor with the Maryland Police Training Commission. After a knuckle-crunching handshake, he leads me to his office. When we sit down, the first thing I ask is, "What do you carry?"

He stands right back up and pulls a Kimber Model 1911 semiautomatic pistol from his holster, clears the firearm, and hands it to me. I like the 1911's bright stainless steel and say how much I admire his sheriff's badge printed on the gun's cherry-wood grips. He smiles and takes a set of white ivory grips from his desk and says he puts these on for special occasions. As for stopping power, it holds eight rounds of .45 ACP. He once had to use that stopping power to kill a bad guy—a drug dealer who tried to run him down with his car.

Though Sheriff Lewis is now busy running his sheriff department, which has eighty deputies, he still likes to do a few traffic stops every morning. He says this keeps him grounded. It reminds him what's going on out there.

As we walk out to his black SUV to cruise around the county, he shifts the topic and tells me, "As gun sales have been surging in the past few years, the murder rate has been falling. The number of officers killed in the line of duty is way down from what it was in the 1970s and before." He adds, "More good guys with guns helps. We can't be everywhere all the time. That's why I feel so strongly that our governor's new gun-control law will only impede the good guys from defending themselves."

As he drives we talk about the guns he finds on the bad guys and where they come from. He says, "We catch criminals with semiautomatic handguns of every make and model. They steal them, buy them on a black market, or have some guy with a clean record buy them from a store. There are too many guns out there to prevent felons from getting handguns. The real solution to gun crime is to let citizens who pass background checks carry concealed if they want to."

The black market in illegal gun sales is hard to quantify because it's illegal; however, the Bureau of Alcohol, Tobacco, Firearms and Explosives (ATF) estimates there were 190,342 guns lost or stolen in the United States in 2012. Most of these guns (177,898) were lost or stolen from private residences and vehicles, but 5,762 firearms were reported as being stolen from Federal Firearms Licensed (FFL) dealers—gun stores, pawn shops, and so on. The ATF says the number of guns stolen from private hands is a guesstimate based on different sources of data. An ATF report explains, "This is raw data that has not been substantively reviewed by the FBI, has not been screened for duplicates or other data entry issues, and does not account for firearms that were subsequently found or recovered."[8] The ATF does, however, say the number of guns stolen from FFLs is a good statistic because in 1994 Congress required FFLs to report the theft or loss of any firearm from their inventories to both the ATF and to local police within 48 hours of discovery. These statistics on stolen guns from 2012 are not an anomaly. Each year the ATF estimates that about 190,000 guns are lost or stolen in the U.S.

The number of guns stolen from Federal Firearms Licensed dealers, however, has another caveat. Gun dealers reported 5,762 guns as being stolen in 2012, but FFLs also reported 10,915 firearms as "lost" from their stores, ranges, and backrooms. Now 10,915 guns aren't just lost in floods or burned in fires. When I asked about this large number of lost guns, ATF agent Tim Graten, the bureau's acting deputy chief of public affairs, said, "I really don't have a good explanation. If we suspect the guns are being sold illegally we'll start an investigation. There are instances where we've revoked Federal Firearms Licenses.

Part of that figure is likely from bad record keeping—our agents work with people who have FFLs to get their records in compliance."

⸻

As I ride along with Lewis, we see two of his deputies who have pulled over a van. There is a woman in handcuffs and a man sitting on the curb with his head in his hands. The van has New Jersey license plates.

Lewis pulls over and steps out. "What's up?" he asks a deputy wearing rubber gloves.

The van had been speeding, but when they pulled the van over they discovered the woman was wanted on an assault charge in Newark (the man was clean). "They must want her bad," says Lewis as he gets back into the SUV, "because they're gonna extradite her."

Lewis takes us back on the road. We go out of town, and as we pass a little house on a quiet country road, he slows down and says, "Good to see he patched up the bullet holes."

"Bullet holes?"

Lewis explains that a felon kept driving up to this house owned by one of his deputies and shooting holes in it with a .30-caliber rifle. "I knew we'd get that guy in a routine traffic stop," says Lewis. "I told all my deputies to be on the lookout for .30 caliber casings whenever they stopped a suspicious vehicle. The guy was using an old military gun—an M1 Garand. It was very unusual. You never see M1s used in drive-bys. That's how we got him, too."

We keep cruising in his black SUV with those cop-standard tinted windows. He says crisply as he passes a sedan and slows to look closely at its driver, "In my twenty-two years as a Maryland state trooper and my seven years here as sheriff, I've never busted a bad guy with a legal gun. The citizens who get concealed-carry permits don't commit crimes with their guns. Each person I've arrested who was later convicted always had their guns illegally."

Studies back Lewis's opinion. A study done by Mark Gius, a professor in the Department of Economics at Quinnipiac University, using concealed-carry-permit and crime data from 1980 to 2009, determined that "limiting the ability to carry concealed weapons may cause murder rates to increase."[9] In his 1998 book, *More Guns, Less Crime*, economics researcher John Lott studied FBI crime statistics from 1977 to 1993 and found that the passage of concealed-carry laws resulted in a decrease in the rates of murder, rape, and aggravated assault, by 8.5, 5, and 7 percent, respectively. The National Research Council, the working arm of the National Academy of Sciences, claimed it found "no credible evidence" either supporting or disproving Lott's thesis.[10] However, James Q. Wilson wrote a dissenting opinion for the National Research Council arguing that all of the committee's estimates confirmed Lott's finding that right-to-carry laws decreased the murder rate.[11]

Lott's findings that more guns equal less crime started a firestorm of research. Over and over again, Lott's research has stood up to analysis from his peers. After losing the empirical debate, the Violence Policy Center, an antigun group, tried to shift the debate by using publicly available media reports from May 2007 through the end of 2009 to look at crimes committed by concealed-carry permit holders in the United States. They determined that people with concealed-carry permits killed at least 117 people, including 9 law enforcement officers during that time period. This number includes people who lawfully killed someone in self-defense and people whose cases were pending, but excludes cases where individuals had been acquitted. That's a sensational number. The Violence Policy Center used this figure to argue that people shouldn't be allowed to carry a concealed firearm. To understand where this ideological group is coming from, you should know they maintain a "Concealed Carry Killers" data-base. But the thing is, there were about twenty-five thousand murders with guns during that period,[12] meaning that even if their statistic is accurate, concealed-carry holders committed less than 0.01 percent of the killings done with firearms. Another very controversial number is how often gun owners use firearms to stop a crime from taking place. Politics makes such an analysis controversial, but it's also a very difficult number to measure. According to Bureau of Justice Statistics (BJS) and National Crime Victimization Survey (NCVS) data from 1987 to 1992, about twenty thousand people each year used guns to protect property. Another source of information on the use of firearms for self-defense is the National Self-Defense Survey. This survey was done in 1993 by criminology professor Gary Kleck of Florida State University. Citing responses from 4,978 households, Kleck estimated that handguns had been used 2.1 million times a year for self-defense, and that all types of guns had been used approxi-mately 2.5 million times a year to scare off bad guys. These and other figures vary by such an extravagant margin because law-enforcement agencies typically don't collect or report how many crimes were thwarted by gun owners. People also often don't report crimes that were avoided. It's difficult even to define what constitutes a crime that has been stopped or avoided.

Sheriff Lewis says, "I can only cite my decades of experience when I say it helps law enforcement when people can utilize their Second Amendment rights."

Though the statistics are problematic, Lewis's experience with guns on the streets runs deep. He started and ran a drug-interdic-tion unit for the Maryland State Police. From Baltimore on down throughout the state, he has busted a lot of bad guys. He is a bull-necked, megaphone-voiced, highly caffeinated cop who grew up in Salisbury, on the Eastern Shore, and saw his friends become stoners and meth heads. He lost good friends to drugs. His response was to buzz-cut his hair and join the state troopers when he was nineteen. He became a star police officer, a hard charger who made one of the nation's largest seizures of crack cocaine out on Maryland's notorious Route 13. He became a national expert on hidden compartments in autos. Later, back at his sheriff's office, he showed me a car with a hidden compartment he'd just seized. To open the compartment, you had to have the cruise control on and the cigarette lighter pushed in. Only then would the compartment rigged under the auto open.

He explains, "Dominicans are masters at making these. When I pulled this car over, I could tell they were lying. So I looked under the car and saw fresh paint." Lewis says he can tell if a man's lying by watching the pulsing of the carotid artery in someone's neck. He's not just a human drug dog; he's also a walking polygraph machine. He pulled them out of the car and soon found drugs and cash.

I ask him, "Why do the two polarized sides of the American gun debate see guns so differently?" He mulls over the question and finally says that he doesn't know how to explain it. But then he adds: "What I can do is show you something that'll make the whole national battle over guns shockingly clear."

He drives into Salisbury. There is this little Mayberry downtown. There are small shops with plate-glass front windows dressed up for window shoppers a month before Christmas. There are quiet walkways that would make a 1950s American feel at home. There are outdoor café tables under small trees planted in red brick boxes. For a moment I see Sheriff Lewis as Sheriff Andy Taylor, a cop with nothing more serious to worry about than Barney's antics and the town drunk who locks himself up after he drinks too much moonshine. Salisbury is a small town. In 2012 it had a population of 31,243 people, according to the U.S. Census Bureau.

Sheriff Lewis turns a corner and drives a few blocks and we're in another time and place. There are young men on street corners outside run-down housing built sometime early in the last century. The teens and young men on the street corners are wearing puffy winter coats, baggy jeans drooping off their rears, hoodies, and expensive high-topped sneakers. They're looking at us with tense expressions. Some move quickly off the street. I see one speaking into a cell phone as he watches us.

"The whole street knows we're here," says Lewis as I feel like we somehow went straight from Mayberry to Yonkers. "They know what this car is."

Sheriff Lewis stops and pushes the button to roll down the window. Two teens nervously walk away, and a third says, "What's up, Sheriff?"

"Why aren't you boys in school?"

"Got my GED," says the boy as he looks at his bright-white sneakers.

"Stay out of trouble."

Sheriff Lewis drives farther down the street. He tells me about the shootings he has responded to here. He stops at a little white saltbox-style house and says, "I took a body out of there. He'd been shot in a local park and crawled here to his mother." He talks about other shootings. He stops at a home on Charles Street and says there had been a drive-by shooting there the previous summer. A car pulled up at 1:40 a.m. and shot this guy as he sat on a porch step. "It was another gang-related killing," says Lewis. "They found the victim face down, brain-dead."

Between 2008 and 2012, an astounding 27.6 percent of Salisbury residents lived below the official poverty line, according to the U.S. Census Bureau.[13] The statewide poverty rate in Maryland in 2012 was 9.4 percent. In 2010 there were 7 murders, 22 rapes, and 575 burglaries in the little town of Salisbury.[14] Before I came to visit,

Sheriff Lewis sent me a YouTube link for a rap video called "Jungle," a video made by a local gang called DDE. "Jungle" was uploaded to YouTube on October 11, 2013, and has since been taken down.[15] It started a police investigation. It featured young men pointing hand-guns at the camera and making hand motions as if they were firing pistols at the viewer. Some of the young men in the video sure don't look twenty-one. "We hear you got that work, we kickin' in the front door," rapped one of DDE's members with a pistol in his hands.

Lewis says all the guns used in the video are illegal. He shows me some of the places where the video was filmed. He explains that the only way to get their illegal guns would be to do blanket and very unconstitutional searches. But, he says, even that wouldn't matter. They'd get guns again. They'd learn to hide them as prisoners hide shivs in the county jail.

He shows me another run-down house and tells me how an eleven-year-old boy, Malik, saw his mother shot multiple times by an ex-boyfriend from New Jersey who came down to murder her. "We caught the guy and he's doing life," says Lewis. "Now I'm the boy's mentor. When I drove Malik to her funeral, he wanted to use my car's police radio. I let him, not knowing what he wanted to say. So he gets on the radio and says, 'I just want to thank all the cops who came to my house and saved my life. I want to thank you all for getting the guy who killed my mother.' Deputies answered him with tears in their voices."

We leave the rough side of town, and I think that's it. I think he's shown me what he wanted me to see. But I've only seen half of it.

He drives about two miles out of town—just one exit on Route 13—and pulls into a driveway in the suburbs.

"This is my father's house," he says. "This is where I grew up."

We walk into the backyard. His father has built a small Western town with a saloon, jailhouse, and everything right here in suburban

Maryland. There's a wooden boardwalk and old-fashioned "wanted" posters nailed to wood walls. His father is into cowboy-action shooting competitions. He has collected this stuff from all over Western America. The saloon is slathered in Old Western movie posters. There are pictures of John Wayne, Gary Cooper, and Roy Rogers. There's a rack of lever-action rifles. There are brass .45 Colt casings and black-and-white pictures of Wild West outlaws. Every inch of the bar and the building's walls are covered in pictures, holsters, and guns.

Mike Lewis's father comes in and gives us a tour that leads back to the main house. In a safe he has more than one hundred single-action Colt revolvers. Some are nineteenth-century relics; others are new and have never been fired. There are more paintings and Western-themed art. One entire wall is a hand-painted mural to the Old West.

After a lot of small talk about guns and the Old West, Mike's father picks up a single-action Colt .45, gets dead serious, and says, "No one is going to take my guns away."

Sheriff Lewis says just as seriously, "I won't let them, Dad."

When we leave, Mike is quiet. He showed me what he didn't have the words to explain. Right there, just two miles apart, are two very different gun cultures. Both are misunderstood and misrepresented by many in popular culture and politics.

This depresses Mike. He doesn't like that society is losing touch with the good part of America's gun culture. He loathes the ignorance that causes some to blame law-abiding gun owners for the actions of killers. "If we don't try to separate the good from the bad, as I do as a cop," Lewis says, "then we'll only make problems worse. When I meet a person who wants all handguns banned, I ask them if they found themselves in a public place with a sociopath determined to kill as many people as possible, would they like the sociopath to be the only one who has a gun? Do they really believe that 'gun-free zones' are smart policy?" According to a survey done by the National Shooting Sports Foundation, 14 percent of urban households have at least one handgun in them, 31 percent of homes in the suburbs have at least one handgun in them, and 27 percent of homes in small towns have at least one handgun in them.[16] Most gun violence is committed with handguns—76.6 percent of murders with guns were committed with handguns between 2006 and 2011.[17] Yet as you move from cities to the suburbs, the rate of handgun ownership doubles even though gun violence is primarily a problem of inner cities. Obviously a difference in gun cultures, which is effected by gun-control policy, is a factor.

The black community commits and suffers from an astonishingly large percentage of this violence. According to the Children's Defense Fund, which certainly is not a pro-gun group, gun deaths among white children and teens decreased by 44 percent from 1979 to 2009, while deaths among black children and teens rose by 30 percent. Blacks made up about 15 percent of the youth population in 2009 in the United States but suffered from 45 percent of all child and teen gun-related deaths. According to FBI statistics used in this report, black males aged fifteen to nineteen in 2009 were eight times as likely as their white peers, and two-and-a-half times as likely as Hispanics, to die from a bullet.[18] These stark figures are often used by advocates of nationwide bans on handguns and popular rifles. But that is to miss the point that these statistics underline that gun violence is far worse where gun-control measures are the most restrictive.

The illegal-gun-ownership rate is impossible to estimate—owners of illegal guns aren't likely to confess their felony to a pollster—but crime data and murder rates tell us illegal guns are common in inner cities. So what does this mean practically and culturally for the people living and working in these urban environments? It means that those with the illegal guns enforce a reign of terror, with respectable citizens, unable to defend themselves, often unwilling to cooperate with the police for fear of gang retaliation. And who, in such an environment, are young people going to look up to? Many will look up to the more powerful members in their communities, the bad guys with guns, because they have few or no examples of good guys who can stand up to them—thanks in part to restrictive gun-control laws that inhibit store owners and law-abiding citizens from protecting themselves.

Advocates for stricter gun-control laws, for federal bans on "assault weapons," and for reductions in the number of concealed-carry permits issued to private citizens ignore this reality.

The murder rate has actually fallen since the federal ban on assault weapons expired in 2004. Meanwhile, during the last few decades, the number of Americans with concealed-carry permits doubled, then tripled and quadruped, and is still rising. Many proponents of gun control act as if these facts don't exist. Instead, they see that Adam Lanza used an AR-15 to murder twenty children in Newtown, but they don't acknowledge that less than 3 percent of murders in the United States are committed with rifles of any type. Those killed by mass murderers represent less than 0.1 percent of all murders. Few know these facts, because the media don't often report these figures.

Lewis says, "People need to realize that if we're going to keep our good, old-fashioned American freedom we need to acknowledge what is good and what is bad with guns in our society."

A short time later, Detroit's police chief, James Craig, surprised a lot of people by saying if more citizens were armed, criminals would think twice about attacking them. While on *The Paul W. Smith Show*, Craig said, "There's a number of CPL [concealed-pistol license] holders running around the city of Detroit. I think it acts as a deterrent. Good Americans with CPLs translates into crime reduction. I learned that real quick in the state of Maine."

Craig repeated this message at a press conference. Craig spent twenty-eight years on the Los Angeles police force. He explained that he started to believe that legal gun owners can help reduce crime after he became the police chief in Portland, Maine, in 2009. "Coming from California, where it takes an act of Congress to get a concealed weapons permit, I got to Maine, where they give out lots of CCWs [carrying concealed-weapon permits], and I had a stack of CCW permits I was denying; that was my orientation. I changed my orientation real quick. Maine is one of the safest places in America. Clearly, suspects knew that good Americans were armed."[19]

In 2013, a survey of police officers by the National Association of Chiefs of Police found that 86.8 percent of those surveyed think "any law-abiding citizen [should] be able to purchase a firearm for sport and self-defense."[20] A survey done by PoliceOne.com of fifteen thousand law-enforcement professionals found that almost 90 percent of officers believe that casualties related to guns would decrease if armed citizens were present at the onset of an active-shooter incident. More than 80 percent of respondents support arming schoolteachers and administrators who willingly volunteer to train with firearms. Virtually all the survey's respondents (95 percent) said a federal ban on the manufacture and sale of ammunition magazines that hold more than ten rounds wouldn't reduce violent crime. [21]

As I drive back out of Salisbury and across the state of Maryland to DC, I pass Beretta's factories and everything comes full circle. After Maryland governor Martin O'Malley signed the legislature's highly restrictive gun-control legislation, Beretta put out a press release saying, "The question now facing the Beretta Holding companies in Maryland is this: What effect will the passage of this law—and the efforts of Maryland government officials to support its passage—have on our willingness to remain in this State?" Beretta then hinted at an answer to this question: "Prior to introduction of this legislation the three Beretta Holding companies located in Maryland were experiencing growth in revenues and jobs and had begun expansion plans in factory and other operations. The idea now of investing additional funds in Maryland and thus rewarding a Government that has insulted our customers and our products is offensive to us so we will take steps to evaluate such investments in other States."

In January 2014, Beretta gave a more conclusive answer. After thirty-five years in Accokeek, Maryland, Beretta announced it would open a $45 million dollar state-of-the-art manufacturing and research and development facility in Tennessee's Gallatin Industrial Park. Jeff Reh, Beretta USA's general counsel and vice–general manager, said, "I think they [Maryland's governor and legislature] thought we were bluffing. But Berettas don't bluff."

PART II

The Politician's View of Your Future

CHAPTER FOUR

Embedded with the Gun Lobby

If you want to protect yourself, get a double-barrel shotgun. Have the shells for a twelve-gauge shotgun, and I promise you as I told my wife, we live in an area that's wooded and somewhat secluded. I said, Jill if there's ever a problem, just walk out on the balcony here, walk out, put that double-barrel shotgun and fire two blasts outside the house.

—Vice President Biden[1]

Great advice, Joe. Not only would that be illegal, but then a woman would face an attacker with an empty shotgun. For tips on safe and responsible gun ownership, ask the NRA, not Joe Biden.

—The voice-over of an NRA ad

Not long after the shooting in Newtown, Connecticut, I stop by the NRA's Capitol Hill offices to speak to Chris Cox, executive director of the NRA's Institute for Legislative Action.

First, I pause outside. There is this young guy with a pierced lip wearing a ski jacket from Patagonia standing in the winter cold on the street outside Bullfeathers, a popular Capitol Hill restaurant. He has this confused look on his face and a sign in his hands held uncertainly at his knees that reads, "Stop Selling Assault Weapons."

I walk up to him and ask, "Who are you protesting?"

"The NRA."

"Why here?"

"Um," he says looking around, "this blog post said to meet here at two this afternoon to protest those baby killers at the NRA."

"Oh," I say, "but why this particular spot? Why not up on by the Capitol Building where some cameras might see you? Or maybe out in Fairfax where the NRA's headquarters is?"

He looks left toward the Capitol Building and asks, "You think everyone else is up there?"

"Could be," I shrug before asking as I point to his sign, "I'm curious, what exactly is an assault weapon?"

"You know, one of those military guns," he says, looking at me like I'm a moron.

"But they're already illegal."

"Huh?"

"Sure," I explain, "machine guns have been illegal, unless someone has a Class III license—which is damn hard to get—since 1934."

"Huh?"

"In 1934 Congress passed the National Firearms Act. One thing it did was basically outlaw machine guns. You see, prohibition had just been repealed and some gangsters had been using Tommy guns— machine guns—in battles with each other and against police. People wanted all that stopped."

"Are you like an NRA spokesman or something?"

"No, I just think we need to make informed decisions."

"Whatever, dude," he says and starts walking toward the Capitol Building.

So I say loudly to his back, "Good luck finding your anti-freedom friends." He doesn't even turn around.

I shrug and go to the NRA's Capitol Hill offices nearby. I'm buzzed in and go upstairs to a boardroom with a cherry wood table surrounded by black cushy chairs. Chris Cox is there to meet me. His tie is off and his sleeves are rolled up. He looks worn out, as he's been running back and forth to the Hill to lobby congressmen. Nevertheless, he smiles pleasantly. Chris has been the chief lobbyist and principal political strategist for the political and lobbying arm of the NRA since 2002. Chris develops and executes independent political campaign and legislative initiatives for the NRA, coordinates national advertising and direct-mail programs, and has administrative responsibility over NRA-ILA's $20 million budget. I ask about the political challenges facing American gun manufacturers. Chris says, "Antigun politicians have been trying for decades to put America's firearms manufacturers out of business through one means or another. They want to hold honest entrepreneurs, along with law-abiding gun owners, responsible for the acts of criminals. This is why the NRA fought for the successful passage of the Protection of Lawful Commerce in Arms Act, which was signed into law in 2005 by President George W. Bush. This was a vital first step toward ending the antigun lobby's shameless attempts to bankrupt the American firearms industry through reckless lawsuits. Still, they keep trying and we keep rallying our members to keep them honest."

Cox pauses, sits back, and adds, "Instead of trying to create good policy that really would help stop murderers, some lawmakers are intent on using this emotionally charged time to legislate their anti–Second Amendment ideology. We're here to stop them from getting away with it and to offer real solutions."

Both gun owners and gun makers were certainly feeling political pressure. In 2013 and early 2014, many gun companies felt forced to take their business to more gun-friendly states. Colt began expanding manufacturing operations in Florida, far from its historic grounds in Hartford, Connecticut. Ruger opted to expand manufacturing in Arizona and in early 2014 was moving its corporate headquarters from Connecticut to Florida. Magpul moved most of its operations from Colorado to Wyoming and Texas. HiViz announced it was moving from Colorado to Wyoming. Shield Tactical said it would move from California to Texas. Kahr Arms decided to leave New York for Pennsylvania. American Tactical Imports decided to move from New York to South Carolina. Stag Arms said it would likely move from Connecticut to Texas or South Carolina. PTR Industries (H&K) said it was moving from Connecticut to South Carolina. Ithaca Gun Company indicated it was moving from Ithaca, New York, to South Carolina.

As I spoke to Cox in early 2013, the Obama administration was working with then–New York governor Michael Bloomberg; Dan Gross, president of the Brady Campaign to Prevent Gun Violence; and others behind closed doors to draft an antigungun wish list that Vice President Joe Biden would take to Congress. At the last minute, Biden's White House task force did meet with the NRA and a variety of other gun groups, a few victims of gun violence, video-game industry representatives, and others, all in the same hectic, politically orchestrated day. Right after those meetings, according to the White House, Biden gave his task force's recommendations to President Barack Obama. The Obama administration then released a broad range of proposals.

As this was happening, Chris Cox didn't seem worried, just worn out. He tells me that "there is still a clear bipartisan majority in both houses of Congress supporting the Second Amendment." Cox explains that politicians listen to the NRA because the NRA has millions of members who vote. "The media likes to insinuate we have some kind of hold on politicians—both Democrats and Republicans. We do, the voting public. Without millions of Americans behind us, we wouldn't have a chance of convincing some politicians to vote for freedom."

When I ask about Congress and their overall Second Amendment leanings, he concludes, "We have a clear majority. Part of the reason we do is we're nonpartisan. We fight for the basic right to keep and bear arms. It's a cornerstone of our freedom."

The idea that the NRA is nonpartisan might make leftists cringe, but Cox is right. The NRA ignores party affiliation when making its congressional "Grades & Endorsements,"[2] and is just as happy to support pro–Second Amendment Democrats as pro–Second Amendment Republicans.

The NRA was founded in 1871 to teach people to shoot, not to fight political battles. Union Army soldiers in the Civil War were such poor marksmen that General Ambrose Burnside (1824–1881) said, "Out of ten soldiers who are perfect in drill and the manual of arms, only one knows the purpose of the sights on his gun or can hit the broad side of a barn."[3]

When William C. Church, editor of the *Army and Navy Journal*, published a series of editorials about the need for better rifle marksmanship just after the American Civil War, these editorials and a subsequent *Manual for Rifle Practice*, written by George W. Wingate, inspired a group of National Guard officers to form the NRA. The NRA subsequently began as a shooting club with a very lofty goal: train Americans to shoot better than anyone else in the world. The NRA didn't form a legislative affairs division until debate began for the 1934 National Firearms Act. The NRA didn't establish its lobbying arm—its Institute for Legislative Action—until 1975.[4]

Though some in the media like to push the narrative that lobbyists act against the interests of the American public, the truth is much of the lobbying done by corporations and associations is waged in self-defense against intrusive regulations, taxes, and, in the case of the

NRA, attacks on the Second Amendment. Lobbying is simply the exercise of the First Amendment right to "petition the government."

I ask another gun lobbyist, Larry Keane, the senior vice president and general counsel for the National Shooting Sports Foundation (NSSF), if any pro-gun organizations had been invited to meet with the White House Office of Public Engagement (OPE). Politico has recently reported that antigun groups had a secret but regular meeting, known as the "Gun Violence Table," at OPE. [5] Keane says, "I wish. There's a lot we could help them with. But they're not interested in our input."

I met with Larry Keane, one of the many faces of the gun lobby, at NSSF's offices in Newtown, Connecticut. He's a mostly bald attorney who seems to have been born in a dark suit, white shirt, and red tie. He serves as the firearms industry's chief spokesperson for legal, legislative, and regulatory matters. He has been appointed to the Defense Trade Advisory Group (DTAG), which advises the U.S. State Department on export policies. He also serves as the general counsel and corporate secretary to the Sporting Arms and Ammunition Manufacturers' Institute (SAAMI), where he is also the chairman of its Legislative and Legal Affairs Committee.

He tells me, "If the Obama administration really wants to do something about illegal guns or gun violence then they'd work with gun manufacturers, the NRA, and the rest of gun-rights groups. There is a lot we all already agree on; such as improving the NICS system [National Instant Criminal Background Check System] and prosecuting more straw purchasers. But President Obama isn't interested in working with us. That, in his view, would legitimize us. He, unfortunately, is only interested in scoring political points. He's in a perpetual campaign. That is unfortunate for the American people."

When I interviewed David Keene, former NRA president and now editorial page editor of the *Washington Times*, before an NRA board meeting in Arlington, Virginia, in January 2014, he agreed with his near namesake, Larry Keane. Keene said, "The Obama administration is treating the gun issue like it's a political race. They want to separate the NRA and to treat the NRA like they do a political opponent during a campaign. The trouble for them is this isn't a new issue. People already have an educated opinion with regards to gun rights and so don't fall for this ruse. I'm not sure President Obama really grasps this."

David Keene says one simple example illustrates the massive misunderstanding the Obama administration has made with regards to the American public and the gun issue.

In January 2013, America's largest outdoor show, the sixty-four-year-old Eastern Sports and Outdoor Show, which regularly attracted two hundred thousand people, fell apart a month before it was about to open, after Reed Exhibitions, a British events organizing company, announced that firearms and products associated with AR-15s ("assault weapons") wouldn't be allowed, not even in pictures.

The backlash was swift and effective. Pennsylvania has about one million active deer hunters, and some of them, along with many other gun owners and outdoorsmen from neighboring states, come to Harrisburg to see new firearms, to book with outfitters, or just to attend seminars on duck calling or fly tying. It's a big deal, and they weren't about to let a British company ruin it with political correctness. The grassroots supporters of the exhibition voiced their displeasure, and soon came reports that companies were pulling out in protest of Reed's action. Cabela's, a major sponsor of the show (Cabela's has a store nearby), was one of the first to announce it was pulling out. Soon, groups like the NRA, the National Wild Turkey Federation, and the Rocky Mountain Elk Foundation, and companies like Ruger, Smith & Wesson, Crimson Trace, Trijicon, and many more started to publicly announce they were canceling plans to attend—despite real costs to their bottom lines.

Chet Burchett, Reed Exhibitions' regional president for the Americas, responded by saying, "Our original decision not to include certain products in the Eastern Sports and Outdoor Show this year was made in order to preserve the event's historical focus on the hunting and fishing traditions enjoyed by American families.... In the current climate, we felt that the presence of [AR-15s] would distract from the theme of hunting and fishing, disrupting the broader experience of our guests. This was intended simply as a product decision, of the type event organizers need to make every day."

Talk about being out of touch. AR-15s are among America's top-selling firearms. Many, such as Remington's R-15, are chambered in calibers used by deer hunters. Predator hunters have long used them. These firearms are mainstream among hunters and in high demand. How would the presence of these firearms "distract from the theme of hunting and fishing"? Saying that is like banning sports cars from a car show while saying sporty, fast, cool, and expensive autos aren't popular, or even particularly useful.

The NRA officially announced: "We had called on Reed Exhibitions to reconsider their decision; unfortunately they have steadfastly refused to do so. As a result, the NRA will not be participating in the upcoming show in Harrisburg or in any other shows hosted by Reed Exhibitions that maintain this policy."

The NRA's announcement was a tipping point. Soon many more companies were pulling out, and then Reed Exhibitions announced the postponement of the show. This very public fight highlights the fundamental mistake Reed Exhibitions made: they failed to note that America's gun owners are sticking together as they fight for the America they know and love.

Meanwhile, other shows across the country began announcing they were *not* banning AR-15s from their shows. For example, the Portland Sportsmen's Show—the second-largest consumer sportsmen's show in the country—contacted The Shooting Wire to say they have "no intention of outlawing any legal sporting product from their exhibit floor."

The issue was further complicated by the fact that Reed Exhibitions had long worked with the National Shooting Sports Foundation to put on the SHOT Show, an annual trade show for firearms and related companies. The NSSF fired Reed Exhibitions and signed a contract with another company.

The Eastern Sports and Outdoor Show wasn't held in 2013. But in 2014 the show went on, thanks to the NRA, which put on the Great American Outdoor Show in Harrisburg from February 1 through February 9. The show featured nearly one thousand exhibitors ranging from shooting manufacturers to outfitters to fishing boat makers spread out over 650,000 square feet of exhibit hall. The event drew an estimated two hundred thousand people and included concerts, fundraising dinners, speaking events, archery competitions, and outdoor seminars.

The attendees represented a broad swath of America largely ignored by the media, derided by the Left, and held in contempt by the Obama administration, though Obama himself feels he has to pretend to be in favor of gun ownership in general and even had his press office at the White House leak a photo of him "shooting skeet" with a shotgun held too horizontal for skeet shooting and with a choke missing from the bottom barrel (it takes two for skeet)—clear signs the shot was a stunt. David Keene says, "Maybe it's not surprising that a British company would be out of touch with Americans' civil liberties, but you'd think the Obama administration would understand America a little better."

CHAPTER FIVE

How Gun Rights Beat the Media

A gun is a tool, no better no worse than any other tool, an axe, shovel or anything. A gun is only as good or as bad as the man using it. Remember that.
—Hero Alan Ladd to leading lady Jean Arthur
in the 1953 western *Shane*

I'm sitting in a trade show booth with three weary, almost identically dressed (dark suits, white shirts, forgettable ties) men who run one of America's largest firearms manufacturers. I ask if they have heard about movie mogul's Harvey Weinstein's comments about the NRA. They nod and laugh.

Weinstein was the executive producer of popular gun-happy films like *Reservoir Dogs* (1992), *Pulp Fiction* (1994), *Kill Bill* (2003), and *Inglourious Basterds* [sic] (2009). The gun company executives tell me they love these movies but find Weinstein's hypocrisy hysterical. The day before, Weinstein said on Howard Stern's radio show, "I don't think we need guns in this country, and I hate it. I think the NRA is a disaster area.... I shouldn't say this, but I'll tell it to you, Howard. I'm going to make a movie with Meryl Streep, and we're going to take this head-on. And [the NRA is] going to wish they weren't alive after I'm done with them."[1]

"Meryl Streep," laughs one of the gun makers. "Can he at least threaten us with Uma Thurman?"

It's January 16, 2014, and we're seated in the back of the company's eight-hundred-square-foot booth at the SHOT Show. Some sixty-seven thousand people from more than one hundred countries are here in Las Vegas to buy and sell guns, optics, ammo, and related merchandise in the Sands Expo and Convention Center. Just down a little hallway are displays of pistols and rifles. There are crowds of people handling them. These people are making orders for their gun stores and catalogs. The gun business is booming. After the 2008 presidential election, these gun makers joked that President Barack Obama is the "greatest gun salesman of all time," but they had no idea just how long the joke would last.

The context of Weinstein's comments actually makes his hypocrisy even worse. He was discussing a project based on Leon Uris's novel *Mila 18*, a book that chronicles a Jewish uprising in German-occupied Warsaw during World War II. As Weinstein explained, "It's not a Holocaust story, as much as it's Jews with guns; it's my whole philosophy.... It's the idea that when injustice is that great you just can't march into the camps." This prompted Stern, who is a gun owner, to ask Weinstein if he owns a gun. Weinstein replied he doesn't, saying, "I don't think we need guns in this country. And I hate it." Weinstein's "I hate it" argument didn't satisfy Stern. When Stern pushed deeper than a three-year-old's "I hate it," Weinstein said he would "find a gun, if [genocide] was happening to my people." Now that's a mind bender. Weinstein thinks people should be disarmed, but he also thinks they should somehow "find" guns if things get really out of hand?

If that's not hypocritical enough, in 2012, following an extortion attempt against Weinstein, a source told the *New York Post* that "[t]he Weinsteins have always had intense security and been on high alert because of the movies they make."[2] The paper also noted that while producing *The Master*, a film the Scientologists didn't like, Weinstein "beef[ed] up his own security." So Weinstein evidently doesn't oppose armed bodyguards protecting him, but he does oppose the right of people who can't afford bodyguards to protect themselves with handguns. Or maybe he thinks that if the government confiscated all private arms, he wouldn't need armed escorts, because before guns were invented people lived in perfect harmony, didn't they?

What I find most astounding, though, is not Weinstein's illogic or hypocrisy, but the fact that these gun makers are not afraid of a Hollywood producer trying to take away their livelihoods, their freedom, their way of life.

This is a big change. A decade ago they would have been gritting their teeth and worrying about their future. But today the editorial board at the *New York Times*, the *Washington Post*, and the other big urban papers; those talking heads on CNN and MSNBC and the once-big three networks; and those producers in Hollywood and the antigun-freedom actors and actresses no longer scare these gun makers. I knew they would laugh because Weinstein had become the joke of the 2014 SHOT Show.

Somehow, despite all those "mainstream" voices manufacturing arguments to take away the Second Amendment of the Bill of Rights, a majority of Americans still want to retain their freedom. In January 2014, according to Gallup polling, just 31 percent of Americans want stricter gun-control laws passed. This was down from 38 percent in 2013.³ Gallup also reported in January 2014 that "the gap between those wanting stricter gun laws and those wanting less strict laws narrowed as a result of a sharp increase in the percentage of Americans who want *less* strict laws, now at 16% up from 5% a year ago [emphasis in original]."⁴

The mainstream media is losing the gun-control argument because of the efforts of men like Stephen Hunter. He's a gun owner and historian who spent his career in mainstream newsrooms. When I meet him at the SHOT Show, he says, "I've always wanted to come to the SHOT Show. It's a rite of passage for any gun owner."

Steve is now sixty-seven years old and retired from the *Washington Post*. In 2003, while at the *Post*, he won a Pulitzer for movie criticism. The Pulitzer committee said Hunter "is forever suggesting that art can be a good, lusty, happy thing, that doesn't always have to be an immersion in a new level of human misery." The Pulitzer Prize's twenty-member board is mostly a who's who of liberal journalists and is administered by Columbia University. It often saves its honors for those advocating the Left's causes, but this time they got it exactly right.

Steve has the look of an aged professor, but he's brimming with youthful mirth. He's cynical and sarcastic, amused with human nature. He cheerily tells me he was once a "leftist hippie with the long hair and all that" and that "he moved by proportions of honesty to becoming a gun owner and shooter." Steve's final transformation into a full-bore gun enthusiast came one fine day in 1985 when he saw an ad for a gun—a bright and lovely stainless Smith & Wesson Model 645 to be precise. He found this semiautomatic pistol to be intriguing and beautiful, and he wanted one. This contradiction within himself needed a final resolution. After some self-evaluation, he decided that "there was something fundamentally dishonest about my anti-gun views."

We find seats in the SHOT Show pressroom—a room crowded with bloggers, magazine editors, outdoor television shows hosts and the proprietors of YouTube channels for gun enthusiasts. We sit down and I ask him about the evolution of his interest in guns.

He says, "When I was a boy the notion that guns were bad stuck in my head. My parents [his father was a professor at Northwestern; his mother wrote children's books], teachers, and the suburban Chicago culture I was in told me guns lead to violence. It took me a long time to move past the notion that owning a gun would corrupt you, that a gun can somehow whisper vile things in your ear until you become a worse person, maybe even a sociopath. I thought that a gun has an aura that acts like alcohol to an alcoholic—that step by step it would make me a bad person.

"There is, of course, an aura surrounding guns," he continued. "There are real, deep reasons why Hollywood glorifies the gun even as many of its producers and actors want guns banned. This feeling comes from holding a gun, from shooting a gun; you get a feeling of a power; you know this mechanical wonder explodes in your hands but when used right won't harm you even as it can do real damage down range. This is why guns are a great responsibility and require a lot of maturity. This is also why Western films resonate. Out there, in the exposed open, is a man with a gun, a true individual who can take care of himself. The gun doesn't make this cowboy good or bad, but it does make him potentially lethal and very independent. That's intoxicating. That's a big part of the reason why all those journalists who oppose gun rights keep losing battles. For generations they had almost full control of the messaging, but still they lost because people are drawn to the gun. When you shoot a gun safely and responsibly you can't help but get this big grin on your face."

Stephen graduated from Northwestern's Medill School of Journalism in 1968. He then served in the military as an honor guard at

Arlington National Cemetery. In 1971 he joined the *Baltimore Sun*'s copy desk. He spent ten years in that role before becoming the paper's first full-time film reviewer. In 1980, while still at the *Sun*, Hunter published his first novel, *The Master Sniper*, about a World War II Nazi assassin. Since then Stephen's novels have won him millions of fans, many of them gun owners. His Bob Lee Swagger thrillers, beginning with *Point of Impact* in 1993, follow a fictionalized Vietnam War sniper loosely based on the real Vietnam War sniper and U.S. Marine Corps legend Carlos Hathcock. Along the way, Hunter got to know his guns. He got to know the gun culture.

In 1997 the *Washington Post* hired him to review films. He tells me most of the editors and reporters at the *Post* thought of him as "crazy uncle Steve." He says, "I was irreverent, sarcastic, and gregarious—I was a voice they understood. They thought I was all right even if I did own and shoot guns. I told them when they're writing about gun control or crime to come and talk to me. I told them I'd save them from technical mistakes and help them with sources. Some took me up on this. During my time at the *Post* the news side went from raving anti-gun to moderately anti-gun. I had something to do with that."

In 2007 his book *Point of Impact* made it to the big screen as *Shooter*, starring Mark Wahlberg. The movie came out just a few days after the Virginia Tech shooting. When Wahlberg was asked about his use of guns he said, "I haven't used a gun anywhere other than on a movie set.... I would love it if they could take all the guns away. Unfortunately, you can't do that so you hope that good people in the world have them to protect the people who can't protect themselves."[5]

Not everyone in Hollywood is antigun. Hollywood great Charlton Heston was president of the NRA for five years, and occasionally a Hollywood type who knows something about guns, like Tom Selleck, an NRA board member, can make headlines, as he did in 2011 for chewing out an extra for unsafe handling of a prop gun on the set of

Blue Bloods.[6] But in general, the culture in Hollywood is not only hostile to guns but ignorant about them.

Stephen told me about the time a Hollywood producer optioned his 1989 novel, *The Day before Midnight*, and Stephen took him to a gun range to get a taste of what characters in the book do.

"It was one of those busy days at the range," Stephen said. "You could smell the testosterone. There were people pounding away with big-game rifles. There were men opening gun cases and slapping each other on the backs. There were guys in the pistol lanes shooting semi-automatics at paper targets. It was loud. It was masculine. You could feel the energy. Before we even got to the firing line the producer started to tremble. He soon became hysterical. Then he broke and ran for the car. Culture shock."

I ask him how we can bust down this cultural barrier.

"Honestly," he says, "you need a guy like me. Someone who has worked with them, someone they trust. A person they've bestowed their major awards on—as they have me—and the gun industry needs to send that person around to speak to them in their own language. Because, really, those editors and reporters don't want to make all the stupid technical mistakes they do. They see themselves as tolerant, worldly, and open-minded intellectuals. They don't really want to only give one point of view, and they certainly don't want to be so factually inept with this issue. But the only way to get them to see that is through a spokesman they trust and understand. I don't know if such a person exists. I'm sure as hell not going to make a life of that—I've done my part."

I ask him how we might reach young reporters before they are indoctrinated with political correctness, how we might open their minds, and he replies, "Liberal reporters believe in consensus. They believe in accord and compromise. Individualism, to them, is akin to becoming an outlier, a person fallen from the inner circles of society.

If they step away from the accepted ethos, they'll be shunned; they won't be promoted. This is often unsaid, but the pressure to conform is profound. Everything they're taught tells them to look for accepted values, to conform to the group, and that anything outside those norms must be shunned. Though as a group they're mostly well educated, they're also mostly looking inward. Reporters speak to each other more than anyone else. They reinforce each other's values and assure each other they're the smartest people in the room. By asking them to accept gun rights, to really accept the idea that an individual can stand apart from the state on their own two feet and defend their own life with a gun, that's asking them to violently assault their foundation. Only a few of them have the courage to do that."

We next talk about the 2007 film *Shooter*, based on Steve's thriller *Point of Impact*, and I want to know if he was happy with it and how we can help Hollywood get guns right more of the time. He says, "The gun handling in *Shooter* is on another level. They listened and got that right. Non-shooters won't see that in the film, but anyone who knows how to handle a gun will recognize this and therefore find it real, authentic. That goes a long way to helping a film resonate. I am mostly happy with the film. The end though, when I saw it for the first time I was cringing and saying, 'No, don't shoot him.'"

In the film, the character Bob Lee Swagger (played by Mark Wahlberg) is a U.S. Marine gunnery sergeant who served as a force recon scout sniper. He reluctantly leaves a self-imposed exile from his isolated mountain home in the Wind River Range at the request of Colonel Isaac Johnson (played by Danny Glover) to help track down an assassin who plans on shooting the president. In the end Swagger kills both conspirators, Johnson and Senator Meachum, as they plan their next move while at the senator's vacation home.

Steve says, "Swagger would never have killed the senator. It's against his code. Hollywood and the urban segment of the audience don't get that, but the millions of former military members and gun owners out there won't, on a deep level, believe or feel good about this ending. Antoine Fuqua did a great job directing the film, but that ending was a big miss. They showed they really don't understand the gun culture in America. Maybe shows like *Top Shots* and the growth in the number of gun owners today will start to seep some of this knowledge of guns and the gun culture into Hollywood and change this over time." Steve shifts to another angle to fill out the picture. He says he remembers when the fairness doctrine was undone by President Ronald Reagan. He says its repeal "unleashed talk radio." Suddenly radio stations didn't have a government bureaucrat wagging their finger and censoring them when they didn't think a station was fair and balanced.

The fairness doctrine was a policy enforced by the Federal Communications Commission (FCC). It was introduced in 1949. It required the holders of broadcast licenses to present controversial issues in a way that was, in the FCC's view, honest, equitable, and balanced. In *Red Lion Broadcasting Co. v. FCC* (1969), the U.S. Supreme Court upheld the FCC's general right to enforce the fairness doctrine where channels were limited, though the Court didn't rule that the FCC had to regulate this speech. Because it regulated frequencies, the government soon snatched the right to regulate content.

Then came FCC chairman Mark S. Fowler. He was a communications attorney who had served on Ronald Reagan's presidential campaign staff in 1976 and 1980. Fowler was appointed by President Reagan to head the FCC. Under Fowler, the FCC soon began to repeal parts of the fairness doctrine. Fowler said the doctrine hurt the public interest by violating free-speech rights guaranteed by the First Amendment. In 1987, the FCC abolished the doctrine by a 4–0 vote; known as the Syracuse Peace Council decision, the FCC decision stated: "The intrusion by government into the content of programming occasioned by the enforcement of [the fairness doctrine] restricts the journalistic freedom of broadcasters ... [and] actually inhibits the presentation of controversial issues of public importance to the detriment of the public and the degradation of the editorial prerogative of broadcast journalists."

On February 16, 2009, Fowler told conservative radio talk-show host Mark Levin that his work toward revoking the fairness doctrine had been a matter of principle, not partisanship. Fowler said Reagan's White House staff thought repealing the policy would be politically unwise. Fowler said that the White House staff thought the fairness doctrine was the "only thing that really protects you [Reagan] from the savageness of the three networks ... and Fowler is proposing to repeal it."[7]

Instead of doing the politically expedient thing, Reagan supported Fowler's fight to repeal the fairness doctrine's gag order on free speech. Reagan later vetoed a congressional effort, led by Democrats, to make the fairness doctrine federal law.

Suddenly, free speech had a chance to flower. Then came Fox News and unrestrained social media. In just a few decades, the mainstream media lost control of the narrative to a diverse universe of blogs, internet forums, e-newsletters, radio, and cable news. Gun-rights group such as the NRA and the Second Amendment Foundation found it easier to mobilize grassroots movements.

"The journalists at the big papers have been confused by these changes," Steve says. "They're for free speech, but they think, for the good of society, they should set and moderate the agenda like they did for so long. But they're guilty of groupthink. They're wed to a very urban and often elitist way of thinking and really are afraid to break away—even when they do recognize this—because the cost to their careers would be too great."

I ask if they're told how to write about the gun issue, and Steve shakes his head no. "There isn't a playbook," he says. "The cultural pressure in the newsroom is to conform to the group's values. The values tend to be anti-gun."

Steve adds, "Regardless, freedom was unleashed. That's how the NRA and others have been able to evolve the argument, to get their point of view across despite the media's reluctance to fairly report this issue."

When I interview David Keene, former chairman of the American Conservative Union (ACU) and a former president of the NRA who still lobbies for the NRA, he picks up this point and says, "After Newtown, in December 2012, the NRA and gun owners in general had to be respectfully silent for a while. It was a time of mourning. Mature and sober debate must come later. But even as the NRA stayed silent, we saw the narrative evolving. A lot of reporters had the knee-jerk reaction of blaming guns, blaming freedom. But soon voices started to point out that these 'gun-free zones' are 'victim zones.' The narrative was changing on a grassroots level and it's all about the narrative. The American people have debated this issue before. They've become educated. They quickly understood that if a good guy with a gun had been there, a lot of what happened might have been prevented."

Keene says, "The only places that saw freedom reduced after Newtown were those areas with single-party politics run by Democrats who railroaded through gun-control legislation. Freedom won in all the areas where there was a real debate."

The fact that the unleashing of the First Amendment has been helping people understand the Second Amendment is not lost on advocates for more gun control. Some politicians see these changes and want to turn back the clock. After a Democratic sweep in the 2008 elections, some Democrats decided it was time to require radio networks to air liberal points of view through a new fairness doctrine, enforced by threat of fines and possibly the revocation of radio licenses.

In 2009 Democrat senator Tom Harkin of Iowa said, "We gotta get the Fairness Doctrine back in law again."[8] Democrat congresswoman, and then House Speaker, Nancy Pelosi of California also called for its return.[9] During an appearance on a radio show in February 2009, former president Bill Clinton said, "Well, you either ought to have the Fairness Doctrine or we ought to have more balance on the other side, because essentially there's always been a lot of big money to support the right-wing talk shows."[10]

In December 2010, Democrat FCC commissioner Michael Copps suggested in a speech that broadcasters should be subject to a new "public values test" every four years to determine if they should be allowed to stay on the air. Copps said news outlets should have to prove they are making a meaningful commitment to public affairs; they should have to show they are committed to diversity programming (such as giving women and minorities more air time); they should have to report to the government what topics they plan to cover on air; and private media companies using "public" airwaves should be required to make greater disclosures about who funds political ads.[11] Basically, Copps wanted the FCC's five-member board to be a means of political control over the airwaves.

President Barack Obama didn't officially come out in favor of this censorship; however, his regulatory czar, Cass Sunstein, is for it. Sunstein wrote a book titled *Democracy and the Problem of Free Speech*. In the book he argues that capitalism has corrupted free speech by giving those with money a louder megaphone that those who don't have the cash to pay for ads. He asserts that James Madison, the "father of the U.S. Constitution," opposed such alleged corruption, though Madison, who lived in a time of freewheeling newspapers, where those with more money could buy more ads or print more pamphlets, specifically believed in limiting the power of the federal government, not the press, not free speech, not the right of wealthy people to spend their wealth as they saw fit. Sunstein argues that the government must muzzle corporations and then decide who gets airtime and how much, which is not a constitutional view at all.

Sunstein argues that "Sites from one point of view [should] agree to provide links to other sites so if you are reading a conservative magazine they would provide a link to a liberal site and vice versa.... If we could get voluntary arrangements in that direction it would be great.... But the word 'voluntary' is a little complicated. Sometimes people don't do what's best for our society.... And the idea would be to have a legal mandate as the last resort and to make sure it's as neutral as possible...."[12]

This effort to curb First Amendment freedom with a new fairness doctrine failed, but the Bipartisan Campaign Reform Act of 2002, popularly known as "McCain-Feingold," silenced corporations, unions, and associations, such as the NRA, the Second Amendment Foundation, and other gun-rights groups, near elections. The U.S. Supreme Court tossed out many of this legislation's restrictions in *Citizens United v. Federal Election Commission* (2010).

Before the *Citizens United* case, the NRA responded to this curb on its First Amendment right to defend the Second Amendment by stating, in 2004, that "NRA News should be deemed a media company and therefore is entitled to distribute news stories, commentaries and editorials that both mention federal candidates and advocate the election or defeat of a federal candidate. Under the relevant campaign finance laws, media companies are permitted to engage in such speech without limitation."[13]

In 2004 the NRA hired Cam Edwards to do an online radio show called *Cam & Co.* "They hired me because I did straight news," Cam tells me. "They didn't want someone to just pontificate. They wanted journalists who could interview NRA leadership, newsmakers, pundits, journalists, congressional leaders, and more. I was a gun owner, but I wasn't known as a gun-rights activist. I was brought in to find and report the truth the media often wasn't reporting. This is the same reason the NRA hired Ginny Simone to investigate and report on what's going on that the media overlooks or ignores."

Cam says, "In the years since a lot has changed. We now have a three-hour show and are on SiriusXM Radio and the Sportsman Channel and, really, too many mediums to do a conclusive count of how many households we reach. What I've been surprised about along the way, as we report on gun-rights-related issues, isn't so much what the media reports, but what they chose to ignore. The NRA estimates that there are now more than one hundred million gun owners in America. These people have more than three hundred million guns. CNN is ignoring and insulting all of those people. CNN isn't fading away because people aren't looking for news or because cable news, and more, have diversified the field; they're losing ground because they're often ignoring the truth.

"Just consider that in May of 2013 the government's Bureau of Justice Statistics reported that homicides involving firearms had fallen 39 percent from 1993 and 2011, but few of the mainstream outlets reported this. Also, during this same time frame, gun sales and the numbers of new gun owners have been surging," Cam says, "but this got so little coverage that a Pew poll found that most Americans think gun violence is going up."

Cam was referring to a May 2013 Pew report that determined that "most Americans are unaware that gun crime is lower today than it was two decades ago. According to a new Pew Research Center survey, [in May 2013] 56% of Americans believed gun crime is higher than 20 years ago and only 12% think it is lower."[14]

Omitting portions of the truth is a form of lying, but the first question is this: Are CNN's reporters and other news outlets aware of what they're missing? To understand how CNN, in particular, became a media outlet only interested in one point of view on guns, I called one of its original seven founding members, Jim Shepherd, now the editor and publisher of The Shooting Wire. Shepherd has held a number of senior news executive positions during his career, including with CNN, the Financial News Network, the Golf Channel, and other television networks. He left CNN in 1985 after he became "disgusted with what they wouldn't report."

Jim says, "Part of what happened to CNN is what happened to Hollywood. The news, like Hollywood, became trapped in creating and fawning over celebrities. Getting Anderson Cooper publicized became more important than breaking the big story. When you have celebrity reporters telling you how they feel about being in Iraq instead of reporting on how our troops are doing, you begin to lose perspective. With guns, instead of going to gun ranges, gun owners' homes, instead of interviewing women who'd stopped an attacker, and instead of really trying to understand the world such women live in and what they're going through, they just tell us how they feel. Katie Couric, Diane Sawyer, and the rest are stars, not reporters. They're not hunting for the truth. They're telling you what they think, and what they think all comes from the cocktail parties on Manhattan's Upper East Side and from conversations with other reporters."

He says, "When I was at CNN, the lead stories in the *New York Times* and the *Washington Post* drove what we covered. They still do that for CNN and network news to a large extent. The cable news reporters and producers are intellectually lazy. They're so busy chasing each other they don't stop to find the truth."

I ask how we break this cycle, and Jim laughs before saying, "It's happening now. CNN's ratings are plummeting. Both the *Washington*

Post and the *New York Times* have seen their staffs cut as their circu-
lations have dropped.... They can't understand how they're being
beaten. They don't want to hear the truth, that they've lost touch. I
tried to tell them once. They invited me to an annual party at CNN.
They invited all the founding members on CNN's twenty-fifth anni-
versary. They asked me to give a speech. I stood up and told them that
they're out of touch. I told them they have to go back to their roots
and question everything. I told them to take off the filter and report
what they find. Yeah, they'll never have me back again."

I want to know how Jim got into guns when he spent his whole
career at CNN and the newsrooms of the network's affiliates, and he
says, "I grew up on a farm in Kentucky. I grew up with guns. But,
yeah, I didn't shoot for twenty-five years. I loved my job and got into
that news culture. I concentrated on business news and international
news, so I didn't have a lot of contact with the gun issue. I didn't get
back into shooting until I noticed, after I'd started the *Golf Wire*, that
the shooting industry needed an online news service. So I started The
Shooting Wire and The Outdoor Wire.

"I didn't know it at the time, but I became a part of alternative
media that was undermining the mainstream media's influence. I was
just trying to provide a needed service," Jim says, "but since we started
The Shooting Wire, in 2002, we've grown so big so fast that I see how
new media is teaching people about what's really going on. We're just
one voice among a lot of new blogs, newsletters, forums, and all that.
We're a big one, but really this is the future. The only way it stops and
the mainstream media regains control of the narrative and so can
dumb down people again by not reporting what doesn't fit into the
liberal narrative, would be by government fiat. A new fairness doctrine
or something."

In closing, Jim says, "A lot of my former colleagues have accused
me of selling out. Really, that's how they think. I tell them no, you

sold out a long time ago. Now you're such a shill you can't even see it."

I next turn to Tom Gresham for some perspective. Tom is the host of *Gun Talk*, a nationally syndicated radio talk show about firearms. His father, "Grits" Gresham Jr. (1922–2008), hosted ABC's *The American Sportsman* series from 1966 to 1979. This exposed Tom to the media from an early age. In the years since, Tom edited for magazines such as *Alaska* and *American Hunter*. He started his radio show in 1995.

Tom says, "I wouldn't have been allowed on the air when that fairness doctrine was in effect. Radio station owners would have been reluctant to stir up the FCC's bureaucrats. And anyway, how would they ever have found an opposing view to gun rights that would draw an audience? Gun owners have a natural constituency. The millions of Americans who join gun clubs to shoot, sight in their hunting guns, and to learn to protect themselves have something in common. They're already at least locally organized. They're a grassroots group all by themselves and there are better than one hundred million of them. All the anti-gun crowd has is emotion after some madman has done something evil. This can stir up well-meaning but dissociated people, but when you combat that emotion with facts, the emotion burns off like rain on hot asphalt and what you have left are gun owners voting their issue."

Keene says this in another way. "Michael Bloomberg has spent millions to fund Mayors against Illegal Guns and still doesn't have any traction. This isn't just because what he's selling runs counter to hard-won American freedom, but also because how do you build a constituency around getting people to become victims? The only way to pull that off is with a state-run media that has a monopoly. No, that might not even work. I recently traveled to Russia to speak to a large and growing gun-rights group. They have a state-run media, but gun rights are such a practical thing it's resonating even in mother Russia."

To fully see what Keene is getting at, it's worth considering where the money is being raised on either side of the gun debate. The NRA's funds mostly come from a large grassroots membership base. This is also true of Gun Owners of America, the Second Amendment Foundation, and other gun-rights groups. According to OpenSecrets.org, gun-rights groups "have given more than $30 million in individual, PAC and soft money contributions to federal candidates and party committees since 1989." Meanwhile, the money from gun-control advocates comes mostly from wealthy liberals. Billionaire and former New York City mayor Michael Bloomberg started a pro-gun-control super PAC, Independence USA PAC, in 2012; it spent more than $8.3 million in several congressional races in 2012. Former congresswoman Gabrielle Giffords started a super PAC in January 2013, Americans for Responsible Solutions (ARS). ARS reportedly raised more than $18 million by January in 2014 from a few well-heeled individuals.[15] OpenSecrets.org says before these antigun super PACs came along, the expenditures of "[g]un control groups, by comparison, have been barely a blip on the radar screen. They've given a total of just under $2 million since 1989."

In 2013 Bloomberg's Independence USA PAC lost big in its attempt to stop a less-well-funded but populist pro-gun movement in Colorado that successfully recalled two Colorado state senators who had voted for a highly restrictive gun law. In 2013 and early 2014, Bloomberg's group, Mayors against Illegal Guns (MAIG), was also bleeding support. On February 7, 2014, the mayor of Poughkeepsie, New York—an upstate city with gang and drug problems—wrote an op-ed to say,

> I'm the mayor of one of the largest cities in the Hudson Valley, just 90 minutes north of New York City. I'm a life

member of the National Rifle Association and a former member of Mayors Against Illegal Guns, or MAIG, started by New York Mayor Michael Bloomberg in 2006. I'm no longer a member of MAIG. Why? Just as Ronald Reagan said of the Democratic Party, it left me. And I'm not alone: Nearly 50 pro–Second Amendment mayors have left the organization. They left for the same reason I did. MAIG became a vehicle for Bloomberg to promote his personal gun-control agenda—violating the Second Amendment rights of law-abiding citizens and taking resources away from initiatives that could actually work to protect our neighborhoods and save precious lives. Gun control will actually make a bad situation worse.[16]

After losses in many states and nationally, gun-control groups decided they had a message problem. To win public support for gun bans, the gun-control movement paid consultants to come up with a public-relations playbook. Completed in 2012, *Preventing Gun Violence through Effective Messaging* is reportedly the result of opinion research done by the firms Greenberg Quinlan Rosner, OMB, and KNP Communications.[17] In a section labeled "Overall Messaging Guidance," the guide lists its number one "Key Messaging Principle" to be "[a]lways focus on emotional and value-driven arguments about gun violence, not the political food fight in Washington or wonky statistics." It further explains this strategy by saying, "It's critical that you ground your messaging around gun violence in prevention by making that emotional connection." Its second key principle is, "Tell stories with images and feelings." The playbook says, "Our first task is to draw a vivid portrait and make an emotional connection. We should rely on emotionally powerful language, feelings and images to bring home the terrible impact of gun violence." They realize they've lost the rational and empirical debates about what really stops gun violence and instead want the debate inflamed by unempirical emotion.

"If the gun-control groups can't control the messaging, they won't even talk to you," says Alan Gottlieb, chairman of the Citizens Committee for the Right to Keep and Bear Arms and founder of the Second Amendment Foundation, when I tell him I can't get Bloomberg's MAIG or the Brady Campaign to Prevent Gun Violence to answer my media requests.

In the end, when it comes to defending our Second Amendment rights, David Keene says, "I'm optimistic. As long as we have our First Amendment intact, I think Americans will push back against these attempts to disarm them. But we can't get complacent. Our freedom is always tenuous."

CHAPTER SIX

Into "Gun-Free" America

She shot him. She's shooting him. She's shooting him. Shoot him again!

—Donnie Herman on the phone with his wife, Melinda, and a police dispatcher as a home intruder opens a closet door where Melinda was hiding with their two children[1]

Just after midnight Dick Anthony Heller steps into a backroom in a federal building on Capitol Hill in Washington, DC. He takes off his holster and revolver. A video camera's unblinking eye watches as he places the Smith & Wesson in a locker in the government building he protects forty hours a week. He grabs his bicycle and pushes it out of the building. As he goes he waves goodnight to the security guard who relieved him. When he steps outside, he pauses to strap on a bicycle helmet. He pulls his socks over the bottoms of his pants. He pushes his bicycle onto a sidewalk under the glare of streetlights. He looks up and down the DC street. People have tried to sell him drugs while he walked home from work in the nation's capital. Others have approached him with bad intentions. He started riding the bike to avoid them. He's seventy years old now and can't carry his gun on these streets for protection. He must carry a gun to protect government officials and property while on duty, but he can't carry one for his own defense even though he went all the way to the U.S. Supreme Court and won.

This is disarmed America in all its contradictions. Dick Heller loves these streets, this city. He doesn't understand why he can't be a good, responsible example of a gun owner on them; after all, in 2008 the U.S. Supreme Court decided 5 to 4 in *District of Columbia v. Heller* that DC's banning citizens from owning handguns was unconstitutional.

After the Supreme Court win, Heller followed the law to get a permit for a handgun. He was fingerprinted, he paid fees, and he waited as DC police did a background check on him. He finally got his permit to own a handgun in DC. Nevertheless, the District still won't let him carry his registered handgun outside his home.

This is why he is again a plaintiff in a case working its way to the U.S. Supreme Court, a case that has been dubbed "Heller II." He is one of five plaintiffs who want the high court to ultimately declare the District of Columbia's gun registry and other gun-control regulations unconstitutional.

The original *Heller* decision declared the Second Amendment to be an individual right. It struck down DC's outright ban on handguns as well as regulations requiring that all firearms, including rifles and shotguns, be kept "unloaded and disassembled or bound by a trigger lock." Those DC laws had made it impossible for a homeowner to use a firearm in defense of his or her life.

He said to me, "I'm just an ordinary guy who decided to make a stand because my constitutional rights have been taken from me. I carry a gun when protecting people in a federal building, but then I have to check in the gun when I leave. I often get off work at midnight. So I have to make my way home disarmed through DC. I've been approached by thugs, but at least I'm a guy. If I were a woman, I wouldn't be able to keep this job. It would be too risky. It's these basic rights to freedom we're trying to win back."

After Heller's first Supreme Court victory, the District of Columbia "obviously grabbed every gun-control restriction they could find from the fifty states and included almost all of them in its hastily written gun-control ordinances," he said. "This is how they created a system so burdensome to the Second Amendment we still don't have our right to bear arms here in DC even though we won that right in court."

The question in "Heller II" is, when does government red tape become so burdensome that it infringes upon the people's right to bear arms?

This challenge to DC's gun laws has been working its way through the courts for a number of years. In October 2011, the U.S. Court of Appeals upheld what it called a "basic" registration of handguns, but questioned whether any registration of rifles and shotguns is constitutional. The court remanded the case to the district court to gather further evidence on whether DC's gun laws are reasonable.

In December 2013 the plaintiffs' attorneys, Stephen Halbrook and Dan Peterson, deposed DC's witnesses and filed a motion in U.S. District Court for the District of Columbia asking Judge James Boasberg for summary judgment on whether DC's gun registration and other laws are "reasonable" based on the evidence.

According to these rules, starting January 1, 2014, every gun owner in DC—even those who have a shotgun or rifle—who has registered a gun since 1976 had to go to police headquarters to be fingerprinted and photographed.

Halbrook said to me, "If DC gets its way, gun owners will have to do this every three years. Even those who have the time and money to make it through this difficult process will find they're never done, as DC is still trying to burden them with expiration and reregistration deadlines that, if missed, would turn them into criminals."

Halbrook also pointed out that long guns are rarely used in crimes and says this clearly shows the laws are only designed to impede people from legally owning guns. The facts back him up. According to data provided by DC to the FBI for 2009, only 2 out of 144 murders in DC were known to have been committed with a long gun. In 2010, out of 131 murders in DC, not one is reported to have been committed with a rifle or shotgun. In 2011, only 1 murder in DC was reported to have been committed with a long gun (a shotgun), out of 108 murders total. Given that less than 1 percent of murders are being committed with long guns, how can DC justify the onerous need for fingerprinting residents every three years? For context, realize that for the same time period (2009–2011) ninety-six homicides were reportedly committed with knives or weapons other than guns and fists.

When questioned about the need for these laws, DC's witnesses weren't able to cite a single study indicating that its firearm registration prevents illegal possession of firearms. Actually, studies show that registration laws haven't had a measurable affect on crime rates or gun violence. During deposition, DC Police chief Cathy L. Lanier even conceded, "It is not clear [to the District] how firearms' registration records could be used to 'prevent' a crime." In fact, she said she couldn't "recall any specific instance where registration records were used to determine who committed a crime," except for possession offenses. Lanier couldn't even provide a single example of a registration record being used to solve a crime committed with a long gun.

Now, every fourth grader knows the First Amendment's protection of the freedom of speech is a fundamental liberty earned on the battlefield and later safeguarded in the Bill of Rights. But few Americans today understand that the First Amendment, the Second Amendment, and the rest of the Bill of Rights are not rights the government is required to enforce, but freedoms government cannot infringe: government has not created these rights; these are rights the government cannot unreasonably take away from the people.

This is what DC is trying to do with the Second Amendment. They are forcing residents to seek permission above and beyond a federal background check for owning any firearm. According to DC, "no person or organization in the District shall possess or control any firearm, unless the person or organization holds a valid registration certificate for the firearm." Possession of an unregistered firearm is punishable by imprisonment for one year and a $1,000 fine. For a second offense, someone can get five years in the pen and a $5,000 fine. "Applicants" wishing to exercise their Second Amendment rights have to be fingerprinted and photographed at a police station; fees have to be paid for each firearm; and restrictions prohibit carrying a gun for self-defense.

DC cites as a legal precedent for registering long guns an 1896 law from the Republic of Hawaii that required a license to possess a firearm. Hawaii, of course, was then an independent country. (Hawaii became a U.S. territory in 1898 and a state in 1959.) DC argues that "laws requiring the registration of certain types of long guns at the federal level has [sic] proven 'highly successful' in reducing the use of such long-guns in crime." DC naturally doesn't cite any data or studies to back up this claim, since there aren't any. DC also cites an 1893

Florida statute that empowered officials to grant a license to carry a pistol or repeating rifle. This law, however, didn't require a license to possess a firearm and, according to background dug up by Halbrook, was only passed "for the purpose of disarming the negro laborers," according to one of the justices at the time.

A logical question is why, after the Supreme Court decided *Heller* in 2008, has DC decided to float a reregistration scheme? Halbrook noted that DC's "own witnesses cite no studies showing that periodic registration renewal or reporting requirements reduce crime or protect police officers."

DC Police chief Lanier and the officers who oversee the Firearms Registration Section are quoted in the brief from the plaintiffs' attorneys noting there were only two handgun applications denied by DC in 2011 and 2012. During this period not a single rifle or shotgun application was refused. This, of course, isn't surprising. Criminals aren't likely to voluntarily troop down to the police station to be fingerprinted and photographed.

The numbers fill in the details. From 2007 to 2013, the police seized twelve thousand unregistered firearms; meanwhile, cops only seized thirty-six registered guns during this same period. Of those thirty-six guns, only seventeen were involved in charges against a registered firearm owner. Of those seventeen cases, only two resulted in convictions for a violent crime. Clearly the good guys with the guns—the ones being burdened by the gun-control regulations—are not the problem.

Actually, this case has also shown that officers responding to calls are not even being informed if there is a registered firearm at a location. Police cars aren't equipped with a computer that can access the firearms registry, and dispatchers can't check the registration database. As of January 2014, the whole system was simply a gauntlet designed to prevent law-abiding citizens from utilizing their Second Amendment rights.

=================

The push against unreasonably restrictive gun laws extends to Chicago, which has some of the most-restrictive gun laws in the country and yet is both America's murder capital and in 2012 ranked dead last for federal prosecutions of gun crimes. A hero of this fight is Otis McDonald. In April 2008, McDonald, a retired maintenance engineer, agreed to serve as the lead plaintiff in a lawsuit challenging Chicago's handgun ban, which had been in place since 1982. McDonald is the child of black Louisiana sharecroppers. He was seventeen years old when he borrowed eighteen dollars from his mother and set off for Chicago in 1951. He was just one of millions of African Americans who fled the South during the "Great Migration." McDonald settled in Chicago's Morgan Park neighborhood. At the time, the neighborhood was bustling and relatively safe. In the ensuing years he got married, raised eight children, and spent a career working at the University of Chicago, where he started as a janitor and worked his way up to become a maintenance engineer. But by the time he retired, in 1997, his neighborhood had been lost to gangs. McDonald told the *Chicago Tribune*, "I know every day that I come out in the streets, the youngsters will shoot me as quick as they will a policeman."

According to police reports, McDonald's house was repeatedly burglarized. On one occasion, McDonald says, three young men surrounded his car and threatened to "off" him.

McDonald decided to become involved in the gun-rights movement in 2005, when Mayor Richard Daley was pushing a statewide ban on "assault weapons." McDonald was concerned that his shotgun might be outlawed under the proposed ban, so he started attending gun-rights rallies. The connections he formed at those events led to his inclusion in the class-action lawsuit against the city of Chicago.

McDonald, a Democrat and longtime hunter, had by then been a law-abiding resident of Chicago for more than fifty years. He wasn't an activist. He was simply a person trying to live the American dream. McDonald explained, "I was feeling the poor blacks who years ago had their guns taken away from them [in the post–Civil War South] and were killed as someone wished. That was a long time ago, but I feel their spirit. That's what I was feeling in the courtroom.... This lawsuit, I hope, will allow me to bring my handgun into the city legally. I only want a handgun in my house for my protection."

McDonald's case went to the Supreme Court, and as with Heller, he won (*McDonald v. Chicago*, 2010). The Supreme Court opinion noted: "[The] number of Chicago homicide victims during the current year equaled the number of American soldiers killed during that same period in Afghanistan and Iraq ... 80 percent of the Chicago victims were black.... If, as petitioners believe, their safety and the safety of other law-abiding members of the community would be enhanced by the possession of handguns in the home for self-defense, then the Second Amendment right protects the rights of minorities and other residents of high-crime areas whose needs are not being met by elected public officials."

The Second Amendment battle with the city of Chicago, however, didn't end with the ruling. To sidestep the Supreme Court decision, Chicago quickly passed a new ordinance. City officials called the new law "the strictest in the nation." As it turns out, it was perhaps the stupidest. The measure prohibited gun stores from opening in Chicago, and it prevented gun owners from so much as stepping outside their homes with a handgun. (In January 2014 U.S. district judge Edmond Chang ruled that the city of Chicago couldn't ban licensed firearm dealers from the city.) The law also prevented citizens from using a firearm on their porches or in their garages. That's right, the law actually explained where you could and couldn't defend your life. Though precisely what a "porch" is under the law remains to be answered. Does screened-in count? How about windows with an air conditioner?

Since passing that ordinance in 2010, Chicago has been forced to allow residents to purchase handguns—but only after they pay fees and navigate onerous restrictions. Officials cite Chicago's murder rate to justify banning concealed handguns. This was the same argument used in Washington, DC, when the *Heller* case was decided. DC's then-mayor Adrian Fenty warned, "More handguns in the District of Columbia will only lead to more handgun violence."[2] Knowing that Chicago's gun laws would soon face a similar legal challenge, Chicago's then-mayor Richard Daley said he was "outraged" by the *Heller* decision and said people "are going to take a gun and they are going to end their lives in a family dispute."[3]

Murders in Washington, DC, however, actually plummeted by an astounding 25 percent in 2009, the year after the *Heller* decision, giving DC its lowest murder rate since 1967. DC's drop was several times greater than that of other similar-sized cities that also registered falling murder rates, says John Lott, author of *More Guns, Less Crime*.

Lott also discovered that jurisdictions with "shall issue" laws, granting concealed handgun permits (subject to certain established criteria), had lower murder rates than those that didn't. Peer-reviewed studies have confirmed Lott's findings. For example, a study by Carlisle E. Moody and Thomas B. Marvell that was published in

Econ Journal Watch in January 2009, determined: "Many articles have been published finding that shall-issue laws reduce crime. Only one article, by Ayres and Donohue who employ a model that combines a dummy variable with a post-law trend, claims to find that shall-issue laws increase crime. However, the only way that they can produce the result that shall-issue laws increase crime is to confine the span of analysis to five years. We show, using their own estimates, that if they had extended their analysis by one more year, they would have concluded that these laws reduce crime."

Despite all the evidence that guns in the hands of law-abiding citizens is a deterrent to crime, Chicago's mayor Rahm Emanuel and police superintendent Garry McCarthy blame the city's high murder rate on less-restrictive gun laws in other states. But Lott's evidence from island states, which are good examples because of their clear and tightly controlled borders, belie this claim: "When handgun bans were enacted in Ireland and Jamaica, in 1972 and 1974, respectively, murder rates doubled over the following decade. And take the more recent example in England and Wales, where handguns were banned in 1997: deaths and injuries from gun crime more than doubled over the next seven years." Closer to home, Chicago's murder rate, which had been falling relative to similar-sized cities prior to 1982, started rising after the gun ban.

I asked Lott what he would do if he were mayor of Chicago. He told me that he would "give law-abiding people the ability to protect themselves in public and in their homes"; hire more police officers, given that Chicago's police department has actually shrunk (he shows how this could be done simply by shifting government resources in his book *Freedomnomics*); and maintain anti-gang units and leave officers on established beats, because it "takes years for [police officers] to get to know who the good and bad guys are on any given street."

In both *Heller* (2008) and *McDonald* (2010), the high court split 5 to 4 in favor of the Second Amendment right of the people to bear arms. This could change with the retirement of a single Supreme Court justice. Anyone who slogs through the minority opinions in either of those cases will find that, with one more vote, the liberal block on the high court is poised to vote the Second Amendment right out of the Bill of Rights.

"I know it's a cliché to say this," Andrew Arulanandam, director of public affairs at the National Rifle Association, tells me, "but this is why we consider the 2014 midterm election and the next presidential election to be the most important elections in the history of our right to keep and bear arms."

The NRA, the Second Amendment Foundation, and many other gun-rights groups have been involved in court battles across the country from Connecticut to California defending an individual's right to own a gun. In an important example, in February 2014 the Ninth Circuit Court of Appeals confirmed that the Second Amendment protects an individual right to carry firearms for self-defense in public. The decision came in *Peruta v. San Diego County*.[4] The majority opinion in *Peruta* said, "We are called upon to decide whether a responsible, law-abiding citizen has a right under the Second Amendment to carry a firearm in public for self-defense." The case was brought by the California Rifle and Pistol Association Foundation on behalf of five individuals who were denied the right to carry a handgun by the San Diego sheriff.

According to California law, a person applying for their Second Amendment right to carry a concealed handgun must: (1) be a resident of their respective city or county; (2) be of "good moral character";

(3) have "good cause" for such a license; and (4) pass a firearms train-ing course. Many rural California counties accept self-defense as "good cause" for a person to get a license to carry a handgun, but some urban sheriffs and chiefs of police disagree, and in these jurisdictions the few who attain permits have to beg, plead, and show imminent danger to their lives before they can exercise their right to bear arms.

The Ninth Circuit's majority opinion attempted to address this problem, stating, "It doesn't take a lawyer to see that straightforward application of the rule in *Heller* will not dispose of this case. It should be equally obvious that neither *Heller* nor *McDonald* speaks explicitly or precisely to the scope of the Second Amendment right outside the home or to what it takes to 'infringe' it. Yet, it is just as apparent that neither opinion is silent on these matters, for, at the very least, the Supreme Court's approach ... points in a general direction."

The Ninth Circuit decided 2 to 1 that the restrictive "good cause" policy of the San Diego County Sheriff's Department was unconsti-tutional. The majority opinion accepts that "the Second Amendment right is 'not unlimited.' It is 'not a right to keep and carry any weapon whatsoever in any manner whatsoever and for whatever purpose.' Rather, it is a right subject to 'traditional restrictions,' which them-selves—and this is a critical point—tend 'to show the scope of the right.'"[5] In this case, the court concluded that the government can ban open carry or concealed carry, but the Second Amendment prohibits the government from banning both. In *Shepard v. Madigan* (2013), the Seventh Circuit Court of Appeals confirmed that a citizen's right to carry a gun is protected outside the home.[6] But *Peruta* was the first appellate decision to affirm that licenses to carry cannot be denied to law-abiding citizens. The majority decision in *Peruta* noted that "Our opinion is not the first to address the question of whether the Second Amendment protects a responsible, law-abiding citizen's right to bear arms outside the home for the lawful purpose of self-defense. Indeed, we are the fifth circuit court to opine expressly on the issue, joining an existent circuit split." The opinion later says, "Our reading of the Second Amendment is akin to the Seventh Circuit's interpretation [in *Shepard v. Madigan*] ... and at odds with the approach of the Second, Third, and Fourth Circuits.... We are unpersuaded by the decisions of the Second, Third, and Fourth Circuits for several reasons. First, contrary to the approach in *Heller*, all three courts declined to undertake a complete historical analysis of the scope and nature of the Second Amendment right outside the home.... As a result, they misapprehend both the nature of the Second Amendment right and the implications of state laws that prevent the vast majority of responsible, law-abiding citizens from carrying in public for lawful self-defense purposes."

The Ninth Circuit then determined that "states may not destroy the right to bear arms in public under the guise of regulating it.... By evading an in-depth analysis of history and tradition, the Second, Third, and Fourth Circuits missed a crucial piece of the Second Amendment analysis. They failed to comprehend that carrying weapons in public for the lawful purpose of self defense is a central component of the right to bear arms."

When circuit courts begin calling each other out on constitutional questions like this, the U.S. Supreme Court usually takes a case to settle the dispute. Whether the U.S. Supreme Court's nine justices will split the same way they did in *Heller* and *McDonald* will depend on the health of the justices and the outcomes of 2014 and 2016 senatorial and presidential elections.

CHAPTER SEVEN

What Happens to Disarmed Peoples

*From available statistics, among the [twenty-seven]
countries surveyed, it is difficult to find a correlation
between the existence of strict firearms regulations and
a lower incidence of gun-related crimes.*
—**Library of Congress**[1]

I didn't set out to embarrass this English journalist. It's just that he had it coming.

Let's call him Stephen Grey, as that's his real name. He's not a bad sort. Grey was educated at England's famed St. Alban's School and studied philosophy at Oxford. He has outsized ears and somehow seems too tall for his boyish face. These features give him a look of young innocence that you soon find is matched by sincerity. Then you run into his intellect and you really like him. He wrote his last book,

Into the Viper's Nest, after being embedded with soldiers in Afghanistan. He saw firsthand what the Taliban did to women. He knows all about the barbaric things al Qaeda has done to a few of his colleagues. He knows jihadists consider civilians to be fair game. Nevertheless, he doesn't think average people should have a right to firearms for self-defense.

Grey was seated across a table from me at a small dinner party in Washington, DC, saying things like, "Americans need to give up their guns. They must become responsible citizens of the world." Meanwhile, the other writers around the table—people who know my background—were glancing at me, bracing for the counterattack.

I stayed quiet as he described his utopian vision of a disarmed world. I didn't think he'd be swayed by crime statistics—though there are some astounding figures we'll get into later. What I needed was something he hadn't heard before. So I started with the story of a particular Springfield Model 1903, which, I told him, "might make you rethink your views."

He eyed me over his whiskey and soda.

This particular rifle, I explained, was owned by Major John W. Hession (1877–1961), an American long-range competition shooter, who probably purchased it in 1906. The rifle, chambered in .30-06, was constructed at the U.S. government's Springfield Armory, which had been started by George Washington. Hession found the rifle was so accurate—he had topped it with a J. Stevens Company riflescope—that he took it to England to compete in the Olympics in 1908 at the Bisley Range. In 1909 he used the rifle to set a world record at eight hundred yards at Camp Perry. At the time the *Piqua Leader-Dispatch* (a newspaper that went out of business in 1919) ran the headline "World's Record Is Broken by Hession" on its front page. The feat made him a star. So much so that the June 1911 issue of *Forest and Stream* reported that when Hession competed at the DuPont Gun

Club, they were "especially pleased to have Mr. Hession with them. He is regarded by critics as the foremost long-range rifle shot in the world. His most remarkable performance, and the one which brought him the most fame, was at Camp Perry during 1909. At this time he made 67 consecutive bullseyes at 800 yds., a record never before equaled nor since broken."

Hession was a top long-range competitor well into the 1940s. He won the Marine Corps Cup Match in 1913 and the British Wimbledon Cup in 1919 and 1932, and in 1925 he managed to set four world records in one day—a day that saw him shoot 102 shots, all of them bull's-eyes. Hession had an understandable attachment to his 1903 Springfield. Such a profound attachment, in fact, that he later did something even more remarkable with this rifle.

After World War I, Britain's Parliament passed gun-control laws that mostly disarmed its citizenry. The belief that there should be "a rifle in every cottage," as proposed by Prime Minister Robert Gascoyne-Cecil in 1900, was finished. According to the 1689 Bill of Rights "subjects which are Protestants may have arms for their defence suitable to their conditions and as allowed by law." This changed with Britain's Firearms Act of 1920. Its restrictions on the private ownership of firearms was partly sold to a war-weary public by politicians fanning fears that a surge in crime might occur because of the large number of firearms available following the war. Another justification for severely restricting firearms ownership was to fulfill a commitment to the 1919 Paris Arms Convention.

Whatever the rationales, the Firearms Act of 1920 passed and required British citizens who wanted to own a firearm to first obtain a firearm certificate. The certificate, which was good for three years, specifically listed the firearm a person was approved to own and listed the amount of ammunition that person could buy or possess. The police even had the power to exclude anyone who had "intemperate habits" or an "unsound mind." Applicants for certificates also had to convince the police they had a good reason for needing a certificate. The 1920 law did not affect those who owned shotguns, but it gave government officials complete control over who could own handguns and rifles.

In 1933, Britain's Parliament passed the Firearms and Imitation Firearms Bill. This legislation increased the punishment for the use of a gun in the commission of a crime. Possession of a real or imitation firearm was also made an offense unless the person could show they had the firearm for "a lawful object." The 1937 Firearms Act extended restrictions to shotguns and granted chief constables the power to add conditions to individual firearms certificates. Clearly the power was in the hands of the state, not the individual.

Predictably, these restrictions reduced the number of firearms in law-abiding citizens' hands. Then came the Battle of Dunkirk in 1940. As the German war machine advanced at this early stage in World War II, the British Expeditionary Force evacuated back across the English Channel. The retreat was costly. In their haste, British troops abandoned most of their equipment, and a disarmed British people awaited an expected Nazi invasion.

Luckily, the British had gun-owning friends across the Atlantic. In 1940 a group of Americans, headed by C. Suydam Cutting, moved quickly to help rearm Britain's citizens. They established the "American Committee for Defense of British Homes" and ran an ad in the November 1940 issue of *American Rifleman* that read in part: "British Civilians, undergoing nightly air raids, are in desperate need of Firearms—Binoculars—Steel Helmets—Stop-Watches—Ammunition." The ad then said, "If you possess any of these articles you can aid in the battle of Britain by sending these materials to American Committee for Defense of British Homes."

Hession, who was then working for Winchester Arms, decided to make a statement. He sent his prized Springfield Model 1903 to the American Committee for Defense of British Homes. Before he did this, he had two plates attached to the rifle's stock. The one on the rifle's butt read: "This rifle was used by Major John W. Hession in winning Olympics Bisley England 1908—Grand Aggregate Camp Perry 1908—Worlds 800 YD. Record Camp Perry 1909." A plate placed on the rifle's forend read: "FOR OBVIOUS REASONS THE RETURN OF THIS RIFLE AFTER GERMANY IS DEFEATED WOULD BE DEEPLY APPRECIATED."

Hession's rifle was shipped to England. Before the end of the war, the NRA alone sent more than seven thousand private firearms to England. The U.S. government, of course, sent many more from the Springfield Armory. Congress passed the Lend-Lease Act in March 1941. Almost immediately, vast quantities of "U.S. Rifle, Cal. .30, M1" were headed across the Atlantic.

Winston Churchill was appreciative. He wrote in *Their Finest Hour*: "When the ships from America approached our shores with their priceless arms, special trains were waiting in all ports to receive their cargoes. The Home Guard in every county, in every village, sat up through the night to receive them.... By the end of July we were an armed nation.... Anyhow, if we had to go down fighting ... a lot of our men and some women had weapons in their hands...."

England, of course, was victorious after American troops entered the war; and wonderfully, after the war, Hession's rifle found its way back from England to Hession. This rifle can now be seen in the NRA's National Firearms Museum in Fairfax, Virginia.

By the time I gave up the floor, Grey had finished his whisky and soda and was staring at the melting ice at the bottom of his glass. I concluded by saying, "Sadly, Britain is again a disarmed nation."

Today, to obtain a firearm certificate in Britain, the police must be convinced that a person has "good reason" to own a firearm, and that he can be trusted with it "without danger to the public safety or to the peace." British firearms licenses are only issued if a person has a recognized sporting, collecting, or work-related reasons for owner-ship. Since 1946, self-defense has *not* been considered a valid reason to own a firearm—nor has national defense.

England's Firearms Act of 1997 banned the private ownership of handguns almost completely. The ban is so restrictive even England's Olympic pistol team had to go abroad to practice before the 2012 Summer Olympics in London. This became such a national embar-rassment that the English government passed a special dispensation to allow the shooting events to be held in England during the 2012 games.

My argument might have been less polished than how it appears here in print, but I still thought it was effective. Grey's response? "The world has evolved."

I took a parting shot: "If your emasculated people ever need to protect their freedom from threats domestic or foreign, Americans will again be there to help rearm your populace."

———

Perhaps that wasn't kind to Stephen, who as I said is a splendid chap and a fine journalist. I begin with him, though, because it's revealing that even an Englishman who has traveled into the world's hot zones, as Stephen has, is still skeptical of the natural right to defend our lives, a right so English it was included in the English Bill of Rights of 1689. This traditional right of an Englishman would later influence the inclusion of what would become the Second Amendment in our own Constitution's Bill of Rights ("A well regulated Militia, being necessary to the security of a free State, the right of the people to keep and bear Arms, shall not be infringed"). Despite England's long history of freedom, the British people have relinquished their fundamental right to self-defense, relying entirely on the protection of their government. History, of course, teaches that freedom can be lost by degrees, with one loss of liberty leading to another.

When this point is raised, gun-rights enthusiasts like to quote, "The strongest reason for the people to retain the right to keep and bear arms is, as a last resort, to protect themselves against tyranny in government."[2] (Though this quotation is often attributed to Jefferson, the real author remains unknown.) The argument is historically grounded, but it makes people wince—and it should make people wince, because armed rebellion should be the last option for a repressed people, especially as we know that few armed rebellions lead to greater freedom, such as was won with the American Revolution.

But to understand what happens to a disarmed nation living in a European-style socialist state, it's helpful to look at the riots that erupted in London in August 2011.

The riots began in Tottenham, a dicey corner of north London, after police shot and killed a twenty-nine-year-old Tottenham resident named Mark Duggan. As typically happens, two competing personality profiles of Duggan were quickly pedaled to the public, each a slave to the politics of the teller: while some said Duggan was a hardened drug dealer, others said he was a beloved family man. Whatever Duggan's moral character, what isn't disputed is that police pulled over a taxi. Duggan was a passenger. Police say they heard a gunshot and that this prompted them to shoot and kill the loveable or cold-hearted Duggan.

The facts of this incident may be in dispute, but the unmanly actions of Tottenham's gangster youth were not. Whether their looting, robbery, and bedlam were childish retaliation for Duggan's death or whether Duggan's death was a hell of an excuse for a lot of rebellious mayhem depends on the view of the teller. Either way, they burned autos, looted stores, and mugged people along the Tottenham High Road and around other parts of London. The most revealing image from the London riots appeared in the August 9, 2011, issue of the *Daily Mail*.[3] The newspaper ran a photo of a skinny young man taking off his pants on the street in bright daylight as an impatient looter waits with the emasculated Englishman's sneakers and shirt already in his greedy hands. Luckily the feeble Englishman chose boxers over briefs, but as I look at this picture I can't help but wonder if men such as T. E. Lawrence, Winston Churchill, and Lord Acton could have stomached the state of manliness in this generation of Englishmen.

To put this cultural shift into perspective, consider the "Tottenham Outrage" of 1909.[4] Two men in Tottenham, Paul Helfeld and Jacob Lepidus, armed with semiautomatic handguns, attempted to rob a payroll truck outside a rubber factory on the corner of Tottenham High Road and Chestnut Road. Helfeld had an FN M1900 pistol, and Lepidus carried a Bergmann 1894 pistol. The truck arrived with the workers' wages, which a guard collected from the car. Lepidus jumped him and tried to grab the moneybag. The guard and the thief rolled onto the ground, each struggling for control of the money. Another guard joined the fight and for a moment restrained Lepidus, but Helfeld then stepped into the fray and fired several shots hitting one of the guards. The guard's heavy coat stopped the bullets from Helfeld's FN M1900, which was chambered in .32 ACP, a light pistol cartridge, comparable to the velocity and power of a .22 Long Rifle used by small-game hunters and target shooters.

Two police officers heard the shots from the nearby Tottenham Police Station and came running. When they arrived they found a local gas stoker beating Lepidus and the others brawling. The two thieves saw the cops and ran with the moneybag.

The chase was on. As they ran one of the officers borrowed a revolver from a bystander and shot four times at Lepidus and Helfeld, but all his shots missed. The criminals returned fire and one of their shots killed a ten-year-old boy, Ralph Joscelyne, who had been helping a baker with his deliveries.

Helfeld and Lepidus ran for a railway footbridge at the end of Down Road leading to a park called Tottenham Marshes. A police officer, William Tyler, cut them off. Tyler shouted, "Come on, give in, the game's up." Helfeld didn't think so. He shot Tyler through the head. Another officer caught up and stayed with Tyler, who died before reaching the hospital.

Lepidus and Helfeld ran to the River Lea. While searching for a crossing, a number of civilian bystanders attempted to arrest them but were scattered when the criminals started shooting. The robbers crossed Mill Stream Bridge but stopped on the other side to gasp for air and to fire more shots at their civilian pursuers, injuring two more. At this point a police officer crawled forward with a revolver, but his borrowed gun failed to fire. Helfeld and Lepidus saw the officer and shot him in the thigh and leg.

The two ran again, this time along the south side of the Banbury Reservoir in Walthamstow. Another civilian, a horse keeper, tried to stop them and was injured. Another police officer caught up with them and fired four shots from a borrowed revolver, but all his shots also missed.

Helfeld and Lepidus fired at more people before reaching Salisbury Farm. They didn't get much rest there, as they were chased by a growing posse of civilians and police.

Helfeld and Lepidus ran again and managed to hijack a tram, wounding another bystander, and headed for Leyton. About forty police boarded and commandeered another tram to give chase. Another police officer, racing after the tram in a horse-drawn carriage, was stymied when the criminals shot his horse and the carriage crashed.

The thieves jumped off their hijacked tram and stole a milk cart. When its owner tried to stop them, they shot and wounded him. They drove the horse and cart along Farnham Road into Forest Road, where it tipped over. They abandoned the milk cart and hijacked another horse and cart. Lepidus was now riding the horse, and Helfeld was firing at the people chasing them. The crowd in hot pursuit was led by a motorcar—remember this is 1909—with two officers in it blazing away with a double-barrel shotgun. The gunfight kept roaring along like a Benny Hill finale with Bonnie and Clyde as guest stars until the robbers' horse and cart swerved and crashed.

Helfeld and Lepidus abandoned the horse and cart and fled to the River Ching. Lepidus climbed over a six-foot-high fence. Helfeld had trouble getting over the fence. As the crowd neared, Helfeld shot himself in the right eye, but survived and was taken to the Prince of Wales Hospital.

Lepidus ran into a home. There was a man, woman, and two children inside. The mother ran out of the house. Two officers and a baker attempted to rescue the children and father. Lepidus looked out one of the front bedroom windows but was driven back by gunfire from police and civilians. A police officer borrowed a civilian's handgun, climbed a ladder placed at the back of the cottage, and opened a bedroom window. He had a clear shot at Helfeld, but he didn't know how to undo the firearm's safety.

Other officers, however, stormed the house and fired through a door into the room where Lepidus was hiding. When the officers busted into the room, they found Lepidus dead. Lepidus had killed himself. The other thief died later in surgery.

The bravery of the officers and civilians involved prompted the creation of the King's Police Medal. The funeral processions for the slain officer and the boy who was killed passed through streets lined with a half million mournful Londoners.[5]

These Londoners wouldn't take their pants off for a looter, and they didn't, unlike many people in the inner cities today, demonize police officers; on the contrary, they were ready to assist them and even loan guns to them.

Something has changed in the English character since 1909. Could it be that the English have been emasculated by losing their right to bear arms, their right to self-defense? Since individuals can no longer combat crime themselves, and are dependent on the state, they increasingly blame the police for not being everywhere all the time, and act helpless when crime strikes.

After jihadists attacked and murdered a British soldier in daylight on the streets of London on May 22, 2013, the English newspaper the *Guardian* obtained a video of one of two of the killers talking to bystanders almost calmly with a bloody knife and meat cleaver still in his hands.[6] The killers weren't worried about the bystanders intervening. Watch the video and you'll see dozens of Londoners in the background watching with craned necks, until the police finally arrive and shoot the killers in self-defense. A disarmed populace is a populace that will cower behind locked doors when a victim is raped or murdered. A disarmed populace is also a populace that will come to resent to the police, as officers are set above citizens, and seem more like masters than servants.

———

There are still guns on the streets in London. A report by the U.S. Library of Congress noted: "Despite [England's] stringent gun laws, newspaper reports indicate that illegal handguns can be purchased for £50–100 (approximately U.S. $70–155). In 2002 a Member of Parliament stated that there are some inner-city areas 'in which it is now easier to buy an illegal gun than to find a taxi in the rain.'"[7, 8]

The source of illegal firearms in England is as diverse as any market. Some guns come from other European Union nations, arriving via ports or the Chunnel,[9] and a few have speculated that after the ceasefire the IRA began selling surplus guns on a black market that leads to England.[10]

An increase in gun crime caused London's Metropolitan Police to start Operation Trident in 1998.[11] Trident was established as a dedicated Operational Command Unit within the Metropolitan Police Specialist Crime Directorate. In 2004 this unit expanded with the formation of Operation Trafalgar, which was designed to investigate all non-fatal shootings in London.

Trident has overstepped on a few high-profile occasions. In 2006, Trident officers raided the home of vintage gun enthusiast Mick Shepherd and seized his gun collection. At the time, press reports claimed a huge gun-smuggling racket had been uncovered, and that guns sold by Shepherd were linked to a number of murders. As he awaited trial, Shepherd was imprisoned in the high-security Belmarsh prison for ten months.[12] Shepherd was, however, finally acquitted of all thirteen firearms offenses filed against him.[13] Moreover, the Kent Police had, ironically, renewed Shepherd's Registered Firearms Dealers license, after visiting his home and inspecting his collection, only a few weeks before arresting him. Shepherd commented on his case by saying that gun owners in Britain "have been persecuted for years to the extent where people now think if they see or hear about guns it is to do with terrible murders and armed robberies.... Why would a killer buy an antique weapon from me for £2,000 when you can get a sub-machine gun or Mac 10 and Uzis for a few hundred quid off the street?"[14]

You might hope that despite such outrages, Britain's strict gun laws would at least result in a lower murder rate—and you would be wrong. Granted, the official number of homicides involving guns, as reported by Britain's Home Office,[15] is extremely low. It was sixty-two in 2000 and fifty-two in 2011, in a country of sixty-three million people.[16] The trick is, that's only a part of the total of Britain's over-all homicide figure, which is hard to compile because the statistics come from local police departments that use different reporting criteria—even different definitions of "homicide," with some counting multiple murders by a single killer as one murder. Because of these discrepancies and others, even the UK's Office for National Statistics (ONS) doesn't stand firmly behind the official homicide figures.[17]

In 2009 an article in Britain's *Daily Mail* ran the sensational headline: "The Most Violent Country in Europe: Britain Is Also Worse Than South Africa and U.S."[18] The article reported that from 1997 to 2007,

> the number of recorded violent attacks soared by 77 per cent to 1.158 million—or more than two every minute. The figures, compiled from reports released by the European Commission and United Nations, also show: The UK has the second highest overall crime rate in the EU. It has a higher homicide rate than most of our western European neighbours, including France, Germany, Italy and Spain. The UK has the fifth highest robbery rate in the EU.... [I]t

is the naming of Britain as the most violent country in the EU that is most shocking. The analysis is based on the number of crimes per 100,000 residents. In the UK, there are 2,034 offences per 100,000 people, way ahead of second-placed Austria with a rate of 1,677. The U.S. has a violence rate of 466 crimes per 100,000 residents, Canada 935, Australia 92 and South Africa 1,609.

This article got a lot of attention, but the fact is, as the article later notes, major differences in how crime is reported and measured make such comparisons problematic.

One of the better studies on comparative murder rates and gun ownership was published in 2007, in the *Harvard Journal of Law & Public Policy*.[19] This study—titled "Would Banning Firearms Reduce Murder and Suicide?"—looked at figures for "intentional deaths" throughout continental Europe and compared them with statistics from the United States. The study's authors were Don B. Kates, an American criminologist and constitutional lawyer, and Gary Mauser, a Canadian criminologist and university professor at Simon Fraser University, in Burnaby, British Columbia, Canada. They determined that "the mantra that more guns mean more deaths and that fewer guns, therefore, mean fewer deaths" just doesn't add up. The authors wrote:

> Since at least 1965, the false assertion that the United States has the industrialized world's highest murder rate has been an artifact of politically motivated Soviet minimization designed to hide the true homicide rates.
>
> Since well before that date, the Soviet Union possessed extremely stringent gun controls that were effectuated by a police state apparatus providing stringent enforcement....

Yet, manifest success in keeping its people disarmed did not prevent the Soviet Union from having far and away the highest murder rate in the developed world. In the 1960s and early 1970s, the gun-less Soviet Union's murder rates paralleled or generally exceeded those of gun-ridden America. While American rates stabilized and then steeply declined, however, Russian murder increased so drastically that by the early 1990s the Russian rate was three times higher than that of the United States. Between 1998–2004 (the latest figure available for Russia), Russian murder rates were nearly four times higher than American rates.[20]

They note that owning a gun in America is common when compared with many other nations, but that countries such as Norway, Finland, Germany, France, and Denmark also have high gun-ownership rates. They found that "[t]hese countries, however, have murder rates as low or lower than many developed nations in which gun ownership is much rarer. For example, Luxembourg, where handguns are totally banned and ownership of any kind of gun is minimal, had a murder rate nine times higher than Germany in 2002."

After looking at areas within England and comparing them with the United States, they found a "a negative correlation" between guns and crime. They determined that "where firearms are most dense violent crime rates are lowest, and where guns are least dense violent crime rates are highest."

They found that it's a "misconception" that low homicide rates are caused by stringent gun controls. They say, "That attribution cannot be accurate since murder in Europe was at an all-time low before the gun controls were introduced." They note that a few studies have dug into this issue. "In 2004, the U.S. National Academy of Sciences released its evaluation from a review of 253 journal articles,

99 books, 43 government publications, and some original empirical research. It failed to identify any gun control that had reduced violent crime, suicide, or gun accidents. The same conclusion was reached in 2003 by the U.S. Centers for Disease Control's review of then-extant studies."

The Harvard report also draws on research done by Professor Joyce Lee Malcolm in her book *Guns and Violence: The English Experience*. Malcolm is a professor at the George Mason University School of Law. Her study of English gun law and violent crime found that:

> The peacefulness England used to enjoy was not the result of strict gun laws. When it had no firearms restrictions [nineteenth and early twentieth century] England had little violent crime, while the present extraordinarily stringent gun controls have not stopped the increase in violence or even the increase in armed violence.
>
> Armed crime, never a problem in England, has now become one. Handguns are banned but the Kingdom has millions of illegal firearms. Criminals have no trouble finding them and exhibit a new willingness to use them. In the decade after 1957, the use of guns in serious crime increased a hundredfold.[21]

In the late 1990s, England moved from strict gun controls to a complete ban of all handguns and many types of long guns. Hundreds of thousands of guns were confiscated. Kates and Mauser concluded: "Without suggesting this caused violence, the ban's ineffectiveness was such that by the year 2000 violent crime had so increased that England and Wales had Europe's highest violent crime rate, far surpassing even the United States."

The authors then reported that in England to "conserve the resources of the inundated criminal justice system, English police no longer investigate burglary and 'minor assaults.'[22] As of 2006, if the police catch a mugger, robber, or burglar, or other 'minor' criminal in the act, the policy is to release them with a warning rather than to arrest and prosecute them."[23] Such a policy would by itself make comparing crime statistics hopeless, as a part of England's nonviolent crime is not being investigated.

Kates and Mauser conclude, "The fall in the American crime rate is even more impressive when compared with the rest of the world. In 18 of the 25 countries surveyed by the British Home Office, violent crime increased during the 1990s.[24] This contrast should induce thoughtful people to wonder what happened in those nations, and to question policies based on the notion that introducing increasingly more restrictive firearm ownership laws reduces violent crime."

The statistical comparisons reported in the Harvard study were revealing. "In Russia, where the rate of gun ownership is 4,000 per 100,000 inhabitants, the murder rate was 20.52 per 100,000 in 2002. That same year in Finland, where the rate of gun ownership is exceedingly higher—39,000 per 100,000—the murder rate was almost nil, at 1.98 per 100,000...."[25] Looking at Western Europe, the study showed that Norway "has far and away Western Europe's highest household gun ownership rate (32 percent), but also its lowest murder rate."[26]

When the Harvard study focused on intentional deaths in the United States compared to Continental Europe, they found that America, which is so often labeled as the most violent nation in the world by gun-control proponents, comes in seventh—behind Russia, Estonia, Latvia, Lithuania, Belarus, and Ukraine—in murders.

The authors say proponents of more gun restrictions in the United States should "at the very least" be able to show "a large number of nations with more guns have more death and that nations that have imposed stringent gun controls have achieved substantial reductions in criminal violence (or suicide)." But after their elaborate study, the authors concluded "those correlations are not observed when a large number of nations are compared around the world."

Kates and Mauser end by quoting Professor Brandon Centerwall, who published his 1991 study on gun-control policies and criminal violence with the following: "If you are surprised by [our] finding[s], so [are we]. [We] did not begin this research with any intent to 'exonerate' handguns, but there it is—a negative finding, to be sure, but a negative finding is nevertheless a positive contribution. It directs us where not to aim public health resources."

That is undoubtedly true, but there's another aspect of the British experience in particular that is rarely talked about. Before the British people were banned from owning guns, it was the people who were armed, while the British took great pride that their police officers were not. Now the reverse is the true: the British people are disarmed but their police force is becoming ever more heavily armed. It is not hard to conclude that in a democratic society, the British tradition of an armed citizenry and a usually disarmed police force is much healthier than the situation today. More guns in the hands of law-abiding citizens not only means less crime, it means more liberty, more courage, and a more self-reliant people.

PART III

Winning the Future of the Gun

CHAPTER EIGHT

The Gun Marketplace of the Future

No longer will we just shrug when faced with a distorted media report about guns.... No longer will we continue to give money to, or do business with, any outfit which in any way labels us as "undesirables." To shrug and just go on is to not just accept the demonization, but it actually agrees with it and supports it. No longer.

—Tom Gresham, host of *Gun Talk*

Don't give all the credit to Barack Obama, or Nancy Pelosi, or Joe Biden, or Eric Holder, or Michael Bloomberg, or George Soros, or Hollywood's hypocrisy, or the biased, anti–Second Amendment news media. Sure, gun-ban rhetoric ignited a blaze of gun sales, but gun sales were rising long before Barack Obama won the presidency in November 2008.

Calls into the FBI's National Instant Criminal Background Check System (NICS)—something gun dealers must do before they can sell anyone a gun—actually rose every year from 2003 to 2013. In 2003 there were 8,481,588 NICS checks. In 2005 the number rose to almost 9 million. In 2006 it surpassed 10 million. In 2007 it grew to just over 11 million. In 2008 it rose to 12.7 million. In 2009 the number of NICS checks passed 14 million. In 2012 the number of background checks called into the FBI topped out at 19.5 million, and in 2013 the number rose to 21,093,273.[1]

This is why attributing the growth in gun sales solely to President Obama's antigun stance is disingenuous, because he was an Illinois state senator when sales started to rise. Nevertheless, many in the media like to say it's all about the Obama administration because that way they can write off rising gun sales as the simple-minded fear from America's gun nuts. As ABC put it in early 2012, Americans are buying more Glocks and Berettas because of "fears that a second Obama administration might restrict gun ownership and the popularity of TV shows devoted to doomsday preparation and killing zombies."[2]

The unreported truth is that most Americans don't think about guns the way the media do; in fact, support for handgun bans has been in steep decline. In 1959, some 60 percent of Americans favored handgun bans, according to Gallup, whereas in October 2013, 74 percent *opposed* handgun bans.[3]

To see this from another angle, consider that according to a report done by the Congressional Research Service, "Per capita, the civilian gun stock has roughly doubled since 1968, from one gun per every two persons to one gun per person."[4]

Other Gallup polls show that the number of women gun owners in America rose from 13 percent in 2005 to 23 percent in late 2013. Also, the number of Democratic households with firearms in their homes rose from 30 percent in 2009 to 40 percent in 2013.[5]

Many factors have changed public opinion about guns, and handguns in particular, since 1959. Advocacy and research from the NRA, the NSSF, the Second Amendment Foundation, and academics such as John Lott (see Lott's 1998 book, *More Guns, Less Crime*) began to show that gun freedom doesn't make communities less safe, but actually can reduce violent crime. Meanwhile, gun-rights groups have been busy fighting for Second Amendment rights in courts and legislatures, increasing the number of gun ranges, and adding courses to train new gun owners all over America. In 2013 the number of NRA-certified firearms instructors in the United States surpassed eighty thousand.[6]

You can see this growth reflected in the number of concealed-carry permits. From the mid-1980s to today, America has become a mostly "shall-issue" nation with regard to concealed-carry permits. (Shall-issue laws typically prevent local governments from arbitrarily refusing to give concealed-carry permits.) Today all or parts of at least forty-one states have "shall-issue" laws. In fact, all fifty states now have laws that, to varying degrees, solidify citizens' right to carry certain concealed firearms in public, either without a permit or after obtaining a permit. (A court forced Illinois to make it unanimous in 2013.) Nationally, the NSSF estimates that in 2013 there were at least nine million concealed-carry holders in the United States. This is up from about one million in the mid-1980s.

All these developments led to more handgun sales. American firearm manufacturers produced about 8.3 million guns for sale in the United States in 2012. This was a record, and up from 6.2 million in 2011, according to the Bureau of Alcohol, Tobacco, Firearms and Explosives (ATF).[7] The American gun market is mostly supplied by U.S.-based gun manufacturers. Today, Stag Arms, Mossberg, Ruger, Smith & Wesson, Colt, and many, many more American companies proudly point out that their firearms are made in the USA. In 2011, an astounding 66 percent of the new firearms for sale in America were made in America. How many other manufacturing industries can boast that two-thirds of their products are American made and creating thousands of new American jobs?

Changes in popular culture have also helped drive gun sales. The History Channel's show *Top Shots* and Discovery Channel's *Sons of Guns* show this wave of interest in guns and shooting. It's difficult to measure how much the video game industry is affecting the cool factor of guns, but it is certainly having some effect. The video game industry made about $9.5 billion in the U.S. in 2007, $11.7 billion in 2008, and $25.1 billion in 2010, according to the Entertainment Software Association. I saw video games' gun influence while at a barbeque in suburban America when I heard kids laughing in the house. I stepped in to see what all the fun was and stopped short.

This twelve-year-old girl had a PS3 Move Assault Rifle Controller, a plastic gun made to look like an M4A1 carbine with a M203 grenade launcher, and she was working the trigger like a soldier in a firefight as she played *Call of Duty: Black Ops 2* on a PlayStation. Three boys and another girl were watching. What floored me wasn't that she was a twelve-year-old girl smiling as she expertly torched video-game enemies. I've reported on the rise of shooting facilities that have weekly "ladies' night at the range" before. What surprised me was this twelve-year-old's parents don't own guns, don't like guns, and are suspicious of guns, as if guns have a malevolent force radiating from them that is capable of corrupting the young and old.

I started talking to the kids watching the girl play. They told me about the weapons systems they like to use. They then debated with one another about the attributes of various assault rifles, such as the SCAR-H, Sig 556, and M8A1. They also talked about tactical shotguns, submachine guns, and sniper rifles by referring to specific makes and models. The game is so realistic they know what all these guns look like and how their actions work, as the game offers all these firearms and more as options. Now, I know my guns, but even I struggled to picture a couple of the models they authoritatively mentioned.

Meanwhile, the twelve-year-old girl gunning down her enemies hadn't learned to play this game at home. She had learned at friends' homes. Parents have a hard time keeping teenagers from these games, as next-generation video-game consoles were used in an estimated 190 million U.S. households in 2012.[8]

Now, social conservatives might fret that such games blur the lines between reality and fantasy. Liberals, like this girl's mother, who stood beside me and frowned, have the same worry. I grew up with guns in my bedroom and spent as much time in arcades as I could then afford, and I don't remember being influenced by video games or Rambo movies to use my .22 rifle or 12-gauge shotgun to harm people. The difference between reality and real life was vivid to me and my friends who also had guns for hunting. While it's certainly up to parents and other adults to teach gun safety and to be good role models, I've always been suspicious of those who think video games and movies lead to violence. The studies on this are vague, as it's nearly impossible to measure how such things affect children. It's interesting to consider, though, how this video-game exposure to guns will shape the attitudes of these children as they grow up.

As we stepped back outside, I told the mother she needed to talk to her daughter about guns. Every child needs to know something about gun safety; and like learning to drive a car, learning to shoot is a serious thing that requires responsibility and maturity. Outside of video games, many groups offer real, safe, and positive experiences with guns. The Boy Scouts of America reported that the number of "shotgun shooting" merit badges increased 27.8 percent from 1999 to 2010, and the Scouts have increased their shooting programs. 4-H's shooting programs have also grown, expounding the view that "[i]n a society that has chosen to possess firearms, all members, regardless of age should be provided adequate training to ensure safe, ethical and responsible interaction with firearms."[9]

The NSSF's "female participation" statistics in the shooting sports show that from 2002 to 2010 an estimated 30.2 percent more women began shooting shotguns. The number of hunters actually increased nationally by 9 percent from 2006 to 2011, according to a report by the U.S. Fish and Wildlife Service.[10] And active-shooting sports, such as 3-gun and sporting clays, have taken off. Another factor is an increase in gun collecting; in fact, here is one statistic that would boggle President Obama's worldview: in 1975, the ATF says, 5,211 people had "Collector Type 3" federal firearms licenses, whereas in 2011 that number had skyrocketed to 60,063 people.

———————

Some savvy entrepreneurs are redefining how new and used guns are bought and sold. They're digitally connecting buyers and sellers through federal firearms licensed (FFL) gun dealers. Chad Seaverns is such a salesman. As the chief operating officer of the National Firearms Dealer Network (NFDN), Seaverns thinks he has a good part of America's gun-buying future in his hands.

"A lot of people don't know about all the deals out there and new buying options for firearms and related products," says Seaverns. "Our company can help them find those deals through live-streaming technology."

When you log on to nfdmall.com, storefronts appear—digital street signs for Smith & Wesson, Remington, Ruger, and most every other gun maker. You can shop by company or firearm type and find all the technical info you need. True, you can't walk out of a virtual mall with a gun, but your order will be sent to a nearby gun dealer that has an FFL and where you can pick up your purchase—after going through a background check, of course.

The local gun store won't mind either, because they get the sale. They simply pay NFDN a monthly fee for the service. A local gun shop might not have a magazine for a Sig Sauer P938, but NFDN's real-time link to the distributors' databases will likely turn up whatever a person is after. Gun owners can even compare prices by using NFDN's site to check the websites of local gun stores as they shop for firearms and accessories.

By having consumers go to local gun dealers to make a purchase, NFDN, and other such companies, stay within federal and state laws. Basically, unlicensed persons are prohibited from buying guns from out-of-state sources, but they can buy if the sale is done through a local dealer. Private citizens are also prohibited from transferring firearms to anyone they have reasonable cause to believe is not a resident of the state the transaction is taking place in. Also, since 1986 it has been a federal offense for anyone to knowingly transfer a firearm to people who can't legally buy a gun.

Slaton White, editor of *Shot Business*, a trade magazine for gun stores, and a deputy editor for *Field & Stream*, says, "The big change today isn't just the growth in gun sales, but that CNC [computer numerical control] machining and other modern manufacturing processes have increased the models, calibers, and types available. Now people can accessorize their guns. AR-type rifles and other tactical firearms can be accessorized with lasers, lights, night vision, ammo holders, and so much other cool stuff. This is the Starbucks generation and people want very personalized products. This has grown the market and created even more interest with all the new gun owners now entering this market."

Such marketplace changes are just the beginning of why Seaverns thinks he has the future of gun sales in his virtual mall. Many local gun shops have gone bust. Those independent little stores with the gun guru behind the counter are often being out-competed by the big-box stores and destination retailers. Well, NFDN works exclusively with these little stores.

"We encourage the stores we work with to have a kiosk in the store so they can help customers look up and order anything they don't have in stock," says Seaverns. "Most products will be delivered within a few days. This helps them compete with the big destination stores."

NFDN has already signed up more than 560 local stores and is growing. As they expand, NFDN is helping to level the playing field for local sporting goods stores. This isn't to say that one type of store is better than another, but rather that more competition—choices for gun enthusiasts—is a good thing.

There are, of course, other online players in this market. There is, for instance, GunBroker.com, an auction site that links private buyers and sellers and uses local licensed firearms dealers as transfer agents, while also selling hunting gear, collectibles, and other goods. And there is GunsAmerica.com, which calls itself the "[l]argest online gun classifieds since 1997." And there are others in this ever-growing field.

Other segments of this marketplace are also growing. MidwayUSA recently expanded to include hunting gear to its popular catalog of gun parts, cleaning tools, and more. Also, OpticsPlanet.com has been expanding fast with a user-friendly website and a growing list of optics, bags, and gun-related gear. Steve Ledin, a director at Optics Planet Inc., says, "We've hired a group of experts with sporting goods backgrounds. They answer consumers' technical questions and more. I'd put their knowledge against anyone's."

In the traditional retail market, Cabela's had fifty stores in 2013 and plans to open thirteen more in 2014. Bass Pro Shops had fifty-nine stores (seventy-seven if you add on its Tracker Marine Centers) with plans to open about a half dozen more in 2014, and estimated foot traffic of 116 million people in 2013. To attain this kind of growth, Cabela's and Bass Pro have turned their retail stores into attractions that bring the outdoors inside with record-book-quality taxidermy, aquariums loaded with monster bass, and indoor mountains and archery ranges. Currently, the largest Cabela's retail facility is in Hamburg, Pennsylvania. It has more than 250,000 square feet of floor space. Bass Pro says its average customer stays two and a half hours and drives an average distance of fifty-plus miles. Cabela's has similar statistics.

In fact, Ralph Castner, Cabela's chief financial officer, says, "A lot of people drive one hundred miles or more to go to our stores. We're expanding to make their drives shorter and to reach new customers. They come a long way because we offer deals on gear, large firearm selections, and because our stores host a lot of events and attractions."

Cabela's founders, Dick and Mary Cabela and Dick's brother James Cabela, began Cabela's in 1961 and took the company public in 2004. About half of Cabela's sales come from hunting-related merchandise, with about a third coming from the sale of firearms, ammunition, and accessories in 2012. About 30 percent of Cabela's revenue comes from catalogs that have long been goody lists for sportsmen.

Bass Pro Shops is a privately owned corporation. In 1971, Johnny Morris rented a U-Haul trailer and took off across the country filling it with the newest premium fishing tackle he could find. When he returned to Springfield, Missouri, he set up shop in his father's liquor store, which was located on the way to Table Rock Lake. The site of the original Bass Pro store in Springfield now brings in over four million visitors annually and is the state's top tourist attraction.

Cabela's and Bass Pro Shops, of course, are hardly the only players in this market for gun dollars. Other big chain stores offer taxidermy, or have gunsmiths on the premises, or hold classes that teach gun safety, handling, and more. Dick's Sporting Goods, Inc., is a good example. It was founded in 1948 when then eighteen-year-old Dick Stack quit an army surplus store in Binghamton, New York, after the storeowner mocked his ideas for stocking fishing tackle. Dick started a tackle store with $300 from his grandmother. Dick's now has more than 450 stores in 42 states.

Gander Mountain, headquartered in St. Paul, Minnesota, currently has 119 Gander Mountain stores in 23 states. Gander Mountain began as a catalog-based retailer in Wilmot, Wisconsin. Gander Mountain sold its mail-order business to Cabela's in 1996, but its stores remain as a private company under the majority ownership of David Pratt and the Erickson family.

Then there's Sportsman's Warehouse, an outdoor sporting goods retailer that operates forty-seven stores in eighteen states. Sportsman's Warehouse calls itself "America's Premier Outfitter." Sportsman's Warehouse offers concealed-carry classes among other gun-related services.

All these competing chains and others are expanding and trying to grab a piece of the hot and growing gun market. According to the research firm Southwick Associates, Inc., shooting accessories were up 30 percent and ammo sales were up 15 percent from 2011 to 2012. In 2013 ammo was so popular that there were wide and prolonged ammo shortages, especially in .223 and 9mm.

"The biggest change I see is that people in their twenties and thirties have become a bigger part of the market," says Rob Southwick of Southwick Associates, Inc. "Those in this demographic are now buying rifles—especially modern sporting rifles—and they're shooting for fun."

The NRA is also taking part in the growth. In August 2013 the NRA National Sporting Arms Museum opened in the Bass Pro Shops flagship store in Springfield, Missouri. The museum has firearms from the 1600s to today, including some historically significant firearms from the NRA Museum Collection. The museum also has firearms and artwork from the Remington Arms Company factory collection. In the Springfield museum, you can see a multimillion-dollar collection of U.S. military sidearms, guns owned by such Wild West outlaws as Jesse James, and firearms once owned by such presidents as Teddy Roosevelt and Dwight Eisenhower. The museum is open every day of the week, and it's free.

New online options and destination stores get most of the national attention, but smaller, independent stores still sell about 40 percent of all guns, and some regional stores have been booming. Take, for example, Gat Guns, in Dundee, Illinois, located about an hour and half west of Chicago. Owned by Greg Torino, Gat Guns has expanded several times since first opening in 1979, and has seen the market change. Randy Potter, the store manager, noted that they used to deal mostly with hunters, but now, "We're catering more and more to suburban moms and dads," as well as "women and young men who want to shoot recreationally and to defend themselves."

Another must-visit regional store is Bill's Gun Shop and Range, which has two locations in Minnesota (Robbinsdale and Circle Pines) and one in Hudson, Wisconsin. John Monson, owner of Bill's Gun Shop, says, "For a while it was challenging just to keep guns and ammo in stock. We ran out of ammo twice…. We have ranges at all our stores, host a ladies' night every Wednesday, and cherish our customers here in Minnesota and Wisconsin. I could sell more guns and certainly more ammo online, but I don't want to do that. I serve the customers who come to our stores."

In Ashland, Virginia, there's Green Top, a fifty-five-thousand-square-foot gun store that's a local landmark. Then there's ATP Guns in Summerville, South Carolina, a store that says it is "The Most Lady-Friendly Gun Shop This Side of the Mason-Dixon Line." They have a "Ladies' Night" every Tuesday and Thursday and explain that these training sessions are designed for "ladies that have never shot a gun" or who were "trained incorrectly by a guy."

One reason shooting sports are growing is because of the growing number of women who participate—now more than five million, an increase of 46.5 percent from 2001 to 2011. Another is the terrific diversity of firearms and accessories that make shooting more attractive to more people. And a third reason is the greater availability of training centers. Not only are gun ranges expanding their number of shooting lanes, but at the Sportsman Shooting Center in Grapevine, Texas, there is a fully enclosed, indoor training center that allows people to practice with simulators and also on a live-fire cinema range with their own rifle and ammunition and computerized scoring.[11] The Sportsman Shooting Center might be unique, but the audience it serves is a growing one.

———————

Meanwhile, gun owners are using technology to defend their civil rights. Chris Walsh, a software designer from Richmond, Virginia, started FriendorFoe.us in 2009 to keep track of businesses and local authorities that allowed him to shop and eat while carrying his concealed handgun. Without really intending it, his website has become a hub for Second Amendment enthusiasts to praise or condemn establishments on the basis of their firearms policies. By early 2014, the site's users had rated more than twenty thousand businesses.

Walsh says, "I never meant for this site to be used to persuade businesses to change their policies, but when a business finds they're losing customers they often clarify or change their policy." He adds, "I'm a big believer in property rights. I don't dispute a business's right to ban firearms on their property. I've just decided to take my business elsewhere. Some other gun owners are choosing to do the same."

When I asked Walsh if he had to give up any favorite restaurants or stores, he said, "I had to give up going to Costco, as they have a corporate policy banning guns. Locally, I also had to stop going to Buffalo Wild Wings. As you educate yourself and try to give your hard-earned dollars only to those who stand with your freedom, you find there are sacrifices. For me though, it's worth it. For the handful of places I've had to give up, I've easily found new places that support gun owners."

Gun Talk host Tom Gresham points out that FriendorFoe.us is only one example of citizens becoming educated consumers. "Gun owners are standing up for a basic human right," says Gresham. "I want to support the companies that also support my constitutional freedoms. Technology is now making it easier for us to do this."

Gresham notes that eBay "blocked firearms from being listed. Paypal blocks the use of its service for buying guns. Google blocks guns, dealers, and makers from searches in its shopping service. We have reports of banks closing the accounts of gun makers simply on the basis that they won't do business with the firearms industry. Each of these is a very public way of saying, 'We don't do business with *those people*.' Each is a way of saying that reasonable and responsible people should have nothing to do with the firearms business. We are being put into the same box as pornography."

Gresham continued, "No longer will we just shrug when faced with a distorted media report about guns. No longer will we just go about our business when a politician makes outrageous claims about

gun owners. No longer will we continue to give money to, or do business with, any outfit which in any way labels us as 'undesirables.' To
shrug and just go on is to not just accept the demonization, but it
actually agrees with it and supports it. No longer."

CHAPTER NINE

The Solution to Gun Violence

If guns are outlawed only outlaws will have guns
**—A bumper sticker retired baseball player
Ted Williams kept on his truck[1]**

At 10:00 a.m. on February 26, 2014, I'm on the thirty-fifth floor of a Manhattan high-rise with three agents who have decades of experience investigating gunrunning and other crimes for the Bureau of Alcohol, Tobacco, Firearms and Explosives (ATF). I want to hear their views on how we can stop sociopaths, gang members, and other criminals from shooting people, though one condition of the interview is that I not ask "policy" questions. ATF agents are enforcers of the laws, not policy makers.

Charles Mulham has been an agent with the ATF since 1989. His hair is buzzed-cop short, and he wears the dark suit, white shirt, and tie. He is New York–blunt and charismatic. He tells me that about 80 percent of the guns found at crime scenes in New York come from out of state. The serial number, make, model, and other data, including forensic information gathered from guns used by criminals in the state of New York, are sent to this ATF Manhattan office. ATF staff enter the information into a comparative database that looks for similarities to see if the gun has been used in another crime.

An ATF report says, "Every firearm has individual characteristics that are as unique to it as fingerprints are to human beings. When a firearm is discharged, it transfers these characteristics—in the form of microscopic scratches and dents—to the projectiles and cartridge casings fired in it. The barrel of the firearm marks the projectile traveling through it, and the firearm's breech mechanism marks the ammunition's cartridge casing."[2] This information is shared among law-enforcement agencies, allowing them to track gun-specific information and link cases throughout the country.

They can only do this with guns taken from criminals or crime scenes, however, as the Firearms Owners' Protection Act of 1986 prohibits the establishment of a registration system for guns or gun owners at the federal level. According to the ATF, "This provision prohibits federal agencies from directly linking ballistic images through a centralized computer database to both the firearms themselves (a firearms registry) and the identities of the private citizens who possess imaged firearms (firearms owners' registry)."[3]

Some groups and politicians argue that all firearms sold should be test-fired and registered in such a national system. To someone who knows little about guns or ballistics, this sounds sensible, but the reality is different. One technical problem is that the science isn't flawless, and even if the ballistics information could be as conclusive as DNA evidence, tracing a gun to its original owner typically accomplishes nothing, because most armed criminals use stolen or illegally purchased guns. Also, a criminal can easily beat the system by changing a gun's barrel or firing pin, or otherwise altering the firearm so it leaves different markings on a cartridge casing or bullet. If the criminal uses a shotgun, there's not much that sophisticated software can do.

Maryland tried instituting a gun-ballistics database in 2000 for all handguns sold in the state and gave up a few years later. A 2004 progress report by the state of Maryland concluded that the program, "for all its good intentions, has not proven to be a time saving tool for the Firearms Examiner or an investigative enhancement to the criminal investigator."[4] In 2005, a Maryland State Police report recommended repealing the law requiring that all handguns sold in the state be registered in their Integrated Ballistics Identification System, because the "program simply has not met expectations and does not aid in the mission statement of the Department of State Police."[5] Maryland suspended the program, and laboratory technicians associated with it were reassigned to the state's DNA database unit. Trying something nationally that couldn't be made to work in the small state of Maryland would be irrational, expensive, and an unnecessary invasion of the privacy of more than one hundred million Americans.

The ATF's more focused "crime gun" database, however, *has* helped investigators. In one example, in September 1995, a bullet fired from a passing car killed a nineteen-year-old factory worker. In August 2003, Chicago police officers at a traffic stop arrested a driver for unlawful possession of a firearm. Using the National Integrated Ballistic Information Network, the Chicago Forensic Science Center of the Illinois State Police matched the firearm to the 1995 murder, and in November 2007 traced the gun to the killer (who had bought it illegally and sold it after his crime)—a felon and alleged enforcer for a street gang. He was convicted of murder and sentenced to fifty years in prison.

ATF agent Jason Zamaloff tells me, "Crime guns come from a lot of sources. Sometimes, though, a gun is used in multiple offenses. One time we found a .357 Magnum revolver that had been used by a bunch of different gang members in the Bronx over several years to kill people. That gun was simply one of the gang's favorite community guns."

"Community guns?"

Agent Zamaloff nods and says, "Gangs often share a stash of illegal weapons. Whoever is guarding the drugs that night gets a gun."

Agent Zamaloff oversees the operations-control center of the ATF's Manhattan office. When multiple guns need to be traced fast to solve a murder or stop more shootings, it is the center's technicians who analyze the data and help law-enforcement agencies' investigations.

In 1991, the ATF estimated that 37 percent of armed criminals obtained firearms from street sales, 34 percent from criminal acts and associates, 8 percent from relatives, 7 percent from dealers, and 6 percent from flea markets and gun shows.[6] More recently, a Bureau of Justice Statistics survey of state prison inmates convicted of gun-related crimes determined that 79 percent of them bought their firearms from "street/illegal sources" or "friends or family." These "illegal sources" includes theft of firearms, black-market purchases of stolen firearms, and straw purchases (purchases where a person without a criminal record breaks the law by buying a gun for someone who can't legally own or possess a gun). The survey also found that 12 percent obtained their firearms from firearms dealers (gun stores, pawn shops) and that 1.7 percent obtained firearms from someone at a gun show or flea market.[7]

The ATF estimated that 190,342 guns were lost or stolen in 2012. Most of these guns (177,898) were lost or stolen from private owners, but 16,667 were reported as being lost or stolen from federal firearms licensed (FFL) dealers. The ATF says the number of guns stolen from private hands is a guesstimate based on different sources of data.[8] The ATF says the number of guns lost or stolen from FFLs is a good statistic, however, because in 1994 Congress required FFLs to report the theft or loss of any firearm from their inventories to both the ATF and to local police within forty-eight hours of discovery. In 2012, FFLs reported to the ATF that 5,762 firearms were stolen and 10,915 firearms were "lost" from their stores, ranges, and backrooms.

Thefts aside, I ask these ATF agents how nearly eleven thousand guns can go "missing" from gun dealers annually, and the three ATF officials sit back, grimace, and try to explain what they're up against.

Agent John Curtis, an area supervisor for the ATF, hands me a sample printout of the records FFLs are required to keep, listing the makes, models, serial numbers, and other data of guns they've sold and have in inventory. Agent Curtis says, "They don't have to keep these records on a computer. They just have to include those criteria in their records. Most do a good job, but the record keeping of a few is less than ideal. We work with them, and if they're consistently not keeping comprehensible records we can start an investigation and possibly revoke a federal firearms license."

"What you're saying is some of those *missing* guns are really just record-keeping errors?" I ask.

"Some of them."

"Do you give FFLs some kind of software they could install on their computers and use if they wish?"

Agent Curtis says, "No. We follow procedures outlined by the law. We encourage them to keep digital records, but we only mandate that they accurately record certain criteria."

"It would be a clever idea," I suggest, "to give them pre-built Excel spreadsheets (or some other program) to help them catalog the flow of guns. I worked in a small gun store when I was kid. The owner scribbled his records in dog-eared, marble-covered notebook. That was back in the '80s. No doubt many of the small stores would welcome such software now. Their databases would then be legible and more easily comparable."

Agent Curtis says, "Whatever we can do to help, we will"—but what they can do to help is prescribed by law.

Agent Zamaloff shifts the conversation by explaining the problem from a policing point of view. He says, "We're still in the pre-digital world with a lot of this. When reporters call, they often assume we can just punch a serial number into a database to trace a gun. We explain to them the law says we can't maintain such a database. What we have to do after a gun is found at a crime scene is first call the manufacturer. The gun maker then goes through their records and tells us which distributor bought the gun with the serial number. We then call the distributor. They tell us which store bought the gun. We call the store. They dig through their sometimes-paper records and tell us who bought the gun.

"Now the average time to crime—the time it takes for a legally sold gun to enter the illegal market and then be found at a crime scene—is about a dozen years in New York. So there are likely various private sales that occurred—these are perfectly legal as long as someone doesn't knowingly sell to someone who can't legally own a gun—before a gun makes it to a criminal's hands, so we often hit a dead end."

Now I'm tempted to ask about the "universal background checks" President Barack Obama and much of the Democratic leadership are arguing we need. A universal background check would make private gun sales illegal unless a background check of the buyer (or the son or daughter inheriting the gun) is performed by the FBI's National Instant Criminal Background Check System. The problem with this idea—other than its imposition of a bureaucrat between every grandfather who wants to give his granddaughter his Model 12 pump shotgun—is that criminals will never participate in the system. They will get their guns as they have always gotten them—illegally. Moreover, it is already a crime to sell a firearm to a person who can't legally own one.

Agent Curtis tells me, "Often private gun owners don't keep records of their guns' serial numbers. So when a theft occurs, they can only give us vague descriptions of the makes and models of the guns stolen. Some gun owners even assume we can plug in their name and give them the serial numbers. We can't. Also, by law most private gun owners don't have to keep such records or even report a theft. Some state laws mandate private gun owners report thefts, but no federal statute docs."

Gun-control groups want to force Americans to register their guns. Meanwhile, gun registries are taboo to gun-rights groups because they treat law-abiding citizens as potential criminals, they empower the state to peek into private gun cabinets, they have sometimes led to gun confiscations (most recently, this happened in England), and they have failed to deter crime, as Canada conceded when it scrapped its gun registry in 2012. Canada's experience, in fact, is a revealing example.

In January in 1994, Garry Breitkreuz (pronounced Bright-Krites) was a new member of Canada's Parliament, representing Preeceville,

Saskatchewan, a town of about one thousand residents. At his first town hall meeting, he discussed the new gun-control bill, C-68, brought in by the Liberal government. It included the creation of a long-gun registry. "I'll never forget that first meeting," says Garry. "Even though it was 39 degrees below zero outside, the place was packed and the people heated."

Now it should be noted that Garry was hardly a gun-rights activist. Not yet anyway. Sure, he grew up in a rural Saskatchewan home and had a .30-30-caliber rifle to hunt deer. "But when it came to the gun issue," says Garry, "I was very naïve."

Naïve indeed. Garry started the meeting off by saying to the crowd that "this long-gun registry seems to make sense. Maybe it'll catch a few criminals...." He had barely started when his constituents made it clear they didn't agree.

"They challenged me," says Garry, "to do some research to find out if forcing people to register their guns will really save lives."

Garry shut up, listened, and promised to research whether requiring people to register their guns really reduces crime.

"After just a few months of digging into it, I did a 180," says Garry. He and a researcher looked at the cost of the gun registry and its effectiveness at reducing crime. To get the answers he needed, he filed "Access to Information" requests (the Canadian equivalent of "Freedom of Information Act" requests). By 2002 he'd filed more than five hundred such requests.

He learned the Canadian government had horribly underestimated the costs of the long-gun registry. In 1995 Canada's Department of Justice told Parliament that the Canadian Firearms Program would cost $119 million to implement and that this cost would be offset by $117 million in fees; however, by 2000, Canada's Department of Justice was estimating that the long-gun registry would cost more than $1 billion.

Garry took his research to the Office of the Auditor General of Canada, which reviewed his data and conducted its own audit. In 2002 the agency reported: "The Department of Justice Canada did not provide Parliament with sufficient information to allow it to effectively scrutinize the Canadian Firearms Program and ensure accountability. It provided insufficient financial information and explanations for the dramatic increase in the cost of the Program."[9]

"This report blew the lid off," says Garry.

He says that before the auditor general's report, even many Conservative politicians wouldn't touch the gun-registry issue. They thought it was a losing battle.

"But the public was ahead of the politicians on this issue," says Garry. "In meetings all over the country I was telling people that with what they were spending on the registry, we could hire five or six thousand police officers."

This resonated.

Gary A. Mauser, a professor emeritus at Simon Fraser University in Burnaby, British Columbia, has also looked deeply into the costs. He says, "John Lott and I added up the costs and found that, in total, the Canadian government spent about $2.7 billion on this failed experiment." That's more than twenty times what it was forecast to cost.

Beyond the financial costs, Garry spoke about the loss of civil liberties that came with having the government invade law-abiding Canadians' gun cabinets, and he cited crime statistics that showed that the gun-owners database wasn't reducing crime rates or helping to solve crimes. Economist John Lott, for instance, reported that "[t] he Royal Canadian Mounted Police and the [Canadian] Chiefs of Police have not yet provided a single example in which tracing was of more than peripheral importance in solving a case."

In 2006, Stephen Harper, a Conservative, became prime minister, forming a minority government; in 2011, the Conservatives had the votes and the will to move against the long-gun registry. When the vote came, on February 15, 2012, something unusual took place. In the Canadian House of Commons, members of Parliament stand to signify their votes. After Garry stood to vote to repeal the long-gun registry, they broke into a cheer: "Garry, Garry…. " This just isn't done in the reserved atmosphere of the Canadian Parliament. But repeal had become a crusade. The *National Post* reported that Canada's public safety minister, Vic Toews, said on the day of the vote that the long-gun registry "does nothing to help put an end to gun crimes, nor has it saved one Canadian life. It criminalizes hard-working and law-abiding citizens such as farmers and sport shooters, and it has been a billion-dollar boondoggle left to us by the previous Liberal government."

I asked Chris W. Cox, executive director of the NRA's Institute for Legislative Action, how this might affect Americans, and he said, "Gun registration in the United States has always been the political fantasy of the gun-ban lobby. The clear lesson from Canada is that registration did not and does not reduce crime; in fact, since Canada's long-gun-registration law went into effect, the U.S. murder rate has dropped almost twice as fast as Canada's. A gun registry only infringes on privacy and has led to the confiscation of law-abiding citizens' firearms in countries around the world, and even here in the U.S. That is why the NRA will fight any registration effort in the U.S. with every fiber we have."

Given the failure of gun registries, I ask the ATF agents what else we can do to stop people from buying guns illegally.

Agent Mulham says, "Sometimes multiple gun sales can be traced to the same straw purchaser. This gives us a chance to build a case."

"Other times," says Agent Zamaloff, "guns out there [on New York City's streets] come in fresh from a store sale where someone who doesn't have a criminal record—a straw purchaser—has bought a gun for someone who does. Sometimes a straw purchaser will learn that a gun has turned up in a crime and will quickly report it as being stolen; either way, this gives us a chance to open and possibly broaden an investigation into what might be a number of individuals involved in a gunrunning ring."

Agent Mulham says, "We can show you some undercover surveillance video of a gunrunner we caught in Brooklyn, as the case has been adjudicated."

I say I'd like that very much. They use a laptop wired to a projection screen to show video of a man from Brooklyn named James Brady, a felon who moved to Alabama and came up with a very stupid criminal scheme. He talked women in Alabama who didn't have criminal records into buying handguns and shotguns for him from Alabama gun stores. He then drove the guns to Brooklyn, New York, to sell them. A contact on the street tipped off Agent Zamaloff.

"We met Brady posing as buyers. He indicated he had multiple buyers and could get us more guns," says Zamaloff. "We took him down fast to keep the rest of his guns off the streets. We ended up busting his straw purchasers as well."

"That's a very good and simple example of an interstate gunrunning operation," says Agent Mulham. "This one was small, others are more complex."

I wonder if those Alabama gun-store employees thought something was funny. One responsibility ATF agents have is checking up on gun dealers to make sure their books are in order and to maintain relationships, so I ask how often they get to the FFLs in their jurisdiction and how they work with them.

Agent Curtis says, "We have a small staff here in New York and we do a lot more than overseeing FFLs. We're also responsible for monitoring alcohol, tobacco, and explosives. In my particular oversight area, we have about one thousand FFLs to check up on. Some are big stores, such as Gander Mountain outlets, and others are small gun shops. To tell you the truth, some establishments might go five or even ten years without a visit from us. If, however, we trace crime guns to a particular FFL, we'll show up at their establishment unannounced and, if we think it necessary, we'll investigate them."

Agent Mulham adds, "Most FFLs are staffed with good, law-abiding people. We maintain strong relationships with them because they sometimes tip us off when a buyer seems to be a straw purchaser or something. Gun-store owners help us a great deal."

I nod. My experience with gun-store owners is that they're almost all conservative men who love their country, see guns as a tool for freedom, and don't want to sell a gun to a criminal. They'd also be foolish to do so, as the few dollars they'd make isn't worth the risk of losing their businesses and perhaps going to jail.

These agents tell me there is no precise formula for what guns cost on the street, but that field agents typically have a good idea. Agent Mulham says, "A quality pistol like a Glock might go for double or triple retail. Lower-quality guns might be worth only $100 or $200 more than retail." Basically, they say, guns are so readily available that the black-market price is typically just a few hundred dollars more than retail.

———

The ATF's reputation has suffered recently from scandals, such as the Fast and Furious operation in which ATF officials in Arizona let semiautomatic rifles, .50-caliber sniper rifles, and other guns be sold to known straw purchasers so the guns could be trafficked to Mexican drug cartels in some kind of crime-fighting technique that no one at the ATF or at their overseer, the U.S. Department of Justice, has ever been able to explain. The ATF let about two thousand guns "walk" without tracking devices secretly hidden in the guns or any realistic surveillance of the firearms in place once the guns were taken from the stores. As ATF agent John Dodson, a congressional whistleblower, said, they let the guns go, fully aware that the next time they saw the guns would be at crime scenes.

When one of the guns—an AK-47—the ATF intentionally allowed to go into the arsenals of criminals was used by a drug runner to shoot down a U.S. Border Patrol agent, the Obama administration, via the U.S. Department of Justice, stonewalled and lied to Congress. After a long congressional investigation helped by ATF whistleblowers— good cops who had argued against the wrongheaded operation from the start—President Barack Obama used executive privilege to shield Attorney General Eric Holder from having to hand over his emails. Holder, of course, runs the Department of Justice, and the ATF is an arm of the Department of Justice. This prompted the House to hold Holder in contempt.

Even though the ATF has drifted into politically incomprehensible adventures that have, on a few occasions, resulted in congressional investigations, I've found that the ATF is mostly staffed with good agents attempting to do what might be an impossible job— keeping America's more than three hundred million guns out of the hands of criminals of all types. The ATF also works closely with the National Shooting Sports Foundation (NSSF), the trade association for firearms manufacturers, on regulations; they annually staff a booth at the NSSF's trade show (the SHOT Show); and they work with gun dealers to help them comply with laws and regulations.

Nevertheless, thanks to Obama administration programs like Fast and Furious, some law-abiding gun owners and dealers are beginning to see the ATF as an adversary, not a partner. Mike Detty, the author of *Guns across the Border*, was a gun dealer in Tucson when the Fast and Furious operation began. He was approached by a straw purchaser who obviously wanted to traffic guns. Detty called the ATF to alert them and was then sucked into the ATF's new crime-fighting technique—letting the bad guys buy and move a lot of guns. "The ATF lied to me," Detty told me at the SHOT Show in Las Vegas in 2014. "A number of Arizona gun dealers assisted them. We were all told the guns would be interdicted. They weren't. A lot of gun dealers look at the ATF differently now."

A similar rift is forming between some law-enforcement agencies and gun owners and dealers because of state laws that now require law-abiding gun owners to report to the police to be fingerprinted, to register their guns, and to meet other mandates. By January 2014 in Connecticut and in the months leading to April 15, 2014, in New York, a grand total of perhaps 1.3 million people had to report to the police to be fingerprinted and register the firearms they own that state politicians deem "assault weapons" for nebulous reasons. Connecticut gun owners of "assault weapons" who submitted the necessary paperwork—including providing the police with a thumbprint and having their signature witnessed by a notary public—after the deadline received a letter stating that they must do one of the following:

1. Render the assault weapon permanently inoperable;
2. Sell the assault weapon to a licensed dealer;
3. Remove the assault weapon from the state; or
4. You may make arrangements to relinquish the assault weapon to a police department or the Department of Emergency Services and Public Protection.[10]

The letter was signed "Sincerely, LT. Eric Cooke, Commanding Officer, Special Licensing and Firearms Unit."[11] However, when a few people who received the letters made their copies public, the Connecticut States Police's Special Licensing and Firearms Unit denied sending them.

Anna Kopperud, the NRA's state lobbyist for Connecticut, called the CSP's Special Licensing and Firearms Unit on February 26 and 27, 2014, to find out and report what options gun owners in Connecticut had. "The CSP spent a day and a half telling me there was no such letter," says Kopperud. "When I asked if a letter had been forged and, if so, how did someone get gun owners' addresses, they said they didn't know."

Questions from me sent to the CSP's Lieutenant J. Paul Vance along with a link to a copy of the letter, however, drew a different answer on February 28. Lieutenant Vance said, "The letter was sent to people who did not register their weapon by the deadline [by Lieutenant Cooke]. It was simply an effort to assist them and advise them of some choices they have."

It wasn't made clear if a gun owner who's in the process of transporting such a firearm out of state or to a gun dealer might be charged with a felony if that gun owner is caught doing so. Would the letter from Lieutenant Cooke give them safe passage? When state legislatures decide to ban commonly owned guns and require tens of thousands of law-abiding citizens to disarm or report to the police, good people can suddenly become "criminals" by simply doing nothing different from what they've done all their adult lives.

Democrat governor Dan Malloy signed Connecticut's gun-control bill (Senate Bill 1160) into law on April 4, 2013. Four days later, President Barack Obama spoke at the University of Connecticut and said, "Connecticut has shown the way, and now is the time for Congress to do the same." CBS reported that "Obama applauded the state legislature and Gov. Dan Malloy for passing 'common sense' bi-partisan legislation last week that calls for widespread restrictions on firearms."[12] The gun-control bill had been written behind closed doors and placed on legislators' desks around 9:00 a.m. on April 3. At about 12:30 p.m. that same day, the state senate started debating the legislation as gun owners chanted outside, "Read the bill." Maybe they're all accomplished speed readers and so did in fact read all the bill's legal language and saw the forty-three times the bill uses the word "felony," mostly as threats to gun owners. Whether they had read it all or not, the senate passed the bill 26 to 10 that same day. Hours later, the House passed it 105 to 44. At noon the next day, Governor Malloy signed the bill. Maybe in their haste they didn't foresee what they were starting. Maybe they didn't understand they would be tempting tens of thousands of citizens to try a little civil disobedience.

The numbers of gun owners who might still have "assault weapons" in Connecticut isn't a guess. The National Shooting Sports Foundation, the trade association for firearms manufacturers, estimates that there were likely 350,000 Connecticut residents with now-banned "assault weapons" as of late 2013. The NSSF told me, "The 350,000 number is a conservative estimate based upon numerous surveys, consumer purchases, NICS background-check data, and also private party transactions." The NSSF used the same criteria to estimate that at least one million New York residents have firearms that are now banned from being sold and that existing owners must register with the police.

As of December 31, 2013, according to Lieutenant Vance, the CSP had received 41,347 applications to register "assault weapons" and 36,932 applications to register "high-capacity" magazines. That means that more than three hundred thousand Connecticut residents decided not to register their "assault weapons," or moved them out of state, or sold them. As this was being written, the NRA was backing a lawsuit, *Shew v. Malloy*, that challenged the constitutionality of several provisions of the Connecticut law, including its expanded bans on semiautomatic firearms and its restrictions on magazine capacity.

Under New York's expansive "assault weapons" category, a semiautomatic Remington Model 1100 shotgun—a shotgun commonly owned by hunters and skeet shoots—with a pistol grip is now an "assault weapon." When I asked how many New Yorkers had registered their weapons, the state responded: "New York State Police cannot release information related to the registration of assault weapons including the number of assault weapons registered. Those records you seek are derived from information collected for the State Police database and are, therefore, exempt from disclosure."

The next question is what the states will do about all those gun owners who now might be committing felonies. Will the CSP ask for search warrants? Connecticut's Department of Emergency Services and Public Protection (DESPP) has been using a "Sale or Transfer of All Firearms" form[13] at the retail level that acts as a de facto registration, as it requires that gun sales, along with make, model, serial number, and the buyer's personal information, be reported to the DESPP and the police; as a result, the CSP has information on which residents might still own unregistered firearms the state considers to be "assault weapons."

When asked if the CSP would use late-registration applications to obtain warrants to seize "assault weapons" and to arrest people, Lieutenant Vance said, "Again, we don't make the laws; our legislature has that responsibility." It was also unclear whether the CSP might use existing gun-registration records to obtain warrants to search the residences of the perhaps three hundred thousand Connecticut residents who might have such unregistered firearms.

I asked a few gun owners in Connecticut who own or used to own so-called assault weapons what they were doing. They told me they had always thought of themselves as good citizens but now found themselves in an untenable position. One told me, "I just came from my local gun store. I had to test a shotgun refitted with a straight stock to make it compliant. It still holds nine rounds, but the world is now a little *safer* without that evil pistol grip."

Another replied, "I have four friends who have either bought homes or property out of Connecticut or are shopping hard. This issue was the final straw for them."

Yet another said, "Gun owners are pissed off and nervous. They don't know if the state will enforce based on long-gun purchase records held by the State Police, but they are encouraged and feel a little vindicated at the level of disobedience."

Several said they had shipped their "bad" guns out of state.

Rich Burgess, president of a pro-gun-rights group called Connecticut Carry, wants to force a public confrontation. He released a letter on March 3, 2014, saying, "A recent media tidal wave based on false reports and bad journalism has proven a few things about the 2013 Gun Ban: people from Connecticut and around the nation are tired of being threatened; are ready to make a stand; and the State of Connecticut does not have the stomach to enforce the edicts and laws with which they threaten gun owners.... Connecticut Carry calls on every State official, every Senator, and every Representative, to make the singular decision: Either enforce the laws as they are written and let us fight it out in court, or else repeal the 2013 Gun Ban in its entirety."

Laws like these can put average guns owners at odds with law enforcement and make the enforcers of such laws seem as adversaries rather than partners in keeping the streets safe. This is compounded by the fact that the state politicians in New York, Connecticut, and other states who voted for recent "assault weapons" bans aren't realistically trying to lower the murder rate; rifles account for less than 3 percent of homicides annually, according to the FBI's "Uniform Crime Reports." The legislators were reacting to the evil deeds of a few mass murderers—though statistically, mass murderers commit less than one-tenth of one percent of all murders, according to research compiled by Grant Duwe, who works for the Minnesota State Department of Corrections and is the author of *Mass Murder in the United States: A History*. Also, according to analysis done by *Mother Jones*, a far-left publication, "Nearly 80 percent of the perpetrators" of mass murders (a total of sixty-seven cases over the last three decades) "obtained their weapons legally."[14] What most of the mass shootings have in common is the murderer has a mental illness. Funding programs to diagnose and treat people in our society who have mental-health issues is the more sensible approach, because *that* is the problem.

Agent Mulham says, "I'm a hunter and gun owner. I get it. I don't care if people like you have a million guns. What we're trying to do is keep guns out of the hands of the bad guys."

———————

The FBI's National Instant Criminal Background Check System (NICS) can be a confusing part of the gun issue. For example, the Brady Campaign, a group that lobbies for gun bans and much stricter controls, sent out a press release in early 2014 saying NICS had "stopped more than 2.1 million would-be gun purchases"[15] since it began, in 1998. The reality, however, is not that 2.1 million would-be criminals were stopped by the background-check system. Some of the people denied instant approval were later approved, as a name similarity or other technical glitch holds up some background checks. In

2010, the FBI referred about seventy thousand NICS denials to the ATF, but the ATF deemed 90 percent of them not worthy of further investigation and found that another four percent were incorrect denials.

When I asked Andrew Arulanandam, director of public affairs for the National Rifle Association, about NICS, he said, "The Brady Campaign is now touting NICS denials, but you know what, the Brady Campaign was opposed to starting the NICS check system in the first place. The NRA lobbied for it. The Brady Campaign wanted long waiting periods for people who wanted to purchase a gun. They were against the whole idea of an *instant system* to approve law-abiding people."

A systemic problem is that in 2010, for example, only 62 out of 72,659 NICS denials led to prosecutions by the federal government, and only 13 of those prosecutions resulted in a conviction. That's a conviction rate of .018 percent.

This prompted Republican senator Lindsey Graham of South Carolina to say on CNN, "There are nine thousand people in 2010 that failed a background check who are felons on the run, and none of them were prosecuted."[16]

Graham was wrong about the "nine thousand" figure. According to the FBI, it was actually about "fourteen thousand" in 2010. The *Washington Post* gave Graham a pass on that figure but gave him three Pinocchios for saying that no felons were prosecuted,[17] as some of the denials are prosecuted at the state level. The Department of Justice, however, doesn't know how many NICS denials are prosecuted by the states, as they don't keep any records of such prosecutions.

As I dug deeper, I found that Pennsylvania, for example, runs its own background-check system[18] and reported that in 2010 "[t]he instantaneous background check process yielded warrant information that led to the arrest of 114 individuals while they were attempting to purchase a firearm last year. The coordinated efforts of PICS [Pennsylvania Instant Check System] staff and law enforcement agencies, who respond to these notifications, have resulted in the arrest of 1,365 fugitives since PICS was established in July 1998."[19]

Federally, a 2004 Justice Department inspector general report that looked at NICS denial prosecution rates explained: "We believe that the number of referrals and prosecutions is low because of the difficulty in obtaining convictions in NICS cases. These cases lack 'jury appeal' for various reasons. The factors prohibiting someone from possessing a firearm may have been nonviolent or committed many years ago. The basis for the prohibition may have been noncriminal (e.g., a dishonorable discharge from the U.S. military). It is also difficult to prove that the prohibited person was aware of the prohibition and intentionally lied to the FFL."[20]

Saying these cases don't have "jury appeal" is another way of saying they're worried about "jury nullification." According to the common-law doctrine of jury nullification, a juror can nullify a law— refuse to convict a defendant despite the law or instructions from a judge—if they believe the law is unjust or that the application of the law in a specific instance is unjust. That should tell prosecutors there's something wrong with the law. Perhaps a fifty-year-old man with a clear record except for the mistake he made of getting into a bar fight when he was nineteen shouldn't be barred for life from having a gun because of that one felony conviction thirty years before.

Also, it is unprofessional for the Department of Justice not to pursue cases that aren't sexy enough or to assume states are prosecuting some bad guys but never confirming this with hard data. This has led some politicians to demand answers.

While testifying before the Senate Judiciary Committee, Attorney General Eric Holder was asked why federal prosecutors aren't prosecuting many criminals who attempt to buy guns. Holder said, "There are reasonable explanations as to why we have those numbers, but I want to make absolutely certain we are prosecuting all the people who we should who have been denied a gun, after failing the instant background system."[21] When Republican senator John Cornyn of Texas pressed Holder by asking, don't "prosecutions work as a deterrence?" Holder replied, "We have limited resources."

Earlier that year, in January 2013, when asked about the Obama administration's lax enforcement of gun laws, Vice President Joe Biden said almost the same thing: "We simply don't have the time or the manpower to prosecute everybody who lies on a form, that checks a wrong box, that answers a question inaccurately."[22]

In 2013, Senators Lindsey Graham, Mark Begich, Jeff Flake, and Mark Pryor—two Republicans and two Democrats—introduced a bill to reform the National Instant Criminal Background Check System. The NICS Reporting Improvement Act of 2013 was written "to clarify circumstances under which a person loses the right to receive or possess firearms based on mental illness." The sponsors of this legislation noted that under current law certain mental incompetency adjudications don't have to be reported to the FBI's NICS.

The NICS Reporting Improvement Act of 2013 would have required states and federal entities to add people to NICS who a federal court ruled were

> an imminent danger to themselves or others; found guilty but mentally ill in a criminal case; . . . not guilty in a criminal case by reason of insanity or mental disease or defect; . . . incompetent to stand trial in a criminal case; . . . not guilty only by reason of lack of mental responsibility under the Uniform Code of Military Justice; required involuntary inpatient treatment by a psychiatric hospital; required

involuntary outpatient treatment by a psychiatric hospital based on a finding that the person is an imminent danger to himself or to others; and required involuntary commitment to a psychiatric hospital for any reason including drug use.[23]

Graham said "Exhibit A" of the need to fix the NICS system is the "Alice Boland case." Boland had made threats against President George W. Bush. She told investigating Secret Service agents: "I would shoot him and the entire U.S. Congress.... If I had a gun I would shoot you too."[24] In 2005 a federal district court judge found that Boland was schizophrenic and legally insane. In February 2013, Boland went to a gun store, passed a background check, and bought a semiautomatic pistol. She then took the gun to Ashley Hall, a private school in Charleston, South Carolina, and attempted to kill two staff members. Though she repeatedly pulled the trigger, the gun wouldn't go off, as she hadn't chambered a round.

Graham wanted to update NICS so that people like Boland could not legally buy guns. The NRA and the NSSF endorsed the legislation. Chris Cox, executive director of the NRA's Institute for Legislative Action, said, "This bill will create accurate definitions of those who pose serious threats and should be barred from the ability to buy or possess a firearm, while protecting the rights of law-abiding citizens and veterans."

Despite the bill's commonsense solution and bipartisan support, Democrats quietly smothered the legislation, presumably because they prefer gun bans to reasonable gun law reforms.

Pro-gun groups, however, haven't given up. The NSSF has been lobbying state legislators to add some mental-health records to the background-checks system. The NSSF calls its initiative "Fix NICS." Thanks to the NSSF's efforts, some states have passed legislation allowing them to report to the NICS people who been found legally insane.

Unfortunately, many Democrats have taken a commonsense idea and turned it into legislation that is a clear violation of civil liberties. For instance, New York's SAFE Act, passed in January 2013, gives healthcare professionals, including nurses and some social workers, the right to submit to the state police the names of people they think should be denied the right to own a gun. The police can then disarm these people without a court order. Others on the Left want to ban anyone who has sought treatment for post-traumatic stress disorder, including honorably discharged veterans, from owning a gun.

In the end, it comes down to understanding the difference between a law-abiding and a criminal gun culture. During a hearing in March 2013, Senator John Cornyn asked what Attorney General Eric Holder meant when, in 1995, he said young people needed to be "brain-washed" about guns. Holder explained that he was then a U.S. superior court judge in the District of Columbia, "the murder capital of the country," and was talking about "young black guys." He wanted "to make them think differently about the possession of guns." He said many of the "black guys" coming into his court "should have been leaders of the community" but instead they had "used guns inappropriately." Holder said he wanted to counter messages they were getting from movies and other parts of popular culture with an advertising campaign to "brainwash" them that guns are bad.

Holder should have asked himself why high legal gun-ownership rates in nearby rural Maryland and Virginia weren't resulting in the same level of gun violence per capita as he was seeing in inner-city DC. If he had, he might have had a better idea than funding an ad campaign to convince young people guns are bad—they know guns are bad; some inner-city youth are drawn to guns because they are bad-ass illegal. An open-minded investigation might have led Holder to the nearby NRA headquarters in Fairfax, Virginia, and to the NRA's gun-safety and youth programs as well as to programs developed by the Boy Scouts, the Izaak Walton League, and more. It would have required him to acknowledge that all gun ownership isn't bad and that if DC hadn't then been living under a handgun ban, maybe those young black men he wanted to save could have seen examples of responsible, law-abiding gun ownership. Maybe that would have helped change the gun culture in DC.

The reality is that the overwhelming majority of American gun owners are law-abiding, responsible people. Their Second Amendment rights deserve protection. It is the criminals who deserve prosecution.

CHAPTER TEN

The Armed Citizen
of the Future

*For better or for worse, the TrackingPoint—or some-
thing very much like it—is where rifles are going.*
—David E. Petzal, rifles editor, *Field & Stream*

The best way to see into the future of gun design is to begin with a
firearms innovator who likes to talk. So I ran down Ted Hatfield—
yeah, one of those Missouri Hatfields whose family used to feud with
the McCoys.

Ted has been a maverick gun builder since the early 1980s. I've
known him for more than a decade and have never seen him without
a swashbuckler's infectious grin. For a brief time in 2004, we had
adjacent offices at the Fairfax, Virginia, headquarters of the National

Rifle Association. The next time I saw him was in 2007 when we ran with the bulls in Pamplona, Spain. Ted was then living in Turkey, where he was designing the shotgun of the future. By January 2014, when I saw him at the SHOT Show, he had a factory outside Chicago. He was about to meet with his design team in Turkey to turn his new tactical pump-action shotgun into a semiautomatic.

His road to making a hip and high-tech shotgun began after a youth spent trying to get himself kicked into an unmarked grave in some hinterland. Ted spent his twenties traveling around the world twice, which included driving a bus through the Khyber Pass, running with those Spanish bulls, and working as a hunting guide in Alaska. All that adventuring paused when, near the end of his twenties, some fool emptied a Colt Model 1911 chambered in .45 ACP at him outside a Houston bar. As he checked himself for leaks, he thought, *Guns, hmm, maybe I'll settle down and make guns.*

Ted came to this decision in 1979—not exactly a high point in the history of American manufacturing, when all the talk was about the "Rust Belt," Jimmy Carter's "stagflation," and how entrenched unions had made America's aging factories uncompetitive. Ted says he didn't think about all that. He says if he had, he "might have just gone back to sea."[1]

Ted had grown up with guns and had always thought of ways they could be tweaked and refashioned. But he didn't want to just make guns. He wanted to make money. This meant he had to make and sell a lot of guns. To do this, he decided to produce guns that would look custom made, as most black-powder rifles then were, but that would be mass produced and so could sell at a more competitive price.

He spent the next few months in his hometown of St. Joseph, Missouri, constructing what became a beautiful replica of a rifle his great-great-grandfather had made before the Civil War. He took the rifle and a box of brochures for his new, actually nonexistent, company to a black-powder shoot in Indiana. Ted handed the rifle around and soon had orders for twenty guns—proving to him that there was indeed a market. Next, he had to figure out how to make the guns at the relatively low prices he had quoted.

He managed to get a loan from a local bank willing to bet on a Hatfield. Ted rented out an old garage and began to learn the hard way what it took to make guns in the early 1980s. Most of the guns then being made in America were coming from large soot-smothered factories in New York and New England. These factories had helped start and then propel the American Industrial Revolution. In the early 1980s, however, they were mostly filled with grease-stained lathes, churning barrel reamers, and an assortment of other large and expensive machines run by skilled machinists.

The machinists in those factories would take a billet of steel and via dozens or even a hundred steps, cut, drill, and grind it into a gun part that would be fit with other gun parts and then assembled into a gun. Making a profit by producing guns in this way on a small scale wasn't feasible. The best a small operator could do was to buy the parts and then assemble, tweak, and expertly fit them together until they became a custom rifle that could, say, shoot a one-inch, three-shot group at one hundred yards—at the time, none of the factory guns could reliably do that.

Ted saw a way between these two extremes. During World War II, engineers innovated large-scale investment-casting techniques using poured steel rather than cut steel, which made detailed design parts easier and more economical to produce. The man who recognized investment casting's potential for the civilian gun business and exploited this technology best was William Ruger.

Ruger come out with his Ruger No. 1, a single-shot rifle, in 1967. Everyone said he was behind the times, as Americans wanted semi-automatics and bolt-actions in the 1960s. Nevertheless, Ruger's elegant and accurate single-shot made at affordable prices created a new segment in the gun market and is still a classic today. Ruger used this success to build his business into one of America's biggest and most renowned gun manufacturers.

Ted discovered that, thanks to Ruger's pioneering work, the parts he needed could be cast in small foundries and made to order. He could then assemble and fit the guns in his rented garage.

"Ruger," he says, "revolutionized the whole business, and some of the big boys never realized or admitted it. They were stuck with those huge factories and all those tools and unions. They got left behind."

Since there was no way to cast wood, Ted bought an old lathe and began turning stocks. This was a slow process, but Ted found another technological development that could help him as it was helping many other manufacturers: computer numerical controlled (CNC) machining, which was more affordable and accurate.

Mark A. Keefe IV, the editor of the NRA's magazine *American Rifleman*, told me that when it comes to making accurate parts, "Depending on complexity, it may take a few different dedicated CNC machines, but not a city block's worth of dozens of steps and hundreds of workers. Parts that were too expensive to be made by individual metal workers can now be made by CNC machines programmed and run by much less-skilled operators."

So Ted found a CNC-operated factory in South Dakota that could turn out stocks and jobbed the work out to them. Interestingly, in a way, Ted was using available technology to turn back the clock. You see, when Eliphalet Remington founded Remington Arms in Ilion,

New York, in 1816, what he did was pull barrel makers, stock fitters, and others into one factory to mass-produce guns. Ted, thanks to new technology, was subcontracting the jobs to experts to lower overhead and other costs. This was something he couldn't have done in 1960, as the technology wasn't then available, but it is something most gun makers, and other manufacturers, now do.

Ted soon began delivering guns and taking more orders.

Other gun manufacturers slowly took notice. Since the 1980s, CNC machining has been propelling the future of the gun. When I toured Beretta's factory in Maryland, Richard Grimes, Beretta's director of manufacturing operations, told me, "It takes a lot less training for workers to run the CNC machines, and the quality is consistently top notch; in fact, all the parts are interchangeable down to thousandths of an inch. Low-skilled workers can assemble them."

In February 2014, Mike Fifer, CEO of Sturm, Ruger and Company said at a sportsmen's club, "Over the past few years I've counted forty-seven truckloads of old machines come out of our plant in Newport, New Hampshire. Those machines have been replaced by CNC machining. I'm proud to say we currently have 2,396 employees here in America making all of our guns for Americans. This includes a new plant we've opened in North Carolina, a plant so high-tech and clean you could eat off the floor. And it includes the last twenty employees we have in Connecticut—workers I'm not moving or laying off despite Connecticut's disregard for your rights, because they've been with us for so long and have too much expertise to let go. Our corporate headquarters, however, is in the final stages of being moved to Florida."

CNC means that many gun manufacturers can affordably outsource work to specialist companies. When I toured the O. F. Mossberg & Sons plant in North Haven, Connecticut, Joseph H.

Bartozzi, Mossberg's senior vice president and general counsel, said, "As far as I know we're the only firearms manufacturer that makes all the parts for our AR-15. All the other companies buy barrels, trigger mechanisms, or something from other manufacturers."

In the 1980s Ted was also at the forefront of stock manufacturing, as CNC would soon revolutionize stock designs. Today, the complex bedding recesses of wooden bolt-action rifle stocks for guns like the Sako 85 and the Browning A-Bolt are inletted in seconds by CNC cutters. Rifle stocks are often still being roughed out by machines that resemble the Blanchard lathe, a machine invented by Thomas Blanchard (1788–1864), but are being finished by CNC machining. These same machines now make synthetic stocks for rifles and shotguns in more configurations than anyone dreamed possible in 1980.

So early on Ted recognized CNC machining was the future. He saw this because he had become a businessman, not just an artisan. He also knew the black-powder market was only so big, so he targeted the classic shotgun market. He began making high-quality, side-by-side shotguns for the average guy. The side-by-side shotgun is favored by rural English gentlemen, and elegant versions are still handmade in the Basque region of northern Spain. In America, the side-by-side shotgun wasn't traditionally associated with an aristocracy; it was a farmer's gun, displaced in the twentieth century by pump-action shotguns and later by semiautomatic shotguns. Ted, however, knew nostalgia runs deep with a portion of America's shotgunners. In 1985, Ted came out with a 20-gauge shotgun with short double barrels and beautiful wood. He soon had orders for all he could make. In the late 1980s, his lowest-grade gun sold for around $2,500, the highest for $6,900—whereas a Spanish side-by-side might cost $20,000. Ted had come in with a classic work of art at a much more reasonable price.

By the early 1990s, Ted's office was in an old brick building that he shared with a bar. He still had his sleeves rolled up and was involved in every facet of the business. He had made a name for himself, but the big manufacturers and other new custom shops were catching up with him. His profit margins were getting smaller as bigger gun manufacturers produced and imported cheaper side-by-side and over/under shotguns. As his business declined and his company went under, he decided he needed to reinvent himself.

He took a job editing for *Sports Afield* magazine, a hunting and fishing magazine founded in 1887 as a "Journal for Gentlemen." But in the late 1990s, its owners at Hearst decided to change the magazine's historic focus from hunting and fishing to hiking, mountain biking, climbing, and other "nonconsumptive" outdoor sports. Because the two audiences couldn't be more different—they shifted from gun-toting, Mossy Oak camo–wearing outdoorsmen who kill their own meat to REI-dressed hikers with granola bars in their Eddie Bauer bags—this publishing misadventure failed fast, and the title was sold in 2000 to the wealthy, self-made publisher Robert E. Petersen.

After the trouble at *Sports Afield*, Ted worked briefly for an advertising company. But a meeting with Turkish gun makers at a trade show in Fort Worth brought him back to gun design. "They were importing Huglu shotguns from Turkey and had a very cool miniature-framed 28-gauge side-by-side at a really cheap price," says Ted. "They saw my name was Hatfield and asked if I had anything to do with the old Hatfield side-by-side shotguns (which of course was my old company). One thing led to another and we formed a partnership to develop high-grade shotguns in Turkey under the Hatfield name."

Before they developed and introduced these guns, however, some American gun companies contacted Ted to see if he would produce shotguns with their names cut into the gun barrels. So instead of Hatfield's, Ted began making side-lock side-by-sides and over/under shotguns for Kimber, as well as shotguns for Smith & Wesson. In 2006 Smith & Wesson told Ted they wanted to create the ultimate police shotgun. Soon thereafter Ted and others started working on what would become the UTS-15 (which stands for "Urban Tactical Shotgun 15-rounds"), a pump-action shotgun that holds fifteen shells and utilizes a lot of new technology. "When the U.S. economy went down the crapper in the fall of 2008," says Ted, "S&W canceled the project. Since S&W had not invested in the original development and our relationship was at an end, we carried on and the UTS-15 is the first product marketed under the UTAS name."

The UTS-15 actually began with a highly unorthodox design first developed by South Africa's Truvelo Armory. UTAS obtained patent rights and samples of the shotgun. After initial evaluation, it was decided to redesign the shotgun almost entirely. They retained its basic configuration and dual over-the-barrel magazines, but changed everything else. All development work was carried out at the UTAS facility in Turkey, with Ted, who was then living in Turkey, leading the way.

After years of tweaks and design modifications, the UTS-15 was unveiled as a tactical, lightweight, short, mostly polymer, pump-action shotgun for a new generation. It is the first shotgun ever produced with a 100 percent polymer receiver. More than 80 percent of the gun is fabricated from carbon-fiber reinforced injection-molded polymer. The UTS-15 is basically a close-quarters combat tactical shotgun with an overall length of just twenty-nine inches and a fifteen-round capacity. It looks like a very fat M4A1, but it's all shotgun. It handles as well as an AR-15 and would be at home in any futuristic war movie.

The UTS-15 also has an optional built-in LED spotlight and laser sight. This is another trend reshaping guns today. Lew Danielson developed the concept of integrating a laser system into pistols back in the 1990s. He began going to gun shows and selling the idea. "They'd send their guns in and we'd fit a laser sighting system into their pistol's frame," Lew told me when I visited his Oregon facility in 2013. The success of this concept led him to start Crimson Trace, today's preeminent laser-sighting-system maker for firearms. You can see his products in movies when someone's gun puts a red dot on a target. Integrating the laser sights manually, however, was too expensive. Crimson Trace soon turned to making laser grips and began expanding to fit most popular handgun models. They're still doing that today, but technology has now been developed for them to work with manufacturers to cost-effectively integrate laser sights and lights into firearms again.

Ted's shotgun is benefiting from this and many other developing technologies. His extensive use of polymer and carbon fiber has also enabled him to keep the shotgun to just 6.9 pounds unloaded. Many firearms now use synthetic stocks, carbon fiber, and even titanium barrels to reduce weight. One trend sure to continue is lighter, smaller firearms in every category as new materials and manufacturing processes are developed and taken from other industries.

Back in the 1980s, Gaston Glock's invention led other gun companies to use polymer. Polymer helped the Glock 17 hold a record 17 rounds of 9 mm Luger without becoming as heavy as a rifle. Engineered plastics and other synthetic materials have been used as major components in firearms dating back to the Remington Nylon 66 (produced from 1959 to 1989). Since Glock came to the market, it's hard to imagine the world of handguns without polymer frames or rifles without synthetic stocks.

Polymer allows very complex detail to be formed into a mold. Molds are expensive to design—they can range from $25,000 to $250,000 or more depending on the part—yet once a mold is finalized, a manufacturer can literally produce hundreds of thousands of complex parts for little more than the cost of the material, the operator, and other incidentals. "With a mold a gun maker can add thirty-line-per-inch checkering with no extra labor cost," Keefe tells me.

It used to be that if a particular handgun didn't fit well in your hands, you simply picked out another model or went down a chambering. Not anymore. Now just about every major maker of a polymer-framed, recoil-operated handgun offers one or more models with an interchangeable grip panel. Now, with guns such as the Beretta Storm, Ruger SR-9, Heckler & Koch P30, Sig Sauer P250, Smith & Wesson M&P, and Springfield XD(M), you can change the contour and depth of the backstrap in seconds. This changes how a pistol rests in a person's hands, which affects trigger reach, the length of pull, and other ergonomic factors. Essentially, you can now have it "your way" with one gun. A former NFL pro and a cheerleader can buy the same model and caliber pistol, and, thanks to the pistol's replaceable grips and other features, both will actually have a good chance of having a gun that fits them well.

Similarly, rifle manufacturers are developing new materials to make lighter rifles. Ever since Winchester released its Featherweight Model 70, in the 1950s, the popularity of lightweight rifles among marksmen and hunters has risen. Most "mountain rifles" now weigh no more than six pounds. Remington, for example, uses titanium in its Model 700 Alaskan Ti. This space-age alloy is half the weight of steel but a lot stronger. Browning's A-Bolt Mountain Ti also has a titanium receiver. Ruger's entry was the M77 Mark II Compact, a rifle with a short, sixteen-and-a-half-inch barrel attached to a stock proportioned accordingly. Kimber designed its own synthetic stock for its 84M Montana so that, in standard, short-action chamberings, the 84M weighs just a touch over five pounds. Weatherby came out with the Mark V Ultra Lightweight and in standard chamberings weighs just five and three-quarter pounds. A lot of custom rifle makers have long specialized in making lighter and very accurate rifles, but their time and expertise is expensive. Because of the entries from major manufacturers, these custom gun makers have seen their share of the light-rifle market shrink.

These manufacturing advances and others—including semisolid metal casting and metal injection molding—have made it possible to design guns anyone can take apart, clean, and put back together. To strip down the UTS-15, for example, you don't need tools—an amateur can take apart the shotgun in less than a minute. It can also be easily modified. The UTS-15 doesn't even come with a standard sight; instead, it has a MIL-STD-1913 Picatinny rail that a consumer can outfit with any type of iron sights or optics. The gun has additional slots for aftermarket Picatinny rails on both sides of the receiver, and a front slot on its hand guard allows someone to attach a tactical flashlight or another device. As with AR-15-type rifles, this platform allows people in this Starbucks age to get what they want rather than just getting a one-size-fits-all design.

"We now have fifteen employees outside Chicago putting this shotgun together for the American market," says Ted. "Back in the 1980s I had to work with engineers on draft boards." These days, like most gun makers, Ted's team works with SolidWorks, a 3-D CAD/CAM engineering program, to design new guns. "Now we can make a part and scan it in with a 3-D laser scanner. We can then tweak the part in SolidWorks. Over in Turkey we have a good Solid-Works draftsman and a couple of engineers as well," says Ted. Design changes that used to take years now take weeks or even days as gun designers tweak prototypes three dimensionally on computer screens. SolidWorks software is attracting a new group of gun designers to the firearms industry. Eric Lichtenberg, president and founder of Lichtenberg Research and Design, for example, says he is a "jack of all trades." He worked in the film industry, but, as many inventors do, he has dabbled in many areas. He has been hired by Kodiak Arms and other gun companies to help their R&D departments. He says, "Technology from the aerospace industry, medical-products field, and others are being picked up by some savvy gun makers to design guns that are lighter and that have other technologies installed. I'm excited. The gun industry can at times be too conservative with design, but nevertheless gun technology is about to take a giant leap into the future. SolidWorks, for example, can show you where the stress points on a new gun design are. It can even actively help you find solutions. What used to take years can now take hours."

Lichtenberg introduced me to a thirty-six-year-old design engineer who works for outdoor sports companies but who used SolidWorks to create a new revolver in his spare time that is simpler to make than a Smith & Wesson J-frame, that has fewer parts than other revolvers, and that's as small as a Derringer, yet packs four shots of 9mm. He decided he didn't want to reveal too much yet on the record, as he wants a gun company to purchase and manufacture his new idea; however, having seen this gun, I have no doubt it'll be on magazine covers as soon as a gun company can tool up to produce it. He says, "I couldn't have done this a few years ago. I would have needed lathes and machinists and more just to get started. Now I'm able to use my expertise to creatively try new concepts digitally."

Ted Hatfield told me, "The pace of innovation is speeding up and we're at the forefront. Now I have what I think is a sound, single, short-stroke, gas-piston design worked out for our new semi-auto shotgun, but we need to turn my wet-bar napkins into engineering drawings. Anyway, that project is now well under way, and with a little luck we'll have our new semiautomatic in production by the end of 2014."

Ted adds, "When I started, in the early 1980s, the business was dominated by a few big manufacturers and some custom shops. Now I order parts made to precise specs worked out on SolidWorks or other software. The parts come in from various manufacturers from all over the world that have the expertise and the cheapest labor costs I can find without compromising quality. My employees then assemble the parts that are perfect to a few thousandths of an inch. Before CNC machining and other advances you still needed skilled labor to use lathes or another tools to expertly fit products together. Not anymore."

Many of the big American gun makers import parts and even guns. CVA, for example, is a gun company formally located in Connecticut, now headquartered in Georgia, and that has a manufacturing facility in Spain. CVA makes rifles, muzzleloaders, and high-quality barrels for a lot of American gun companies. I toured their factory in Bergara, Spain, in 2007. CVA calls the barrels coming out of its plant "Bergara Barrels." They are cut and polished to a perfection only custom barrels could once reliably attain. They are an example of how, during just the last two decades, CNC machining and other advances have improved the accuracy of factory rifles and ammunition to the point where "minute of angle" groups and smaller, can be attained with medium- and low-priced hunting rifles that have not been modified by a gunsmith. "This was unheard of twenty years ago," David Petzal, rifles editor for *Field & Stream* magazine, tells me. "Now we have no shortage of rifle manufacturers who guarantee one-inch groups at one hundred yards."

Increased accuracy from factory rifles hasn't been the only big change. Remington, CVA, and other gun makers have developed proprietary coatings for metal that make them impervious to the elements. Thompson/Center Arms uses Weathershield on its Icon, a coating that makes stainless steel even more impervious to the elements. Remington uses a proprietary TriNyte Corrosion Control System to produce its XCR (Xtreme Conditions Rifle) with scratch and corrosion resistance superior to stainless steel. Ruger has All-Weather Grey on its M77 MkII, and Mossberg has MarineCoat on its 4x4.

Mark Hendricks, CVA's vice president of technical development, says, "We wanted to see if our new muzzleloaders with a nitride finish could take the elements. So we shot a few, didn't clean them, and left them out in the snow for weeks. This should rust out and destroy a muzzleloader, especially one that was fired. Thanks to the finish, when we cleaned them, they looked and performed like new."

The manufacturing process itself is now less focused on the assembly line than on the craftsman. Aitor Belategui, the director of innovation at CVA's plant in Spain, told me in March 2014, "We're now making employees responsible for individual guns. They see a barrel through the cutting and polishing processes and then take the barrels through the other steps of manufacturing and assembling. This makes them responsible for the quality of fit, finish, and accuracy with *their* guns."

"It used to be," adds Mark Hendricks, "that someone made a lot of barrels that then sat in racks until they were carted over by someone else to the next stage. But now our employees are more like old-fashioned gun artisans, as they're individually building guns and are then responsible for their products' quality. This is taking our guns to another level of performance—if that's possible."

"Right," says Aitor, "this also makes it easier for us to complete small orders faster and to keep our inventory in step with demand."

———————

American-based manufacturers with Federal Firearms Type 7 licenses (manufacturer of firearms and/or ammunition) increased by 282 percent, from 1,941 in 2002 to 7,423 in 2012, according to the Bureau of Alcohol, Tobacco, Firearms and Explosives (ATF)—in 1980 there were only 496 American manufacturers with Type 7 licenses.

Relatively new gun makers include companies like Stag Arms, which was founded in 2003. Stag Arms has about two hundred employees making AR-15s in Connecticut; however, as this is being written, Stag Arms was looking to move to a more gun-friendly state. Another example is Magpul Industries, a company that began making AR-15 accessories in 1999. Magpul's quick growth and political troubles are a timely example of some of the forces shaping the future of the gun. In December 2012 Magpul Industries had been preparing to break ground on a new state-of-the-art facility in Colorado. Magpul's PMAG magazines, AR stocks, grips, and other products were in high demand. Started in a home basement in 1999, by 2012 Magpul had more than two hundred employees, and the future looked bright. But then the state's Democrat governor John Hickenlooper and Democrat-led legislature pushed for a series of gun-control restrictions. In early 2013 the Colorado State Senate's president, John Morse, stood on the state's senate floor and argued that new gun restrictions were needed as a way of "cleansing a sickness from our souls."

Magpul and other companies said they would take their jobs out of Colorado if the state banned them from selling some of their products.

The legislature and governor, however, banned so-called high-capacity magazines (no magazine can be loaded with more than ten rounds); required "universal background checks"; forced gun buyers to pay for their own background checks; and more.

In January 2014, Richard Fitzpatrick, chief executive officer of Magpul, announced that the company was relocating its manufacturing, distribution, and shipping operations to Cheyenne, Wyoming. "Moving operations to states that support our culture of individual liberties and personal responsibility is important," he said, giving full credit to Wyoming governor Matt Mead, the Wyoming Business Council, and the group Cheyenne LEADS for supporting the relocation. Magpul's corporate office, meanwhile, will be moved to Texas. Texas governor Rick Perry gave Magpul a big Texas welcome, saying, "In Texas, we understand that freedom breeds prosperity, which is why we've built our economy around principles that allow employers to innovate, keep more of what they earn and create jobs."

Gun manufacturers are not only moving out of states that are restricting gun rights, they are moving to states that allow them the freedom to pursue new technology. One of these emerging technologies is 3-D printing. Many people find 3-D gun printing controversial, because, arguably, it allows anyone to make a homemade gun. But people already make homemade guns. I know a well-traveled hunter who bought several homemade handguns in rural parts of Africa; none of these homemade handguns took more than a hacksaw, an open fire, and some scrap metal.

These guns are primitive, but the human ingenuity behind them is no different from the stainless steel Model 1911 semiautomatic pistol with carbon-fiber grip printed out by Solid Concepts on a 3-D printer in 2013.[2] Solid Concepts, a company based in Austin, Texas, chose the Model 1911 because the design is in the public domain. The company posted YouTube videos of employees shooting their 3-D-printed pistol. Kent Firestone, a vice president at Solid Concepts, says, "As far as we know, we're the only 3D Printing Service Provider with a Federal Firearms License. Now, if a qualifying customer needs a unique gun part in five days, we can deliver. It's a common misconception that 3D printing isn't accurate or strong enough."[3]

The worry that people might soon print their own 3-D guns to evade authorities is mostly media hype. That fear made headlines in 2013 after Cody Wilson, a Texas law student and leader of a group called Defense Distributed, made available on the internet blueprints for a 3-D-printed gun. The group says it exists "to defend the civil liberty of popular access to arms as guaranteed by the United States Constitution and affirmed by the United States Supreme Court, through facilitating global access to, and the collaborative production of, information and knowledge related to the 3D printing of arms."[4] The files to print out the gun, known as "the Liberator," were downloaded more than one hundred thousand times before the Bureau of Alcohol, Tobacco, Firearms and Explosives (ATF) took the 3-D-gun plans off the internet.

The thing is, traditionally manufactured guns—well-designed firearms that aren't likely to blow up in your hands—are readily available at relatively low costs, so there is, for now, a limited market for quality 3-D-printed guns. (Ironically, an underground market for such guns could be created by stringent gun-control laws.) There's also a misconception that 3-D-printed guns are more dangerous than other guns because they can allegedly evade a metal detector. But barring a major leap forward in ammunition, 3-D-printed guns will likely still need metal firing pins, not to mention metal ammunition; and, if they were going to shoot a cartridge much heavier than a .22 LR, the guns would have to use some steel to contain the pressure.

If people are worried 3-D-printed guns will be made in shapes that don't look like guns, that's not a new problem either. "Pen guns" (guns that resemble ink pens) designed to fire a single .22 LR or other light cartridge have been around for a long time, as have guns made to resemble Zippo liters, stopwatches, and cameras. These inventions are neat to see in spy movies—some people buy pen guns for that reason—but they've never been a problem for the criminal-justice system, because easily concealable small pistols and revolvers pack a lot more lead, are more accurate, and have been available at affordable prices since the late nineteenth century.

The real future of 3-D-printing technology isn't scary—it's about helping manufacturers make hard-to-find parts for custom guns or firearms that have gone out of production. 3-D printing is just another aspect of the industry using high tech to help customers have the firearms they want.

One of my favorite gun nuts is Bryce Towsley. He has a snow-white beard, an encyclopedic knowledge of guns, and a libertarian's penchant for personal freedom. A few summers ago, he took a road trip to Maine to look at a used lathe for making his own gun parts and came back with the lathe, a barrel reamer, and so many thousands of additional pounds of machinery that he blew out the tires on his trailer—at least that's his story. Upstairs in his barn is his "ammo room," an entire floor filled with stacks of ammo. In the basement of his home, he has a gunroom with a vault door. Inside are more than six hundred rifles, pistols, and shotguns from AR-15s to Colt .45s. He writes about guns. He competes in more than a dozen competitions—from 3-gun to Cowboy Action—every year.

So I ask Bryce to lead me through the crowded aisles at the 2014 SHOT Show to see the latest innovations in gun design and alterations. We check out the new Glock 42. At just under six inches long, the G42 is simple, elegant, and the smallest Glock ever made. It is chambered in .380 and weighs just 14.36 ounces when loaded with 6 rounds.

Glock isn't the only manufacturer making carry pistols that are smaller and lighter. Two of the smartest new designs of 2014 are from Remington.

We have to wait for a turn to handle the 9mm R-51 pistols that are attached to tethers in the Remington Outdoor Company booth. This little pistol comes with a laser grip from Crimson Trace and a suppressor (where these are legal). Its grip angle is slanted to lower muzzle jump and optimize target acquisition. It's just 6.67 inches long. It has a lightweight aluminum frame and is so easy to load that my mother's arthritic hands could work this pistol.

Nearby is a cutting-edge AR-15 from DPMS (another Remington company). An engineer shows us the DPMS GII. The semiautomatic rifle is chambered in .308 (7.62 NATO). Stripped down, this rifle weighs about 6.45 pounds—about 2 pounds less than similar rifles chambered in .308. It also has dual ejectors, a monolithic bolt carrier with an integral gas key, and an improved extractor made from a new alloy.

As we handle these guns and visit other manufacturers, even a person unfamiliar with firearms would quickly notice how much AR-15s are being tweaked and accessorized to meet demands of law enforcement and civilians who might use an AR-15 for home defense, for fun at a range, or to compete in fast-growing 3-gun competitions.

Every year the pace of innovation seems to speed up, and the selections become more diverse. There is no use in outlining all the new guns of 2014 here, because by the time this book is published, the next generation of guns will be ready for the 2015 SHOT Show. The point is the market is big and growing and driven by well-tested technological advances and an ever-increasing focus on customization.

A good way to see how innovation is changing the gun industry is to look at how triggers have changed over the last two decades. Jim Carmichel, the now-retired shooting editor of *Outdoor Life*, used to call triggers from the big gun makers "lawyer triggers." Gun manufacturers were worried about lawsuits if a gun went off too easily, so most fitted their rifles with triggers so hard to pull they were nearly impossible to shoot accurately under real conditions. Any decent rifleman had to buy and install (or have installed) an aftermarket trigger from Timney Triggers or another company.

This changed in the early 2000s when Kimber, a medium- to high-end gun maker founded in 1979, started putting exceptional triggers on its center-fire rifles. In 2003, engineers at venerable Savage Arms found a way to make a trigger both lawyer-proof and light enough to pull without jerking a rifle off target. Savage called it the Accutrigger. This trigger let shooters adjust the trigger pull from one pound, eight ounces, to six pounds without any help from a gunsmith. The innovation gave shooters a fabulous system in an economical package, and it gave Savage a remarkable competitive advantage. Since 2003, Thompson/Center, Marlin, Mossberg, Weatherby, and others have incorporated user-adjustable triggers on a lot of rifles; also, Remington (X-Mark Pro), Ruger (LC6), Winchester (MOA), and Browning (Feather) named new trigger designs in an attempt to win back some of the market share they had lost to Savage.

The marketplace is still pushing engineers to evolve new triggers. For example, in January 2014 during a media day at a gun range in

Las Vegas—an event held annually the day before the SHOT Show begins that allows writers and editors to see and shoot new gun introductions—I thought I heard a machine gun being fired and thought *cool, a gun with a fun switch*. When I got over to shoot the "machine gun," however, I found it was an AR-15 fitted with a Tac-Con 3MR Trigger System from a new company called Tactical Fire Control, Inc. Every year, arms makers and others in the firearms industry show off their smartest designs at the SHOT Show, and it always seems there are a handful of standout new guns and products. The Tac-Con 3MR Trigger System is such an invention. It is "a drop-in, 3-mode fire control system consisting of Safe, match-grade Semi-Automatic, and the Tac-Con patented 3rd Mode of operation." The third mode provides a positive reset that dramatically reduces the time between shots. An experienced trigger finger can make this thing fly.

The trigger's reset is achieved by transferring the force from the bolt carrier through the trigger assembly to assist the trigger back onto the front sear. The Bureau of Alcohol, Tobacco, Firearms and Explosives (ATF) follows guidelines to approve new gun designs. If a gun falls into a category that requires a special license to own (such as a machine gun), then it can only be sold to someone with such a hard-to-get license. The ATF approved this trigger for the general market, but to stop worries on ranges, the manufacturer is putting a letter from the ATF stating as much into every box.

To understand the trends pushing guns into the future, however, "you also must continue to acknowledge the nostalgic streak that runs deep and wide in almost every class of firearms," says Mark A. Keefe IV, the editor of the NRA's magazine *American Rifleman*. "Maybe it's the appreciation for history, maybe it's a desire to return to a simpler time or to reach back in time. But, in my view, it's those things and more. Mostly, it's the fact that good design and performance are simply timeless. But innovation is what drives the industry. So we're forever pushing forward into the past so to speak."

An example of this is the M1 Garand and the M16, two standard-issue rifles of the U.S. military whose semiautomatic civilian derivatives dominate the American marketplace for rifles. Indeed, civilian AR-15-type rifles have so many new options for sights, lights, grips, triggers, and other accessories that former Special Forces soldiers have told me that technological advances in the American civilian gun market drive the development of battlefield rifles as well.

Keefe says it's uncertain when a new service rifle for the U.S. armed forces will displace the M4 carbines—lightweight versions of the Vietnam-era M16—and thereby propel the gun market in a new direction, but the search for a better rifle is never ending. Many sources tell me the U.S. Army won't replace the M4 until a new infantry rifle makes a technological "leap ahead." In 2014 the U.S. Army had about a half million M4s and was reluctant to make a big and expensive change without a very good reason for doing so.[5]

Some of the M4's critics have been very vocal. For example, U.S. Army Senior Warrant Officer Russton B. Kramer, a twenty-year Green Beret, told the *Washington Times* that if you want to improve your chances of surviving on the battlefield, you have to modify your M4 with over-the-counter products.[6]

Other active and former U.S. soldiers tell me the M4 is fine, but that soldiers improve the weapons with civilian triggers, sights, and grips. Steve Adelmann, a retired SOF Operator who spent twenty-two years in the U.S. Army and who currently owns Citizen Arms, told me, "I can't speak for everyone, but my experience was that aftermarket parts were purchased to upgrade, not to keep guns running. I consulted several current armorers and grunts about the *Washington Times* article to see if my recollections were incorrect. To a man they backed up my observations."

The *Washington Times* also reported that "U.S. Special Operations Command in 2001 issued a damning private report that said the M4A1 was fundamentally flawed because the gun failed when called on to unleash rapid firing." Also, in "2002, an internal report from the Army's Picatinny Arsenal in New Jersey said the M4A1 was prone to overheating and 'catastrophic barrel failure.'" That makes the M4 sound like a flawed product, but the M4 carbine remains a proven and versatile platform that has yet to be surpassed in a range of categories.

The chief criticism of the M4 is whether the "direct impingement" gas-operated recoil system lets in sand and dust that jam the carbine in desert environments. Republican senator Tom Coburn of Oklahoma has been pressuring the Pentagon to test M4 alternatives since at least 2007. He has even used his senatorial leverage to put some army nominations on hold to force the army to listen to him. (The first hold was on Peter Geren, for secretary of the army, in 2007; the second on Heidi Shyu, for army acquisition chief, in 2013.)[7]

Criticism with the army's current small arms doesn't stop with the M4. In 2006, the Center for Naval Analysis made a report public that said more than a third of all soldiers using the M249 squad automatic weapon (SAW) in combat in Iraq and Afghanistan were dissatisfied with its reliability. Also, "30% of these soldiers experienced stoppages with their M249 while engaging the enemy in combat…. The same survey noted that nearly half of all users of the M9 pistol were dissatisfied with its use. There is no plan for the Army to issue replacements for the Army's decades-old designs for M9 pistols, M16 rifles, or M249 machine guns," said Coburn. Coburn and other critics think the armed services should encourage private manufacturers to present the army with new options.

Coburn stepped into a related gunfight when he wrote that "ballistic testing going back to World War I … show that the current 5.56 mm ammunition that is the Army and NATO standard is not the ideal ammunition for our troops engaging targets greater than 300 meters." Coburn argued that the army should be "conducting robust research and analysis on the possibility of intermediate caliber ammunition that would be effective at long ranges."

Adelmann says, "From a purely logistical standpoint, it's much easier to upgrade or replace uppers and other parts of the M4 than it is to develop and procure an entirely new system." Adelmann now builds AR-15s for private customers. He adds, "New caliber and bullet options are pushing guns into the future, and I see that as a good thing. New guns will have to adapt to the advantages they offer."

What would surprise a firearms engineer from 1880 wouldn't be all the new metals, powders, and other advances, but the basic fact that we're still using the self-contained cartridge. As we fly on jets, microwave our food, and send text messages from smartphones, we're still using the same nineteenth-century concept of a primer placed at the end of a brass cartridge loaded with gunpowder and topped with a bullet.

Drew Goodlin, director of new product development for ATK Ammunition Systems Group, which includes Federal Premium, Speer Bullets, CCI Ammunition, Fusion, and more, tells me, "We have some patents on emerging technologies utilizing electricity and chemicals, but I don't see the bullet going away as the choice for hunting, the military, or even personal defense for a long time. What's exciting is how much we've been able to engineer bullets and shot to more accurately and ethically kill game faster without bullet failures. Though there are some emerging alternatives in personal defense, the bullet will be the go-to option until something comes along that is as affordable and reliable as traditional guns and ammo."

Bullet design is, of course, an ancient art. From about 1500 to 1800 AD, lead bullets changed very little, as they were good. Any frontiersman with a bullet mold could melt lead over a fire, cast a round ball of a certain caliber, and stuff it into a muzzleloader. Then came the percussion cap (priming with a fulminating powder made of potassium chlorate, sulfur, and charcoal, which is ignited by concussion) in the early nineteenth century, and it was good. Muzzleloaders could suddenly be fired in any weather. Finally, during the nineteenth century, the self-contained cartridge was developed, and they became really good. Cartridges could be loaded, levered, bolted, and even driven into place by gasses bled off from a fired cartridge. Firearms had entered the modern era.

The next big advance came in 1882 when Major Eduard Rubin, director of the Swiss Army Laboratory, made the first copper-jacketed bullet. The copper jacket was added because the surface of a lead bullet fired at high velocity can melt due to hot gases behind it and friction as the bullet travels down a rifle's bore. Because copper has a higher melting point and greater specific heat capacity and hardness than lead, copper-jacketed bullets allow greater velocities without bullet deformities and other issues.

A copper-jacketed lead bullet is a versatile and efficient killer. Such bullet designs work well on medium-sized game (and people) in most situations, but they aren't reliable when they hit hard bone or large game. Copper-jacketed lead bullets changed slowly until, in 1946, John Nosler had a bullet fail to penetrate far enough into a moose in British Columbia. At the time, there were two basic copper-jacketed lead bullet options available. The military used full-metal-jacket bullets—a single copper alloy envelope around a lead alloy core. These bullets achieved good penetration but often failed to expand and so zipped right through, leaving a wound only as wide as the pointy bullet. The other type was the soft-nose hunting bullet, such as the one Nosler was using. It has a copper jacket over the bullet's base, but the top is open to expose the softer lead. These bullets "mushroom" when they hit a target to leave a large wound channel, but they sometimes break apart and fail to penetrate through heavy bone or muscle tissue. Copper-jacketed, soft-nose bullets are still used by hunters for deer and other medium-sized game. The Remington Core-Lokt is such a design and is still an economical and popular choice for deer today—though a bonded (a process that chemically bonds metals together) Core-Lokt is now available.

Nosler decided hunters needed a more humane alternative for big, tough game. He went to work, and by 1947 he was testing his first Nosler Partition.[8] He designed the bullet with two lead cores separated by a "wall" of jacket metal. In a cross-section, the jacket on a Nosler Partition looks like an "H" with a lump of lead in its top and bottom. The nose of the jacket was made to be fragile. When a Partition hits, it expands. Its rear stays intact (the bottom of the H) and penetrates, but its front disintegrates. Soon the Nosler Partition became the standard all other bullet designers measured their ideas against.

Hunters still use and swear by Partitions, but many don't like that half the bullet falls apart. Maximum weight retention, they point out, is fundamental to a bullet's performance. So other bullet makers went to work. Petzal says, "When I started big-game hunting in the late 1960s, I could look forward to seeing at least one dandy bullet failure every season. Either a slug would zip right through the animal, not expanding at all, or it would blow up and fail to penetrate far enough. Not anymore. Now premium bullets do pretty much what they're designed to do."

The Swift A-Frame was introduced in 1984, by Kansan Lee Reid. The A-Frame resembles the Nosler Partition, but an A-Frame's front core is bonded to the jacket, so the A-Frame retains its weight—usually better than 90 percent. Also in 1984, Nosler introduced the Ballistic Tip—a bullet with a plastic tip—to stop bullet damage in rifle magazines. At the time, the engineers at Nosler didn't realize what this tip would do to a bullet's ballistics or performance; however, when the design turned out to be accurate and make bigger wound channels, the engineers realized they had something special. Polymer tips now grace a lot of premium bullets.

In 1989 Barnes came out with the X-Bullet. Randy Brooks of Barnes Bullets decided that really big game required an all-copper bullet. The X-Bullet he designed would become one of the most-imitated big-game bullets on the market. It's a solid copper bullet with a small, but deep, hollow point in the tip. When the bullet hits a target, its tip folds open into four petals, forming an "X." Under normal conditions it retains 100 percent of its weight, and its penetration is extreme.

Hunting bullets that expand as an "X" and hold together became the standard measurement of premium big-game bullets. In 2003, Barnes advanced the technology of the X-Bullet with the introduction of the Triple-Shock X (TSX), which has rings cut in the shank for higher performance.

Meanwhile, Steve Hornady developed a long list of remarkable hunting bullets. Hornady's InterBonds have earned a solid reputation, as have Nosler's AccuBonds, and Swift's Sciroccos. These are all bonded bullets, meaning the metals in them are chemically bonded together so the bullet is much less likely to come apart. Another excellent bonded bullet is the Trophy Bonded Bear Claw. It was originally designed by Jack Carter, a Houston-based big-game hunter and bullet inventor. When Federal Premium Ammunition began making this bullet, they swapped Carter's pure-copper jackets with gilding metal and made other design tweaks. They now market it in their Vital-Shok line as the Trophy Bonded Tip.

Mark A. Keefe IV, the editor of *American Rifleman*, put these and many other advances in bullets this way: "Bullets are now an engineering problem. A bullet can be made to expand and hold together through hide and bone, through armor, or even cinder blocks. Thanks to a lot of engineers, all you need today is the right bullet for the job. Just a few decades ago you didn't have controlled-expansion bullets that held their shape after their initial upset. Now the marketplace has developed specific bullet/caliber options for very specific problems."

On this topic, Steve Hornady, president of Hornady Manufacturing Company, tells me, "It's not easy getting a bullet to expand and hold together at very different velocities. Our .30-06 Springfield Superformance load, for example, sends a 180-grain bullet out the muzzle at 2,820 feet per second. This bullet slows to about 2,100 feet per second at 400 yards. We need that bullet to reliably expand and to hold together on impact at both those velocities. We've solved those problems. Hunters and others just need to pick the right tool for the job. If we don't have it, we'll design a better option for them."

Hornady's Superformance line of ammo, which was introduced in 2011, has custom blends of powders made for specific rifle cartridges and bullets. Hornady says its Superformance ammunition increases rifle muzzle velocities by one hundred to two hundred feet per second over average factory loads and are more accurate.[9] People have long hand-loaded their own rifle ammunition, but now Hornady and other companies are filling the need for customized ammunition. Needs for specialized ammunition range from Federal Premium's subsonic .22 LR for small-game hunters who don't want to disturb their neighbors to new calibers and cartridge options to help hunters and long-range marksmen extend their range. David Petzal, rifles editor for *Field & Stream* magazine, says, "The development and improvement of such cartridges as the .338 Lapua, .50 BMG, and the various tactical .416s have made shooting long even more possible. Before their use, shooting to and beyond one thousand yards was more of a stunt than serious shooting, but combined with the other technology available, they have extended the range of an expert shooter from roughly one thousand yards to twice that."

———

Increasingly, electronics are changing firearms. I knew we were at the beginning of a new era in small arms in 2006 when a pair of binoculars allowed me to outguess Pete Dube, a smart outfitter and guide. Pete and I were lying prone atop a ridge in north-central Wyoming glassing a mule deer buck that was looking to bed down for the day.

"That buck's big, but he must be over a thousand yards off," said Dube.

"No, it's not quite that far," I challenged as I watched the mule deer through a pair of Leica Geovid BRF 8x42 binoculars.

"Oh, just how far is it then?" he asked incredulously, knowing people who don't live in the wide-open West can't judge distances on the plains.

"Oh, about 830 yards," I shot back.

He pulled out his rangefinder, took the range, and blurted, "What! How the—?"

I didn't tell him. When you get one up on a savvy guide, you don't give up the advantage easily. You see, the binoculars I carried housed the top-quality optics Leica is famous for, but he had no way of knowing that it also contained a laser rangefinder.

The buck we were watching bedded down into a shadow and out of our sight.

"We'll have to back off and come around the ridge, down that coulee eight hundred yards over there," whispered Dube.

"Six hundred forty," I interrupted.

He checked the range and his eyes narrowed.

After crawling out onto the ridge, we started glassing for the buck. "I see him," I said. "He's one hundred forty-two yards straight ahead."

Pete searched for the buck, but the sun's low angle was reflecting light across his old binoculars' lenses, washing out the image. The glass on the Leica I was using had been treated and smoothed to an astounding degree to prevent refraction and reduce glare.

Finally, Pete found the buck and, after using his rangefinder to get the exact distance, he winced again and said, "Let me see those!" And then he laughed so hard he would have spooked the buck, if not for a stiff Wyoming wind.

The next big leap began in 2010 when digital video scopes began to hit the market. Raytheon's Elcan Optical Technologies offered a video riflescope that could switch reticles and record shots. It was the talk of the gun magazines, but today the Elcan already seems quaint. Everything changed when TrackingPoint hit the market, in 2013.

Field & Stream's David Petzal says,

> Ten years ago I was told by a ballistician who worked for the army that the next thing was "guided" small-arms munitions that could be directed to their targets much in the manner of smart bombs or cruise missiles, and that these would be of 25mm. These have yet to appear. What has evolved is the integrated rifle system with the software in the TrackingPoint rifle that is intended for big-game hunting. It comes in .300 Win. Mag. [Winchester Magnum] and .338 Lapua, and incorporates a scope, laser range-finder, ballistics computer, and WiFi transmitter. It also mostly eliminates the shooter from the equation, since all that person does is put the reticle on what they want to hit

and pull the trigger. The electronics decide when the rifle will fire.

Petzal adds, "If the past is any indicator, the size and weight of the TrackingPoint rifle system will come way down in the future, as will the price. The other questions—concerning the sportsmanship of using such a firearm, and if it should be in civilian hands at all—will also be resolved, or forgotten, at some point. But for better or for worse, the TrackingPoint—or something very much like it—is where we're going."

John Snow, the shooting editor for *Outdoor Life*, tells me, "I don't think TrackingPoint will even be around in a few years. The technology might get picked up by someone else and turned into something cheaper, but like ArmaLite's experience developing the AR-15, I don't think TrackingPoint will realize the benefits from its technology. People just aren't ready and the system they're selling needs improvement."

TrackingPoint calls its shooting system "precision-guided firearms." But Snow compares the TrackingPoint to Remington's failed Etronix rifle, which was announced in 1999 and discontinued a short time later. Etronix had an innovative battery-operated trigger system. Jim Carmichel, former shooting editor for *Outdoor Life*, noted that though electronic triggering "has been brilliantly successful in military rapid-fire weaponry, it has fizzled in sporting applications. Back in 1985 I authored *The Book of the Rifle*. In it I wistfully described a simple ignition system in which the complexities, complications and un-reliabilities of traditional percussive ignition were eliminated and replaced with a simple circuit that would work somewhat like an ordinary electric dynamite cap."[10]

Carmichel was pleased to see his vision come to be, but a lot of gun owners weren't impressed or ready for a battery-operated trigger mechanism. Remington went to the trouble because a rifle with an electronic firing system has some remarkable advantages. It has a virtually instant lock time (the time between pulling the trigger and the gun going *bang*). This means when you pull the trigger, the gun goes off faster. This matters when marksmen are shooting at long range, where every problem is magnified. The electronic system is also more repeatable than a mechanical system. What killed the idea were the costs, some marketing mistakes from Remington, worries that cold weather would kill the battery, and the fear that a person in a self-defense scenario would find himself helpless thanks to a dead battery—sometimes when someone needs a gun to go *bang*, he really needs the gun to go *bang*.

After gun owners refused to accept Remington's electronic-ignition system, Carmichel wrote, "Let's suppose that firearms had always been fired by electricity when suddenly a gunmaker decided to introduce a new ignition method in which a complicated series of levers and sears—all prone to breakage and disorder—released a spring-driven rod (which had to be reset with each firing) that smashes into an explosive chemical to ignite a flash of fire. Do I hear anyone say that it would be barely a step beyond starting fire by banging two rocks together?"

Meanwhile, Snow certainly has a point that the high cost of TrackingPoint's "fighter jet technology" is pricing out a lot of consumers. In early 2014 TrackingPoint did show they are trying to find a larger segment of the private market. They introduced a new line of AR-15s—the 500 Series, manufactured by Daniel Defense. These AR-15s come in three calibers—7.62 (.308), .300 BLK, and 5.56 calibers (.223). These AR-15s use TrackingPoint's Tag Track Xact technology and are priced at $9,950—about half the cost of TrackingPoint's long-range, bolt-action rifles. These ARs can lock onto and hit moving targets at distances up to five hundred yards. TrackingPoint says,

"With stabilized target selection, target tracking and guided firing the 500 Series semiautomatic AR products enable anyone to be an expert marksman out to the 500 yard effective range of the firearm, even from difficult firing positions, such as kneeling, standing, or even lying beneath an automobile."

At the 2014 SHOT Show, Oren Schauble, TrackingPoint's director of marketing, told me as he held one their Series 500 AR-15s, "We're reluctant to advertise some of the things this semiautomatic system can do. You can tag targets at say four hundred yards and then use a mode, the Fire Free Mode, to quickly engage those targets. A soldier could use this to quickly, in the heat of battle, take out multiple targets without having to think about where to hold the rifle's sights—enemy combatants wouldn't have a chance of accurately returning fire at medium to long range in enough time to matter."

To conceptualize how big of an advantage this is, realize that in the second Gulf War ("Operation Iraqi Freedom") U.S. M1 Abrams tanks could shoot Iraqi tanks from much greater distances than the Iraqis' tanks could, and U.S. tanks could do this as they drove at high speeds thanks to a fire-control computer than calculates shooting solutions. This TrackingPoint-type system theoretically gives infantry soldiers the same advantages. A soldier could be running and shooting accurately as he maneuvers. They could also tag a target and then shoot while undercover, as the rifle won't go off until it's in line with the tag.

These electronic shooting systems also appeal to today's soldiers and younger marksmen who can't imagine life without smartphones and iPads—or many without their PlayStation or Xbox. The TrackingPoint system, for example, has built-in Wi-Fi and ShotView that streams video. A mobile app lets shooters share their experiences with others in real time with a smartphone or tablet. The scope also records each shot with video and audio that can be downloaded to an iPhone or Android device and shared on social media like Facebook and Twitter. Anyone who doesn't get how all that will help establish this technology isn't in touch with this generation. Schauble already envisions internet forums and chat rooms set up for marksmen to share data and video they recorded at ranges. He says, "It's Wi-Fi capable, so someone shooting a 3-gun competition could live-stream video from his rifle as he moves along and shoots in the competition. Of course, soldiers can do this too. This way people at a control center can watch live and give the soldier advice on enemy combatants to come—it's the future."

So next I ask TrackingPoint's CEO, John Lupher, if the system could use facial-recognition software to target a certain person at long range. Lupher is a Texas A&M– and Stanford-educated engineer who has filed numerous patents for the company on target tracking, fire control, heads-up-display integration, and networking capabilities. Prior to TrackingPoint, he founded Evermore Systems, an Austin, Texas, product-development company.

Lupher smiles and says, "Now you're starting to grasp what the future of this technology can be. We're not there yet though."

"Could soldiers one-day carry a chip or other device your TrackingPoint system could sense and thereby read as good guys in a combat zone?" I ask.

Hollywood screenwriters thought of this for the 1973 movie *Westworld*. In the movie there are guns that can be fired only at humanoid robots. They use temperature sensors to keep the guns from shooting people. In the movie the robots rebel, override the restrictions, and begin shooting people with the guns. In another example of fiction meeting reality, science-fiction thinkers took this to another level in the videogame series Metal Gear Solid. In the game there are "nanomite computers" in peoples' bloodstreams that have an imprint of who the person is. "Smart guns" in the game can read a certain person's information.

Lupher says, "That would be more difficult, as a lot of factors can affect signals. Such things will one day be possible though. Perhaps the scope could read something on the soldier's uniform." He gets quiet a moment as his minds runs over the possibilities before adding, "Right now what's exciting is TrackingPoint can make shots safer and more ethical."

"And it can help a person used to video games to use those skills in real life, I suppose?"

"Yes, now an novice shooter can, within minutes, begin to hit targets beyond ten football fields," say Lupher.

Long-range marksmen I interviewed, however, told me they're excited but skeptical about the development of these "precision-guided firearms" from TrackingPoint. They think it would be better if a military or police sniper could switch to traditional optics if the electronic system fails. Many hunters feel the same way, as they're reluctant to rely too heavily on technology. *Field & Stream*'s David Petzal says he thinks they're the future, but also says, "In real life bullets go where they damn well please, not where computations say they should. I've been fooled badly, many times, going by the book." I interviewed former Special Forces snipers who underlined Petzal's point, telling me that sure, TrackingPoint would help a novice, because it takes away the need to control your breathing, to have good trigger control, and more. But a novice shooter would still need an expert to read the wind—with TrackingPoint, a shooter has to manually dial in wind speeds to adjust for a bullet's wind drift—and have experience of other factors that go into making a shot at long range.

The U.S. Armed Forces certainly see the potential in this technology and are looking to improve it. In 2007 the U.S. Defense Advanced Research Projects Agency (DARPA) in Arlington, Virginia, funded Lockheed Martin to develop a technology that can automatically account for wind speed and other factors. It's called the "One-Shot" program. In 2008 Lockheed Martin acquired fiber laser specialist Aculight Corporation, located in Bothell, Washington, to help build this system. They say a sniper will one day be able to use fiber-laser technology to illuminate a target at night more than a mile away. The fiber laser could even theoretically measure bullet drift caused by wind, as it would use light reflections from moving particles between the sniper and the target to determine wind direction and speed.[11] It's not, however, all about long-range snipers. To help soldiers shoot more accurately at shorter distances—ten feet to two thousand feet— Lockheed Martin is using One-Shot technology to build a rifle sight called the "Dynamic Image Gun Sight Optic" (DInGO).

In 2012 DARPA granted a $6 million contract to Cubic Corporation, a San Diego–based company, to develop a compact targeting system to help snipers hit targets at the "maximum effective range of current and future weapons" with their first shot.[12]

DARPA is reportedly interested in applying One-Shot technology to a program called the "Autonomous Rotorcraft Sniper System." This program would have spotters find and track targets with a drone or even a manned helicopter. The drone would have a rifle mounted in a stabilized turret. The gun would be controlled by a trained operator. It could fly over a battlefield and take out targets inside buildings or behind cover.

Meanwhile, TrackingPoint announced that the U.S. military purchased six TrackingPoint models to test and evaluate.[13] To win a military contract, TrackingPoint will need to compete with Lockheed Martin and other companies in this fast-developing sector.

Retired Special Forces operator Steve Adelmann, who has consulted for companies building these electronic sighting systems, says, "When I was a sniper I always critically considered new technologies. They can offer a lot of benefits, but their capabilities can often be overhyped or just theoretical. I was in the army in the mid-1990s when we were using GPS to do things the commercial market only became capable of five or so years ago. Despite GPS technology, however, the army still trains soldiers to use traditional maps and compasses. This is because when technology fails, you don't want your personnel to be helpless. So I see these coming digital optics systems as the future of small arms, but continuing to train on core sniper skills with mechanical backups will always be vital."

However it works out for TrackingPoint and Lockheed Martin, guns of the future seem irrevocably linked to digital technology. A low-end Nikon digital camera can now find a human face in the frame and set the exposure for that face. An electronic sight on a pistol linked to its firing mechanism could do the same thing. It could find someone's heart, or it could be set to wound. The possibilities are just starting to present themselves.

———

Another developing area is so-called "smart-gun" technology. Smart guns theoretically offer a way for a firearm to be personalized so it will only work for an "authorized person." Engineers working on smart guns have already tried things like radio-frequency identification (RFID), fingerprint-recognition systems, and magnetic rings to keep an unauthorized person from firing a gun. Smart guns have long been used in science fiction. The "Lawgiver" gun, for example, in the Judge Dredd comics is linked to the DNA of an authorized shooter.

The benefit of smart-gun technology is its potential to reduce or eliminate accidental use and misuse of guns. Theoretically, a villain couldn't take a gun from a police officer or armed citizen and then use that gun. Also, a parent wouldn't have to worry about a child getting their hands on and firing a self-defense gun. The trouble is none of the designs work all the time—batteries go dead, temperature or moisture can affect electronics—and most require a person to wear a bracelet or other device. Gun owners are understandably critical of guns that might go *click* when that big buck is sighted or when a cop has to return fire.

Some antigun groups actually oppose this technology—though for very different reasons. In a long list of criticisms of smart guns, the Violence Policy Center worries that "[p]ackaged with a strong sales pitch, [smart-gun] technology could penetrate new markets for [the] gun industry."[14] As if making gun ownership safer is a problem.

A bigger problem is politics. Larry Keane, senior vice president and general counsel for the National Shooting Sports Foundation, told me, "We're not opposed to smart-gun technology. We're opposed to government mandates. Most firearms manufacturers have been reluctant to invest R&D dollars in smart-gun technology because gun-control advocates want to make the technology mandatory. If that happens, new guns will become prohibitively expensive, which is part of what these groups want. This then raises the question what would happen to the three hundred million guns now owned by Americans that don't use such a safeguard? If history is any indicator, such ideological groups would next say guns without this capability should be banned.

"Here's another dilemma: If a gun company develops a smart gun and adds it as an option in their line of firearms, they'd open themselves up to lawsuits. Here's why: If someone steals a gun made by that manufacturer that doesn't have the smart technology installed and then that criminal uses that gun to rob or kill someone, a trial attorney could then file a lawsuit saying that person wouldn't have been robbed or shot if the manufacturer had just installed the safeguards it had available on more expensive models. They'd tell a jury 'the greedy gun maker doesn't care.' Some juries might buy that argument. Why would gun makers want to expose themselves to that liability in our litigious system?"

The political worries are, unfortunately, real; for example, in 2002 the "Childproof Handgun Bill" was signed into law in New Jersey. This law mandates that when smart-gun technology becomes available, all new handguns sold must be smart guns. In 2013 a German manufacturer, Armatix, announced they had developed such technology. Armatix says its Armatix iP1 pistol is a viable smart gun that uses radio frequencies to identify an authorized shooter—for the pistol to go *bang*, a person must be wearing the company's "intelligent iW1" wristwatch that broadcasts a specific frequency. The New Jersey law states that the technology will be required on all new handguns sold three years after the state attorney general determines that a smart gun is commercially available. (Weapons used by law-enforcement officers would be exempt.) As this was being written, New Jersey's attorney general had not declared such technology to be commercially available.

In April 2013 Attorney General Eric Holder said while testifying before a U.S. House of Representatives Appropriations subcommittee:

> One of the things we learned when we were trying to pass those common sense reforms last year, Vice President Biden and I had a meeting with a group of technology people and talked about how guns can be made more safe by making them either though fingerprint identification, the gun talks to a bracelet that you might wear, how guns can be used

only by the person who is lawfully in possession of the weapon. It's those kinds of things that I think we want to try to explore so that people have the ability to enjoy their Second Amendment rights while at the same time decreasing the misuse of weapons that lead to the kinds of things we see on a daily basis, where people, kids especially, are struck down.[15]

When Holder talked about how smart-gun technology could be mandated and regulated during a closed-door meeting at the Justice Department's National Institute of Justice, W. P. Gentry, the president of Kodiak Arms, tells me, "I looked Holder right in the eyes and told him if he mandates my technology I'll burn it down. I told him I'd destroy my smart-gun technology before I let the government use it against the American people. Other gun manufacturers backed me up."

Kodiak Arms is a Utah-based manufacturer that has developed what they call the "Intelligun."[16] As this book was being written, pre-orders for the Intelligun were being taken. This first version of the Intelligun is a conversion kit for standard Model 1911 pistols. Gentry says, "We don't make a Model 1911. The Intelligun is a conversion kit that is easy to install on a 1911 pistol. It's as simple as changing out the grips and the mainspring. If someone isn't comfortable doing this, they can hire a gunsmith or they can send their pistol to us—for a small charge—and we'll install it. Within the next year we'll have Intelligun conversion kits available for other popular handguns. We started with the 1911 because it's the most popular pistol ever made. We'll soon have something for 'J-frame' revolvers and eventually for Glocks and more."

The Intelligun uses biometric scanners on a gun's grips. It doesn't read a fingerprint. It actually takes a series of photos and overlaps them. It then looks for enough points that match an algorithm. It does this in less than a second. If the person is authorized—the gun can be programmed to authorize as many as twenty people—it unlocks the gun's firing mechanism. "We use state-of-the-art technology that exceeds U.S. Department of Defense requirements. Our biometric scanners can see right through sweat and even blood," says Gentry.

When you pick up the gun, your fingers naturally touch the biometric scanners. A pressure sensor keeps the gun "turned on." If you put it down, the gun locks within a second. The consumer model does have a manual override—a key a person can use to unlock a firearm that has a dead battery.

Gentry says, "We think our main market is new gun owners. There are a lot of parents out there who would like to have a gun for self-defense in their home, but they're reluctant to purchase one because they're afraid little Johnnie or Susie might get their hands on the gun. This technology offers another line of safety."

The Intelligun uses a lithium-ion battery in its grip. There is an indicator that tells how much battery life is left. In the consumer model, if the battery is dead, the Intelligun locks. Models being made for police departments, however, activate if a battery dies. "Police departments have asked for this tweak," says Gentry. "They're afraid a dead battery might leave a police officer in harm's way."

Eric Lichtenberg, president and founder of Lichtenberg Research and Design, worked as a contractor on the Intelligun. He tells me, "The grip on the Intelligun for the Model 1911 is a little thicker than standard grips. This is an issue with the batteries that are now available on the market. That is something that's changing fast. As we develop Intelligun conversion kits for more models this will change."

Gentry thinks the possibilities for the Intelligun are considerable. "We've even sold some to schools," says Gentry. "A few schools have quietly put some teachers through firearms-training courses. These teachers have Intelliguns. A few schools—I can't tell you which ones, as they want it kept quiet—have installed gun safes in various parts of schools. They're hidden in the walls. They have biometric scanners. If an authorized person touches the scanner, the box opens, giving them access to an Intelligun. If they're also authorized to use the gun they can respond to a school shooting in seconds, not minutes."

When the Intelligun gun safe is opened, it sends a text message to other teachers and school administrators, and it calls 9-1-1 to let the police know a gun has been accessed and that a teacher is now armed on the premises. This takes the idea of having good guys with guns as first responders to an entirely new level.

Gentry says, "We think this is the future. This potentially can safely arm good guys right away. And the gun doesn't send or receive any signals. It can't be turned on or off by anyone in some government office. It puts the power in the hands of the individual. This is the key to our future. We can use this technology to create a safer country, but as we do we have to make certain the technology won't be twisted into something that can be used to reduce the rights of the citizenry by empowering the government with mandates and other controls. If the government stays out of our way, we are going to save lives and enhance freedom."

Lichtenberg says the biggest obstacle to getting the Intelligun into the hands of police officers has been "police unions," which fear the "oversight" this technology could have on their members' actions in the field. Lichtenberg says, "Technology is now available that goes beyond authorization. A smart gun could also use a time stamp to record when a gun is drawn and if it is fired. GPS technology could keep track of where a cop's gun is and could record everything they do with it. Cell phones already do this. It wouldn't be hard to install such technology in the polymer frame of a pistol. This information could be available in trials, investigations, and so on. Combined with a small camera, such as are found on iPhones, this could give detailed accounts of police actions."

Kodiak Arms is at the forefront of this technology, but others have been dabbling in it for years. In 1999, Mossberg, through its subsidiary Advanced Ordnance and an electronics design contract with KinTech Manufacturing, developed a smart shotgun called the iGun that used radio frequency identification technology.[17] RFID technology is used in a lot of industries; for example, an RFID tag attached to an automobile can be used to track its progress through the assembly line. The iGun couldn't be fired unless its owner had a device that activates the gun. The gun, however, never made it to market. More recently, TriggerSmart, an Irish company, patented what it says is a working prototype of a personalized gun that works using RFID technology; and Biomac Systems, a U.S. and Austrian company, is also working on biometric sensors molded into a gun's grip.

In 2012, in the James Bond movie *Skyfall*, Bond is given a Walther PPK by Q that has a biometric palm-print scanner on its grip. Kodiak Arms president W. P. Gentry says that this "is basically the product we offer." In the Bond films, this concept actually began in the 1989 movie *License to Kill*, when Q provides Bond with a gun (disguised as a camera) using the same idea. In both movies the feature saves Bond's life when an enemy attempts to use his gun.

In the end, whatever technology brings us, the future of the gun will be driven, as it always has been, by the needs of hunters, soldiers, and individuals exercising their right to self-defense. Ultimately, it's all about that fundamental right. Imagine a woman walking alone, at midnight. Under a streetlight's glare are two men watching her. She doesn't pause. Her hard heels keep tap, tapping along on the sidewalk. She shows not a tinge of hesitation or fear. She is alone, sure. Her friends say she shouldn't go down these streets at night, not without a man. But tight behind her belt is something small, but powerful. She has a gun of the future, a small, light, but deadly equalizer that takes fear from the night. She has a smart gun with a laser grip that knows her personally. She doesn't live in a place where might makes right, where cops come along later to probe and put up yellow tape around a victim's body. She lives in a free society, a city that gives her the ability to be equal to anyone. So she only shifts her eyes at the idle men as she passes. They've seen her before. She isn't afraid. They nod respect. She's free. Truly free. Truly equal. They know they can't use her gun against her. She knows ultimate freedom is freedom from predation. That is the future of the gun. It is the future of freedom.

The Evolution of Freedom's Tool

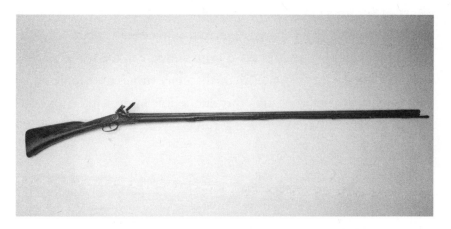

The American Long Rifle: Also known as the Kentucky and Pennsylvania Rifle, this flintlock design is most likely a descendant of the German Jaeger ("hunter")–type flintlock. In the New World, gunsmiths evolved this rifle throughout the seventeenth century into a longer-barreled firearm with a wooden stock extending the full length of the barrel and butt stock with a graceful downward curve. American long rifles became so accurate they were formidable tools for snipers in the American Revolution.

Muzzleloader with Percussion Cap: The phrase "keep your powder dry" was coined because before the percussion cap was invented (around 1820), wet weather often made guns unreliable. The percussion cap changed this. It contains a small charge of chemical in a small copper cuplike holder that can be quickly pressed onto a nipple in the rear of a gun barrel. When the trigger is pulled, the hammer strikes the cap, igniting the chemical that sends sparks through a hole in the nipple into the gunpowder in the barrel, firing the gun.

Colt Walker: After Samuel Colt went bankrupt and his Patterson Revolver went out of production, in 1847 a Texas Ranger named Samuel Walker asked Colt to make a new and more powerful revolver. Walker wanted the guns to arm his men for the Mexican-American War. Walker helped Colt get a government contract for one thousand such revolvers. The new revolver was dubbed the "Colt Walker." It remained the most powerful repeating handgun until the introduction of the .357 Magnum nearly ninety years later.

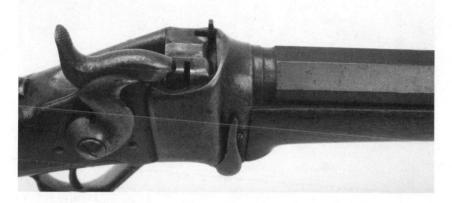

Sharps Rifles: The Sharps became known as the "Buffalo gun." They were a series of large bore, single-shot rifles that began with a design by Christian Sharps in 1848. Sharps Rifles were renowned for accuracy.

Smith & Wesson Model 1: First sold in 1857, this was the first revolver that fired a fully self-contained cartridge. Earlier revolvers from Colt were a big advance, but a downside was that reloading required jamming loose gunpowder and a lead bulled into each chamber, then placing a percussion cap on the nipple of each chamber. S&W's Model 1 used a self-contained cartridge with the primer, powder, and bullet all in one neat and weatherproof package.

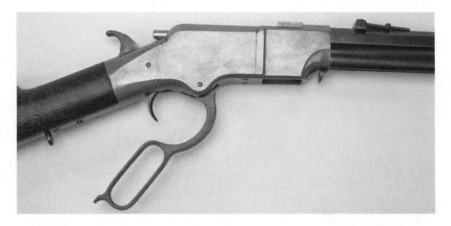

Henry Rifle: The original Henry rifle was a .44 caliber rimfire, lever-action, breech-loading rifle designed by Benjamin Tyler Henry in 1860. Only a few were purchased and used during the American Civil War, but this rifle became one of the iconic guns of the West.

Winchester Model 1873: The 1950 movie *Winchester 73* with James Stewart shows what a big deal this rifle was. The Winchester Model 1873, manufactured between 1873 and 1919, was a big advance because it was chambered in the heavier .44-40 cartridge—later models, the 1876 and 1886, were made strong enough to handle true big-game cartridges in the .45-70 class.

Colt Peacemaker: The most famous revolver is undoubtedly the Colt Single Action Army, introduced in 1873, and also known as "the Peacemaker." It was chambered in Colt .45 and was the standard military service revolver from 1872 until 1892.

Mauser 98: The perfection of the bolt-action rifle design is believed by many to be the Mauser 98, introduced in 1898. Its design became the new standard, and it has influenced bolt-action rifle design ever since. The U.S. Model 1903 bolt-action rifle, which served with distinction through two world wars in its .30-06 chambering, is basically a

modified Mauser 1898. Current production sporting rifles such as the classic Winchester Model 70 and bolt-actions by Remington, Ruger, and others can trace their lineage to the 98.

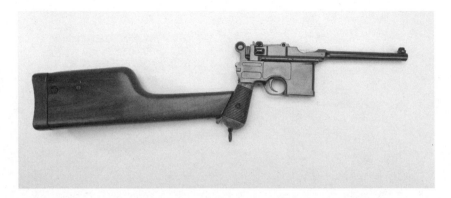

Mauser Broomhandle: The first auto-loading pistol designs to go into production were the German Schoenberger and Borchardt designs in 1893 and '94. In 1896 the Mauser firm began manufacturing the first semi-auto pistol to gain widespread acceptance, the Model 1896, nicknamed the "Broomhandle" for its slender oval cross-sectioned grip—a design that inspired the look of Han Solo's blaster.

Colt Model 1911: John Moses Browning's greatest creation is certainly the Model 1911 pistol. It was rapidly adopted by the U.S. military and only slightly modified over time, remaining the primary U.S.-issue sidearm through the Vietnam War. Colt and many other gun makers still make the 1911 today, as they are still used by some in the military, by law-enforcement, and by millions of Americans.

Winchester Model 12: The Model 12 became the standard for pump shotguns. It was made from 1912 to 1964. It was used in both world wars and by sportsmen for a half century. The Remington Model 870 pump-action shotgun, first sold in 1951, is its successor.

M1 Garand: The M1 Garand is a semi-automatic rifle chambered in .30-06 Springfield. General George S. Patton called it "the greatest battle implement ever devised." The Garand officially replaced the bolt-action M1903 Springfield as the standard service rifle of the U.S. Armed Forces in 1936.

AK-47: First made in 1949, there have now easily been one hundred million AK-47s made in factories all over the world. The AK-47 is a select-fire (semi-auto or full-auto) carbine with a detachable round-box magazine. Though not known for accuracy, the AK-47 has a reputation for being relatively cheap to produce, and for reliability even in the nastiest environments.

S&W Model 29: This was the first revolver from S&W chambered in .44 Magnum, a cartridge championed by famed gun writer Elmer Keith. It was first sold in 1955. Clint Eastwood popularized a Model 29

chambered in .44 Magnum as "the world's most powerful handgun" in the Dirty Harry movies.

AR-15: The U.S. version of the assault-weapon configuration was introduced in 1963. It was originally known as the AR-15 and was designed by Eugene Stoner in the late 1950s. It was ultimately adopted as the M-16 and manufactured by Colt and chambered for the 5.56 NATO, a military twin of the .223 Remington cartridge. Its rear sight is mounted on a distinctive integral carrying handle. Early on it had reliability issues, but many of these were fixed. Its design is still the basis for the service weapon used by U.S. armed forces.

Beretta 92: The Beretta 92 (also Beretta 96 and Beretta 98) is a series of semi-automatic pistols designed and manufactured by Beretta. The model 92 was designed in 1972, and production of many variants in different calibers continues today. The U.S. armed forces

replaced the Model 1911A1 pistol in 1985 with the Beretta 92F, the M9.

Glock: In 1982, the semi-auto pistol market was turned upside down by a new Austrian manufacturer offering a radically different design with the frame made from plastic-like polymer. Traditionalists initially scoffed at the 17-round design that doesn't have an external manual safety other than a lever on the face of trigger. Tupperware jokes abounded. Antigun-rights activists called it "plastic gun" and wanted it banned. The Glock quickly proved itself as a simple and reliable pistol as its popularity took off. It took years for other pistol makers to catch up with Glock's advances.

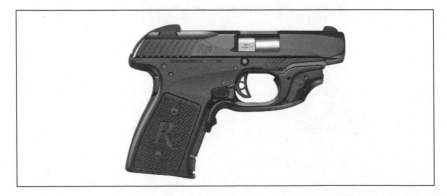

Remington R-51: This little pistol has ray-gun looks and a Luger-like shape. The R-51 is a light-carry gun in 9mm. Its grip angle is also slanted to lower muzzle jump and optimize target acquisition. It's just 6.67 inches long. It has a lightweight aluminum frame and is one of a new trend in light, easy-to-use carry guns. Glock's G42 is another example in how new technology is making it possible to make pistols that pack a punch lighter and smaller.

Notes

Chapter One: Every American Should Hear This

1. "Guns Advertisements," Vintage Ad Browser, http://www.vintageadbrowser.com/guns-ads.
2. William Hosley, *Colt: The Making of an American Legend* (Amherst: University of Massachusetts Press, 1996).
3. S.C. Gwynne, *Empire of the Summer Moon* (New York: Scribner, 2010).
4. R. L. Wilson, *Colt: An American Legend* (New York: Abbeville Press, 1991).
5. "Colt 1839 Revolving Percussion Rifle," National Firearms Museum, http://www.nramuseum.org/the-museum/the-galleries/the-prospering-new-

republic/case-31-the-age-of-industry/colt-1839-revolving-percussion-rifle.
aspx.

6. Jeffery Robenalt, "The Battle of Walker's Creek and the Colt Paterson
Revolver," TexasEscapes.com, http://www.texasescapes.com/
JefferyRobenalt/Battle-of-Walkers-Creek-and-Colt-Paterson-Revolver.htm.

7. E. B. Mann, "Colt: The Man behind the Gun," *Field & Stream* 86, no. 4
(1982).

8. Wilson, *Colt: An American Legend.*

9. The armory was founded by Eli Whitney. See "The Family," Eli Whitney
Museum and Workshop, http://www.eliwhitney.org/museum/eli-whitney/
family.

10. Dennis Adler, *Colt Single Action: From Patersons to Peacemakers* (Edison,
NJ: Chartwell Books, 2008).

11. Joseph Poyer, Craig Riesch, and Karl Karash, *The Model 1911 and Model
1911A1 Military and Commercial Pistols* (Tustin, CA: North Cape Publications, 2008).

12. Ibid.

13. Chapter 2 and Conclusion in Violence Policy Center, *Assault Weapons and
Accessories in America* (Washington, DC: 1988), http://www.vpc.org/
studies/awacont.htm.

14. Richard Lowry, *Legacy: Paying the Price for the Clinton Years* (Washington, DC: Regnery Publishing, 2003).

15. "Expanded Homicide Data Table 8," Crime in the United States, 2011,
Federal Bureau of Investigation, http://www.fbi.gov/about-us/cjis/ucr/
crime-in-the-u.s/2011/crime-in-the-u.s.-2011/tables/expanded-homicide-
data-table-8.

16. National Research Council, *Firearms and Violence: A Critical Review*
(Washington, DC: 2005).

17. See "Uniform Crime Reports," Federal Bureau of Investigation, http://
www.fbi.gov/ucr/ucr.htm.

18. "A Historical Review of Armalite," ArmaLite, Inc., January 2010, http://
www.armalite.com/images/Library/History.pdf.

19. Alexander Rose, *American Rifle: A Biography* (New York: Delacorte Press,
2008).

20. D. T. McElrath, "Golden Days at ArmaLite," *American Rifleman*, December 2004.

21. "The Aluminum Rifle," *Time*, December 3, 1956.

22. T. L. McNaugher, *The M16 Controversies: Military Organizations and
Weapons Acquisition* (New York: Praeger, 1984).

23. Rose, *American Rifle*.

24. "The Armalite AR-15 Rifle," *American Rifleman*, June 1959.

25. Rose, *American Rifle*.

Chapter Two: The Rifle Grows a Brain

1. The Remington 2020 website can be found at http://shoot2020.com/.

2. Matt Richmond, "As NY Institutes New Gun Laws, Focus Shifts to Gun Industry Subsidies," WNYC News, February 5, 2013, http://www.wnyc. org/story/267157-ny-institutes-new-gun-laws-focus-also-shifts-its-gun-industry-subsidies/.

3. John Christie, "States Have Subsidized Makers of Assault Rifles to Tune of $19 Million," Pine Tree Watchdog, January 2, 2013, http://pinetreewatchdog.org/states-have-subsidized-makers-of-assault-rifles-to-tune-of-19-million/.

4. "Schumer: 40–50 New Jobs Coming to Remington's Manufacturing Plant in Ilion," press release, Office of Senator Charles Schumer, March 22, 2011, http://www.schumer.senate.gov/record.cfm?id=332104&.

5. "*Face the Nation* Transcripts, December 16, 2012: Newtown Tragedy," December 16, 2012, http://www.cbsnews.com/news/face-the-nation-transcripts-december-16-2012-newtown-tragedy/.

6. Eliot Spitzer, "It's Time to Target Cerberus, the Private-Equity Firm That Dominates the Gun Industry," Slate.com, December 12, 2012, http://www.slate.com/blogs/spitzer/2012/12/17/newtown_shooting_it_s_time_to_target_cerberus_the_private_equity_firm_that.html.

7. Walter H. B. Smith, *Mannlicher Rifles and Pistols: Famous Sporting and Military Weapons* (Harrisburg, PA: Military Service Publishing Company, 1947).

8. Philip Cook and Jens Ludwig, *Guns in America, 1996* (Police Foundation: 1996); Bureau of Alcohol, Tobacco, Firearms, and Explosives, *Annual Firearm Manufacturer and Export Reports, 2012*, available online at https://www.atf.gov/sites/default/files/assets/pdf-files/afmer_2012_final_web_report_17jan2014.pdf; and Bureau of Alcohol, Tobacco, Firearms, and Explosives, *Firearm Commerce in the United States, 2011*, available online at http://www.atf.gov/files/publications/firearms/121611-firearms-commerce-2011.pdf.

9. "Report Advises against New National Database of Ballistic Images," press release, National Academies, March 5, 2008, http://www.nssf.org/share/legal/docs/030508-NatlAcadPR.pdf.

10. David Howitt, Frederic A. Tulleners, and Michael T. Beddow, "What Laser Machining Technology Adds to Firearms Forensics: How Viable Are Micro-Marked Firing Pins as Evidence?," draft paper, University of California at Davis, available online at http://www.nssf.org/share/legal/docs/0507UCDavisStudy.pdf.

11. Aaron Smith, "In Remington's Gun Town, Jobs Are No. 1 Concern," CNNMoney, April 10, 2013, http://money.cnn.com/2013/04/10/news/companies/remington-guns-jobs/index.html.

12. "Crime Rate in Herkimer, New York," City-Data.com, accessed May 2014, http://www.city-data.com/crime/crime-Herkimer-New-York.html.

Chapter Three: Technology Perfects the Pistol

1. "U.S. Army Awards New Beretta M9 Pistol Contract," press release, Beretta USA, September 2012, http://www.berettausa.com/usarmyawards newberettam9pistolcontract/.

2. James Michener, *Iberia* (New York: Random House, 1968).

3. Patrick Sweeney, *The Gun Digest Book of the Glock*, 2nd ed. (Iola, WI: Krause Publications, 2008).

4. Daniel Horan, "Pistol-Packing by the Millions," *Wall Street Journal*, January 17, 2012.

5. Peter Kasler, *Glock: The New Wave in Combat Handguns* (Boulder, CO: Paladin Press, 1992).

6. See the timeline of Glock's history one the Glock website: http://us.glock.com/heritage/timeline.

7. Paul M. Barrett, *Glock: The Rise of America's Gun* (New York: Crown Publishing, 2012).

8. Bureau of Alcohol, Tobacco, Firearms and Explosives *2012 Summary: Firearms Reported Lost and Stolen*, U.S. Department of Justice, Office of the Director, Strategic Management (Washington, DC: 2012).

9. Mark Gius, "An Examination of the Effects of Concealed Weapons Laws and Assault Weapons Bans on State-Level Murder Rates," *Applied Economics Letters* 21, no. 4 (2014), http://www.tandfonline.com/doi/pdf/10.1080/13504851.2013.854294.

10. Charles F. Wellford, John V. Pepper, and Carol V. Petrie, *Firearms and Violence: A Critical Review* (Washington, DC: National Academies Press, 2004), http://books.nap.edu/openbook.php?isbn=0309091241&page=2.

11. James Q. Wilson, "Appendix A: Dissent," in Wellford, Pepper, and Petrie, *Firearms and Violence*.

12. "Uniform Crime Reports, 2008 and 2009" Federal Bureau of Investigation, http://www.fbi.gov/about-us/cjis/ucr/crime-in-the-u.s/2009/crime2009.

13. "Salisbury, Maryland," State and County Quickfacts, U.S. Census Bureau, accessed May 2014, http://quickfacts.census.gov/qfd/states/24/2469925.html.

14. "Crime Rate in Salisbury, Maryalnd," City-Data.com, accessed May 2014, http://www.city-data.com/crime/crime-Salisbury-Maryland.html.

15. Kody Leibowitz, "Rap Video Alarms Community, Chief 'Can't Arrest Out of Problem,'" WMDT 47, October 24, 2013.

16. *Consumer Handgun Ownership Report, 2011*, National Shooting Sports Foundation.

17. "Expanded Homicide Data Table 8," Crime in the United States, Federal Bureau of Investigation, http://www.fbi.gov/about-us/cjis/ucr/crime-in-the-u.s/2010/crime-in-the-u.s.-2010/tables/10shrtbl08.xls.

18. DeWayne Wickham, "Wickham: Gun Violence Threatens Young Blacks," *USA Today*, February 11, 2013, http://www.usatoday.com/story/opinion/2013/02/11/dewayne-wickham-on-blacks-and-gun-violence/1906819/; and Children's Defense Fund, *Protect Children, Not Guns, 2012*, http://www.childrensdefense.org/child-research-data-publications/data/protect-children-not-guns-2012.pdf.

19. George Hunter, "Detroit Police Chief: Legal Gun Owners Can Deter Crime," *Detroit News*, January 3, 2014, http://www.detroitnews.com/article/20140103/METRO01/301030038#ixzz2r425mp5E.

20. "25th Annual National Survey Results," National Association of Chiefs of Police, 2013, http://www.nacoponline.org/25th.pdf.

21. "PoliceOne's Gun Control Survey: 11 Key Lessons from Officers' Perspectives," PoliceOne.com, April 8, 2013, http://www.policeone.com/Gun-Legislation-Law-Enforcement/articles/6183787-PoliceOnes-Gun-Control-Survey-11-key-lessons-from-officers-perspectives/.

Chapter Four: Embedded with the Gun Lobby

1. Glenn Kessler, "The NRA's Claim That Joe Biden's Gun Advice Is Illegal," *Washington Post*, February 25, 2013, http://www.washingtonpost.com/blogs/fact-checker/post/the-nras-claim-that-joe-bidens-gun-advice-is-illegal/2013/02/25/854b8ca2-7df3-11e2-9a75-dab0201670da_blog.html.

2. NRA Members can view the Grades & Endorsements section of the NRA website at http://www.nrapvf.org/grades-endorsements.aspx.

3.   John Houston Craige, *The Practical Book of American Guns* (New York: Bramhall House, 1950).

4.   Glen H. Utter, *Encyclopedia of Gun Control and Gun Rights* (Westport, CT: Greenwood, 2000).

5.   Reid J. Epstein, "Joe Biden on Sidelines in Gun Control Talks," Politico, October 28, 2013, http://www.politico.com/story/2013/10/joe-biden-on-sidelines-in-gun-debate-98966.html.

Chapter Five: How Gun Rights Beat the Media

1.   "Howard Stern Show: Harvey Weinstein Interview," YouTube video, recording of interview on *Howard Stern Show*, January 15, 2014, uploaded by "M076n7," January 15, 2014, http://www.youtube.com/watch?v=lig_yRICAro.

2.   Emily Smith, "Aspiring Actor Busted for Trying to Extort Millions from Harvey Weinstein," *New York Post*, August 23, 2012, http://nypost.com/2012/08/23/aspiring-actor-busted-for-trying-to-extort-millions-from-harvey-weinstein-feds/.

3.   Rebecca Riffkin, "Americans' Dissatisfaction with Gun Laws Highest since 2001," Gallup Politics, January 30, 2014, http://www.gallup.com/poll/167135/americans-dissatisfaction-gun-laws-highest-2001.aspx.

4.   Ibid.

5.   "Gun Control: Where Do Stars Stand on Firearms?," Celebuzz.com, http://www.celebuzz.com/photos/gun-control-where-do-stars-stand-on-firearms/mark-wahlberg-6/.

6.   "Tom Selleck Loses Temper with Gun-Toting Extra," ShowBizSpy.com, April 1, 2011, http://www.showbizspy.com/article/229667/tom-selleck-loses-temper-with-gun-toting-extra.html.

7.   Mark S. Fowler, interview, *The Mark Levin Show*, February 16, 2009.

8.   Michael Calderon, "Sen. Harkin: 'We Need the Fairness Doctrine Back,'" Politico, February 11, 2009.

9.   John Gizzi, "Pelosi Supports 'Fairness' Doctrine," *Human Events*, October 25, 2008.

10.   John Eggerton, "Bill Clinton Talks of Re-Imposing Fairness Doctrine or at Least 'More Balance in Media,'" *Broadcasting & Cable*, February 13, 2009.

11.   Sara Jerome, "FCC Push to Regulate News Draws Fire," *Hill*, December 6, 2010.

12.   "Uncovered Audio: Obama's Regulatory Czar Pushes Creepy Plan for Legally Controlling Internet Information," BlacklistedNews.com, http://www.

blacklistednews.com/_Uncovered_Audio%3A_Obama%E2%80%99s_
Regulatory_Czar_Pushes_Creepy_Plan_for_Legally_Controlling_Internet_
Information_/8740/0/21/21/Y/M.html.

13.   Nancy Watzman, "NRA Fights Campaign Finance Reform, Disclosure,"
       Sunlight Foundation, January 15, 2013, http://sunlightfoundation.com/
       blog/2013/01/15/nra-fights-campaign-finance-reform-disclosure/.

14.   D'vera Cohn, Paul Taylor, Mark Hugo Lopez, Catherine A. Gallagher,
       Kim Parker, and Kevin T. Maass, "Gun Homicide Rate Down 49% since
       1993 Peak; Public Unaware," Pew Research, Social and Demographic
       Trends, May 2013, http://www.pewsocialtrends.org/2013/05/07/gun-
       homicide-rate-down-49-since-1993-peak-public-unaware/.

15.   Jennifer Bendery, "Gabby Giffords' Gun Control Group Outraises All
       Other Super PACs," Huffington Post, February 4, 2014, http://www.
       huffingtonpost.com/2014/02/03/gabby-giffords-gun-control-
       fundraising_n_4718939.html.

16.   John Tkazyik, "ICYMI: Valley View: Mayoral Group's Gun Agenda Is
       Wrong," *Poughkeepsie Journal*, February 7, 2014, http://www.
       poughkeepsiejournal.com/article/20140207/OPINION04/302070047/
       ICYMI-Valley-View-Mayoral-group-s-gun-agenda-wrong.

17.   "There Is a 'Gun Control Playbook' versus Washington Gun Owners,"
       Washington Examiner, August 1, 2013, http://www.examiner.com/article/
       there-is-a-gun-control-playbook-versus-washington-gun-owners.

Chapter Six: Into "Gun-Free" America

1.   Robin Reese, "Georgia Mom Shoots Home Invader, Hiding with Her
       Children," ABC News, January 8, 2013, http://abcnews.go.com/US/
       georgia-mom-hiding-kids-shoots-intruder/story?id=18164812.

2.   Editorial, "Handguns Supreme," *Washington Post*, June 27, 2008, http://
       www.washingtonpost.com/wp-dyn/content/article/2008/06/26/AR2
       008062603605.html.

3.   John Lott, "Court's Gun Decision an Important Win for Americans Who
       Want to Defend Themselves," Fox News, June 28, 2010, http://www.
       foxnews.com/opinion/2010/06/28/john-lott-supreme-court-guns-ban-
       washington-chicago-daley-kagan-sotomayor/.

4.   Peruta v. San Diego documents available at http://michellawyers.com/
       guncasetracker/perutavsandiego/.

5.   *Peruta* opinion available at http://michellawyers.com/wp-content/
       uploads/2010/11/Peruta-Opinion.pdf.

6.　　Mary E. Shepard, et al., v. Lisa M. Madigan, et al., No. 13-2661, FindLaw (7th Cir. 2013), http://caselaw.findlaw.com/us-7th-circuit/1648621.html.

Chapter Seven: What Happens to Disarmed Peoples

1.　　Library of Congress, "Firearms Regulations in Various Foreign Countries," May 1998.

2.　　For a discussion of this quotation's origin, see Monticello's research on it at http://www.monticello.org/site/jefferson/strongest-reason-people-to-retain-right-to-keep-and-bear-arms-quotation.

3.　　"Forced to Strip Naked in the Street: Shocking Scenes as Rioters Steal Clothes and Rifle through Bags as People Make Their Way Home," *Daily Mail*, August 9, 2011, http://www.dailymail.co.uk/news/article-2024001/UK-riots-2011-London-Birmingham-people-forced-strip-naked-street.html.

4.　　"An Outrage That Appalled a Nation," BBC News, January 23, 2009, http://news.bbc.co.uk/2/hi/uk_news/magazine/7844916.stm.

5.　　Mike Waldren, "The Tottenham Outrage," Police Firearms Officers Association, http://www.pfoa.co.uk/193/the-tottenham-outrage.

6.　　Vikram Dodd, "Man Killed in Deadly Terror Attack in London Street," *Guardian*, May 22, 2013, http://www.theguardian.com/uk/2013/may/22/police-respond-serious-incident-woolwich.

7.　　"Firearms-Control Legislation and Policy: Great Britain," U.S. Library of Congress, http://www.loc.gov/law/help/firearms-control/greatbritain.php.

8.　　"Gun Law Off-Target," *Daily Telegraph*, Aug. 13, 2002, http://www.telegraph.co.uk/comment/telegraph-view/3580332/Gun-law-off-target.html.

9.　　Ian Burrell, "Legitimate Firearm Users Think That Tougher Restrictions Miss the Target," *Independent* (London), January 15, 2001, http://www.independent.co.uk/news/uk/this-britain/legitimate-firearm-users-think-that-tougher-restrictions-miss-the-target-702162.html.

10.　　Paul Lashmar, "Gun UK: A Teenage Girl Is Dead and a Baby Wounded," *Independent* (London), October 17, 2004, http://www.independent.co.uk/news/uk/crime/gun-uk-6159840.html.

11.　　Jason Bennetto, "Drug Gangs Force Police to Increase Firearms Officers," *Independent* (London), January 30, 2004.

12.　　"'I Was Portrayed as One of Britain's Biggest Illegal Gun Dealers,'" *Bromley Times*, July 11, 2007, http://web.archive.org/web/20071020094850/http://www.bromleytimes.co.uk/content/bromley/times/news/story.aspx?

brand=BMLYTOnline&category=news&tBrand=northlondon24&tCat
egory=newsbmlyt&itemid=WeED11%20Jul%202007%2013:08:29:253.

13. Chris Summers, "When Is a Gun Not a Gun?," BBC News, June 29, 2007.

14. "'I Was Portrayed as One of Britain's Biggest Illegal Gun Dealers.'"

15. The Home Office's statistics on firearm violence can be found at www.
homeoffice.gov.uk/ publications/science-research-statistics/research-
statistics/crime-research/hosb0212/hosb0212snr?view=Binary.

16. "2011 Census: Population Estimates for the United Kingdom," Office for
National Statistics, March 2011.

17. "Homicide," chapter 2 in *Crime Statistics: Focus on Violent Crime and
Sexual Offences, 2012–13* (London: Office for National Statistics: 2014),
http://www.ons.gov.uk/ons/rel/crime-stats/crime-statistics/focus-on-
violent-crime-and-sexual-offences—2012-13/rpt—chapter-2—homicide.
html.

18. James Slack, "The Most Violent Country in Europe: Britain Is Also Worse
Than South Africa and U.S.," *Daily Mail*, July 2, 2009, http://www.
dailymail.co.uk/news/article-1196941/The-violent-country-Europe-
Britain-worse-South-Africa-U-S.html.

19. Don B. Kates and Gary Mauser, "Would Banning Firearms Reduce Murder and Suicide? A Review of International and Some Domestic Evidence,"
Harvard Journal of Law and Public Policy 30, no. 2 (Spring 2007), http://
www.law.harvard.edu/students/orgs/jlpp/Vol30_No2_KatesMauseronline.
pdf.

20. William Alex Pridemore, "Using Newly Available Homicide Data to
Debunk Two Myths about Violence in an International Context: A
Research Note," *Homicide Studies* 5, no. 3 (2001), 267.

21. Joyce Lee Malcolm, *Guns And Violence: The English Experience* (Cam-
bridge: Harvard University Press, 2004).

22. Daniel Foggo, "Don't Bother about Burglary, Police Told," *Sunday Telegraph*, January 12, 2003.

23. Steve Doughty, "Let Burglars Off with Caution Police Told," *Daily Mail*,
April 3, 2006.

24. "International Comparisons of Criminal Justice Statistics, 1999," Home
Office Statistical Bulletin, 2001.

25. Awr Hawkins, "Harvard Study: No Correlation between Gun Control
and Less Violent Crime," Breitbart, August 28, 2013, http://www.
breitbart.com/Big-Government/2013/08/27/Harvard-Study-Shows-No-
Correlation-Between-Strict-Gun-Control-And-Less-Crime-Violence.

26. Kates and Mauser, "Would Banning Firearms Reduce Murder and Suicide?"

Chapter Eight: The Gun Marketplace of the Future

1. See the "Reports and Statistics" page for the National Instant Background System on the Federal Bureau of Investigation website: http://www.fbi.gov/about-us/cjis/nics/reports.

2. Alan Farnham, "Gun Sales Booming: Doomsday, Obama or Zombies?," ABC News, April 5, 2012, http://abcnews.go.com/Business/gun-sales-booming-doomsday-obama-zombies/story?id=16073797.

3. Lydia Saad, "U.S. Remains Divided over Passing Stricter Gun Laws," Gallup Politics, October 25, 2013, http://www.gallup.com/poll/165563/remains-divided-passing-stricter-gun-laws.aspx.

4. William J. Krouse, "Gun Control Legislation," Congressional Research Service, November 14, 2012.

5. Saad, "Self-Reported Gun Ownership in U.S. Is Highest since 1993," Gallup Politics, October 26, 2011, http://www.gallup.com/poll/150353/Self-Reported-Gun-Ownership-Highest-1993.aspx.

6. Kyle Jillson, "NRA Reaches 80,000 Certified Instructors," *NRAblog*, September 29, 2011, http://www.nrablog.com/post/2011/09/29/NRA-reaches-80000-instructors.aspx.

7. "Annual Firearms Manufacturing and Export Report, Year 2012" Bureau of Alcohol, Tobacco, Firearms and Explosives, https://www.atf.gov/sites/default/files/assets/pdf-files/afmer_2012_final_web_report_17jan2014.pdf.

8. This estimate comes from GrabStates.com, accessed May 2014, http://grabstats.com/statmain.aspx?StatID=25.

9. "Kids 'n' Guns: National 4-H Shooting Sports Committee Position Statements," National 4-H Shooting Sports, http://www.4-hshootingsports.org/Kids'N'Guns.php.

10. *2011 National Survey of Fishing, Hunting, and Wildlife-Associated Recreation: National Overview* (Washington, DC: U.S. Fish and Wildlife Service, August 2012), available online at http://www.doi.gov/news/press-releases/upload/FWS-National-Preliminary-Report-2011.pdf.

11. See the Sportsman Shooting Center website at www.sportsmanshooting center.com.

Chapter Nine: The Solution to Gun Violence

1. Richard Ben Cramer, "What Do You Think of Ted Williams Now?," *Esquire*, June 1986.
2. "The Bureau of Alcohol, Tobacco, Firearms and Explosives' National Integrated Ballistic Information Network Program," Bureau of Alcohol, Tobacco, Firearms and Explosives, June 2005, http://www.justice.gov/oig/reports/ATF/a0530/intro.htm.
3. Ibid.
4. Senate Bill 584, Maryland General Assembly, 2014, available online at http://mgaleg.maryland.gov/2014RS/fnotes/bil_0004/sb0584.pdf.
5. "Ballistics Statute Faulted," *Washington Times*, January 17, 2005, http://www.washingtontimes.com/news/2005/jan/17/20050117-102901-2749r/?page=all.
6. "Protecting America: The Effectiveness of the Federal Armed Career Criminal Statute," ATF, March 1992.
7. Caroline Wolf Harlow, "Firearm Use by Offenders," Bureau of Justice Statistics, November 2001, https://www.ncjrs.gov/App/Publications/abstract.aspx?ID=189369.
8. Bureau of Alcohol, Tobacco, Firearms and Explosives *2012 Summary: Firearms Reported Lost and Stolen*, U.S. Department of Justice, Office of the Director, Strategic Management (Washington, DC: 2012).
9. Office of the Auditor General of Canada, "Deparmtent of Justice: Costs of Implementing the Canadian Firearms Program," chapter 10 in *Report of the Auditor General of Canada* (Ottowa, Canada: Minister of Public Works and Government Services, December 2002), http://www.oag-bvg.gc.ca/internet/English/parl_oag_200212_10_c_12404.html.
10. Jim Hoft, "CT Sends Out Letters to Gun Owners: 'Surrender, Destroy or Sell' Your 'Assault Weapons,'" Gateway Pundit, February 27, 2014, http://www.thegatewaypundit.com/2014/02/ct-sends-out-letters-to-gun-owners-surrender-destroy-or-sell-your-assault-weapons/.
11. Ibid.
12. "Obama Calls On Congress to Follow CT and Pass 'Common Sense' Gun Laws," CBS Local, April 9, 2013, http://newyork.cbslocal.com/2013/04/08/obama-in-conn-to-promote-gun-legislation/feed/.
13. "Connecticut Law Requiring Permit for Certificate for Sale, Transfer of Long Guns Takes Effect," *New Haven Register*, April 1, 2014, http://www.nhregister.com/general-news/20140401/connecticut-law-requiring-permit-or-certificate-for-sale-transfer-of-long-guns-takes-effect.

14. Mark Follman, Gavin Aronsen, and Deanna Pan, "A Guide to Mass Shooting in America," *Mother Jones*, February 27, 2013, http://www.motherjones.com/politics/2012/07/mass-shootings-map.

15. "Brady Campaign Releases a Report Analyzing 20 Years of Effective Background Checks," Brady Campaign to Prevent Gun Violence, http://www.bradycampaign.org/brady-campaign-releases-a-report-analyzing-20-years-of-effective-background-checks.

16. *State of the Union*, "Interview with Senator Lindsey Graham," CNN, March 31, 2013.

17. Glenn Kessler, "Lindsey Graham's Claim That No Fugitives Have Been Prosecuted after Gun Background Checks," *Fact Checker* (blog), *Washington Post*, April 4, 2013, http://www.washingtonpost.com/blogs/fact-checker/post/lindsey-grahams-claim-that-no-fugitives-have-been-prosecuted-after-gun-background-checks/2013/04/03/5d20c1fa-9ca9-11e2-a941-a19bce7af755_blog.html.

18. "About PICS," Pennsylvania State Police, http://www.portal.state.pa.us/portal/server.pt?open=512&objID=4451&&PageID=461119&mode=2.

19. *Pennsylvania State Police Annual Firearms Report, 2010*, Bureau of Record and Identification, available online at http://www.portal.state.pa.us/portal/server.pt/document/1102470/pennsylvania_state_police_2010_firearms_annual_report_pdf.

20. "Review of the Bureau of Alcohol, Tobacco, Firearms and Explosives' Enforcement of Brady Act Violations Identified through the National Instant Criminal Background Check System," U.S. Department of Justice, July 2004, http://www.justice.gov/oig/reports/ATF/e0406/exec.htm.

21. To see Attorney General Eric Holder's testimony from March 6, 2013, visit "Cornyn Presses Holder on Obama Administration's Failure to Prosecute Gun Crimes," YouTube video, uploaded by "Senator John Cornyn," March 6, 2013, http://www.youtube.com/watch?v=WLZqPnR1t_k.

22. Caroline May, "Biden to NRA: We 'Don't Have the Time' to Prosecute Gun Buyers Who Lie on Background Checks," Daily Caller, January 18, 2013, http://dailycaller.com/2013/01/18/biden-to-nra-we-dont-have-the-time-to-prosecute-people-who-lie-on-background-checks/.

23. Tate, "Graham, Begich, Flake and Pryor Introduce Legislation on Mental Illness and Gun Violence," Lindsey Graham official website, March 6, 2013, http://www.lgraham.senate.gov/public/index.cfm?FuseAction=IssueStatements.View&Region_id=&Issue_id=96fef72b-802a-23ad-4948-c27807a16ef1,7926d5be-cd20-43bf-ab15-d33f725d02f6,c8935458-

2345-49e6-afcf-3bb47eafd453,ca167d00-81ac-4794-a23b-eb3a093f19
2d&Month=3&Year=2013&CFId=93893406&CFToken=91674884.

24.   "Alice Boland Gets a Gun (Timeline)," press release, Office of Senator
      Lindsey Graham, February 13, 2013, available online at http://www.
      scribd.com/doc/125350089/Alice-Boland-Gets-A-Gun-Timeline.

Chapter Ten: The Armed Citizen of the Future

1.   Geoffrey W. Norman, "The Real Hatfield," *Inc.*, http://www.inc.com/
      magazine/19901001/5391.html.

2.   See the Solid Concepts website at http://www.solidconcepts.com/3d-
      printing/.

3.   "World's First 3D Printed Metal Gun Manufactured by Solid Concepts,"
      news release, Solid Concepts, http://www.solidconcepts.com/news-
      releases/worlds-first-3d-printed-metal-gun-manufactured-solid-concepts/.

4.   This mission is quoted in Alexis Kleinman, "The First 3D-Printed Gun
      Has Been Fired (VIDEO)," Huffington Post, May 7, 2013, http://www.
      huffingtonpost.com/2013/05/06/3d-printed-gun-fired_n_3222669.html.

5.   Sydney J. Freedberg Jr., "Army Killed New Carbine Because It Wasn't
      Twice as Reliable as Current M4," Breaking Defense, June 14, 2013,
      http://breakingdefense.com/2013/06/army-killed-new-carbine-because-it-
      wasnt-twice-as-good-as-current-m4/.

6.   Rowan Scarborough, "Troops Left to Fend for Themselves after Army
      Was Warned of Flaws in Rifle," *Washington Times*, February 19, 2014.

7.   "Amendment #3186: The Need for Small Arms Modernization by the
      U.S. Army," available online at http://handbook5.com/a/amendment-
      3186-the-need-for-small-arms-modernization-by-the-us-army-w40903.
      html.

8.   "Nosler: History," Nosler.com, http://www.nosler.com/nosler-history/.

9.   "Superformance," Hornady.com, http://www.hornady.com/store/Super
      formance.

10.   Jim Carmichel, "Electronic Rifle Revisit," *Outdoor Life*, September 2009,
      http://www.outdoorlife.com/articles/gear/2007/09/electronic-rifle-revisit.

11.   John Keller, "Lockheed Martin Relies on Aculight Fiber Laser Technology
      for One-Shot Program's Sniper Targeting System," *Military & Aerospace
      Electronics*, December 1, 2010, http://www.militaryaerospace.com/
      articles/print/volume-21/issue-12/electro-optics-watch/lockheed-martin-
      relies-on-aculight-fiber-laser-technology-for-one-shot-programs-sniper-
      targeting-system.html.

12. John Keller, "DARPA Chooses Cubic to Move One Shot Sniper Targeting Technology to the Next Level," *Military & Aerospace Electronics*, August 14, 2012.

13. "TrackingPoint and the XM 2010," TrackingPoint Labs, March 10, 2014, http://tracking-point.com/labs/military/.

14. "'Smart' Guns Backgrounder," Violence Policy Center, http://www.vpc.org/fact_sht/Smart%20Gun%202013.pdf.

15. "Eric Holder Wants Gun Owners to Wear 'Smart Gun' Bracelets," Daily Caller, April 7, 2014, http://dailycaller.com/2014/04/07/eric-holder-wants-gun-owners-to-wear-tracking-bracelets/#ixzz30H847aj3.

16. See the Intelligun website at http://intelligun.com/.

17. "iGun Technology Corp.," http://www.iguntech.com/tech.html.

Index